CW00794262

THE Rorke's Drift Men

THE Rorke's Drift Men

HEROES OF THE ZULU WAR

JAMES W. BANCROFT

SPELLMOUNT

First published 2010 by
Spellmount, an imprint of
The History Press
The Mill, Brimscombe Port
Stroud, Gloucestershire, GL5 2QG
www.thehistorypress.co.uk

© James W. Bancroft, 2010

The right of James W. Bancroft to be identified as the Author
of this work has been asserted in accordance with the
Copyrights, Designs and Patents Act 1988.

All rights reserved. No part of this book may be reprinted
or reproduced or utilised in any form or by any electronic,
mechanical or other means, now known or hereafter invented,
including photocopying and recording, or in any information
storage or retrieval system, without the permission in writing
from the Publishers.

British Library Cataloguing in Publication Data.
A catalogue record for this book is available from the British Library.

ISBN 978 0 7524 5692 8

Typesetting and origination by The History Press
Printed in Great Britain
Manufacturing managed by Jellyfish Print Solutions Ltd

Contents

Foreword

On 22 January 1879, a garrison of British soldiers successfully defended the storehouse and field hospital at Rorke's Drift against an army of Zulu warriors. This heroic stand has been written about extensively and inspired the epic film *Zulu!* Yet, surprisingly, information about the soldiers who took part has not been so readily available. The main bulk of the troops who defended the post came from 2nd Battalion 24th Regiment, particularly B Company, with some men from the 1st Battalion, men of the Royal engineers and the Royal Artillery. There was also a sergeant from the 3rd Regiment and a corporal of the 90th Light Infantry, and there were colonials from the Natal Mounted Police and the Natal Native Contingent. There were also several men from the Army's Medical and Commissariat departments, a member of the general staff, a chaplain and a civilian ferryman.

Most of the rank-and-file soldiers in the garrison were rough-and-ready lads from the coal mining and cotton manufacturing communities in and around city slums, and their only alternative to the highly-disciplined life in the British Army was the precarious environment and drudgery of the pit and mill. In addition to this there were a number of men present who had gained a great deal of experience serving in various campaigns around the world. This combination, and their staunch loyalty to their regiment made them a formidable fighting unit, and the rifle in their hands gave them a decisive advantage! The Zulu warriors who fought at Rorke's Drift were undoubtedly a fearless foe, who expected to face little resistance from the small garrison. However, the British fought for their lives with great gallantry, and held the Zulu assaults back so stubbornly that the warriors lost heart and retreated back across the river border. Sixteen gallantry medals were awarded to defenders, one being cancelled at a later date. Seven were presented to soldiers of the 24th Regiment, which was the most ever given to one unit for a single action. There have been attempts to devalue what is considered by some to be a high number of recognitions, but it was no more than they deserved. In fact, the important part some men played was definitely overlooked.

More than 125 years after the campaign the names Rorke's Drift and Zulu are still immediately recognised and stir great passion. However, many Rorke's Drift men returned to a life of poverty, and a struggle for survival equal to that which they had endured on active service, and in some cases their lives were rocked by heartbreak and terrible tragedy. Most had faded into obscurity until now. *The Rorke's Drift Men* contains biographical tributes to all the defenders known to me, with information drawn from eyewitness accounts, official reports, military service records, census returns and other official civilian documentation. I have tried to present the work in the form of biographical tributes as opposed to lists of facts and figures. The basis of the work has been my own files concerning British courage and achievement compiled over the past 35 years, with additional help from numerous Zulu War enthusiasts and family descendants of defenders, particularly Kris Wheatley, a great-granddaughter of Caleb Wood, whose enthusiasm for the subject and standard of research concerning the defenders of Rorke's Drift must be applauded. I also acknowledge the help of the Royal Corps of Transport, the Royal Army Medical Corps, both museums being in Aldershot; and Alun Baynham-Jones, the curator and associates at the South Wales Borderers Museum at Brecon, which should be the first visit of anyone wishing to further their knowledge of the subject.

James W. Bancroft, Eccles, 2010

The Defence of Rorke's Drift

Tension between British authority and various factions in South Africa had been building up for years prior to 1879, especially concerning the independent-minded Boer farmers and the warrior nation of the Zulu. Because of this, many British Army units were already in South Africa taking part in the ninth of a series of Cape frontier wars. The 2nd Battalion had embarked on the troopship *Himalaya* on 1 February 1878, for active service at the Cape. This campaign consisted mainly of sweeping skirmishes to flush rebel natives out of the bush, and the rebel leaders were captured and dealt with by mid-1878. However, the main threat to stability in the region came from the highly-disciplined army of fearless Zulu warriors. In order to deal with the Zulu threat the British issued a deliberately harsh ultimatum to the Zulu king, Cetshwayo. British forces began to build up at strategic places along the border with Zululand, and when Cetshwayo failed to comply to the ultimatum, they invaded in three main columns on 11 January 1879. The 3rd (Central) Column, under the Commander-in-Chief, Lord Chelmsford, crossed the Buffalo River into Zululand at a commandeered mission-station known as Rorke's Drift. The main bulk of this section of the invasion force was made up of soldiers of the 24th Regiment, which left B Company of the 2nd Battalion to garrison the storehouse and field hospital which had been established there, along with some men from other imperial and colonial units.

The main invasion force set up camp in enemy territory on the slopes of a rock feature called Isandlwana. However, Lord Chelmsford considered this to be a temporary base, so on the morning of 22 January 1879 he took half his force forward to find a suitable site for an advanced base camp, and to try to locate the enemy; leaving over a thousand British and colonial troops to guard the ill-prepared camp. Later that day a vast Zulu army swarmed down from the hills around Isandlwana in a devastating surprise attack. In the initial stages of the battle firepower from the British ranks kept the Zulus back, but the 24th Regiment were eventually overwhelmed by the enemy's superior numbers and

Cetshwayo ka Mpande was crowned king of the Zulus in 1873, and was said to be more intelligent, and at times equally as ruthless as the great Zulu chief, Shaka. When he failed to respond to the harsh ultimatum put to him by the British Government – which included that he should disband his army – British troops invaded Zululand and war began.

were forced to stand and fight in hopeless disorder. They were massacred almost to a man, but the few survivors of the battle, and the warriors themselves, told how the British soldiers stood back-to-back and fought bravely for their lives until they 'fell like stones'. A wing of the Zulu army, consisting of four regiments of warriors about 4,000-strong, who had not 'washed their spears', advanced into Natal seeking additional blood at Rorke's Drift.

Under the command of Lieutenant John Chard, Royal Engineers, and Lieutenant Gonville Bromhead, 24th Regiment, the hundred or so able-bodied men in the garrison had been warned of the Zulu advance, and with orders to stand and fight, they hastily built a makeshift barricade with bags and wooden boxes to form a compound between the two buildings, and six men were posted in the hospital having been told to barricade the entrances and windows and defend the patients as best they could.

The first Zulu onslaughts were met by withering British rifle fire, and many warriors fell 'as if they had been cut off at the knees', but they eventually rushed the barricade and the defenders were forced to use their bayonets in fierce hand-to-hand combat. After setting fire to the roof of the hospital the Zulus forced their way in, killing some patients, while others were rescued by being passed through holes cut in partitions and then helped out of a window. Most

Having received orders to stand and fight, British soldiers began to empty the storehouse of anything they could use to build a barricade. The men worked with a sense of urgency knowing that their lives might depend on whether they could complete a perimeter wall before the Zulus attacked. (Richard Scollins)

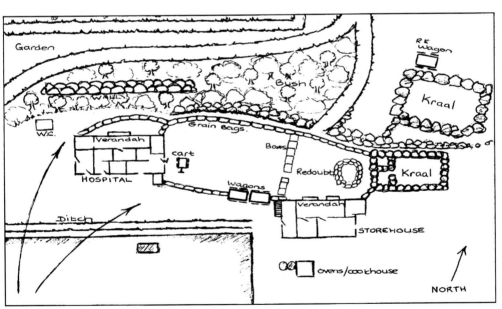

A wall of grain bags three units high was constructed, enclosing the front of the hospital and running along the ledge of the rocky terrace to the stone wall of the kraal, and also coming from the far end of the storehouse down to the edge of these rocks. Two wagons were utilised to form part of the defensive wall connecting the right hand front corner of the storehouse with the left hand back corner of the hospital. The arrows indicate the initial Zulu attack. (Tracey Bancroft)

A Zulu onslaught against the barricade.

of them reached an inner redoubt where they joined their comrades in the desperate fight for survival.

With good foresight, Lieutenant Chard ordered two piles of mealie bags which had been left outside the storehouse to be built up into a high redoubt as a second line of fire, and from where he could get an elevated view of the perimeter on all sides. It would also be the place where they would make a last stand if the Zulus pushed them back from the original barricade. However, the British fought with exceptional bravery and the Zulus eventually lost heart and moved off. When a relief column arrived on the following morning fifteen defenders had been killed, two were dying, and ten were badly wounded. The Zulus had suffered about 500 casualties.

The tragedy at Isandlwana was one of the worst disasters in British military history, and sent a shockwave across the nation. Lord Chelmsford requested reinforcements from Britain, and a new invasion was planned. On 28 March 1879, a British column assaulted a strategic Zulu stronghold at Hlobane Mountain, only to suffer a serious reverse. However, on the following day, the Zulu army attacked the British camp at Khambula and suffered such heavy losses that it never recovered. On 4 July a large British force, in square formation, moved on the Zulu capital at Ulundi, and was attacked by about 20,000 warriors. British firepower cut them down in their thousands, and imperial cavalry put them to flight. The Zulu capital was burnt, and the campaign came to a close when Cetshwayo was captured a few weeks later.

The Biographies

Corps of Royal Engineers

John Chard

John Rouse Merriott Chard was born at Boxhill, Plymouth, on 21 December 1847. He was the second son of William Wheaton Chard (1819–1873) of 'Pathe', in the village of Othery, Somerset, and Mount Tamar, Plymouth, and his wife Jane, daughter of John Hart Brimacombe, of Stoke Climsland, Cornwall. They had married at Launceston in the December quarter of 1839. His older brother, Wheaton, followed family tradition and became a colonel in the 7th Royal Fusiliers, while his younger brother, Charles, became a vicar. There were five

John Chard of the Royal Engineers had fame reluctantly thrust upon him. He was at Rorke's Drift to work on a ferry which had broken down, and he found himself as the senior officer at the post when news arrived that an army of Zulus was on its way to attack the garrison. He was awarded the Victoria Cross for his cool leadership throughout the engagement. Queen Victoria was an admirer, and he became known as the Hero of Rorke's Drift.

sisters, and the family worshipped at St Budeaux Church in Plymouth. His great-nephew, Lieutenant-Colonel Michael Chard, regimental secretary of the Royal Regiment of Fusiliers in 1979, stated: 'All my family are Royal Regiment of Fusiliers and he was the black sheep because he became a sapper – but he ended up doing rather well.'

He was educated at the Plymouth New Grammar School, and received some private tutorship. He attended the Royal Military Academy at Woolwich, where he was remembered for always being late for breakfast. He passed-out in 1868, and was commissioned as a Lieutenant in the Royal Engineers on 15 July 1868. After two years at Chatham he sailed to Bermuda in October 1870, being employed in the building of fortifications at the Hamilton Dockyard. His father died at Plympton near Plymouth in 1873, and he returned to England in January 1874. In the following month he was posted to Malta, where he was again employed in the construction of defences. He returned to England in April 1876, and after a short stay at Chatham, was appointed to the Western District at Exeter.

As the situation in South Africa worsened he was ordered to report to Aldershot to join the 5th Company, Corps of Royal Engineers for active service at the Cape. The unit set sail from Gravesend on 2 December 1878, arriving at Durban on 5 January 1879. His vaccination injection had become inflamed and his right shoulder was very sore, but British troops were already assembling on the Natal-Zululand border, so with no time to recover he was ordered to take a small party of engineers to join the 3rd Column at Rorke's Drift. For almost the entire journey the tracks were bad, and by the time he arrived at his destination on 19 January the column had already invaded enemy territory. One of the ponts which was used to ferry the troops across the Buffalo River had broken down, so Chard and his men set up camp on the Natal bank to work on repairing it.

Two days later he received orders to take his party of engineers to the British base camp at Isandlwana, about eight miles away, and he set off with them on the morning of 22 January. While he was there he saw enemy activity on the distant hills, some movement being in the direction of Rorke's Drift, so he set off back to report what he had seen, arriving at the post by midday. The officer commanding the post, Major Spalding, did not seem too concerned about the situation and informed Chard that he was leaving him in charge while he went to Helpmekaar to hurry forward a company of regular infantry which was overdue, uttering the immortal words 'nothing will happen!' as he left.

Lieutenant Chard then returned to the river with a guard of seven regular soldiers and about 50 natives, and just after three o'clock he was in his tent catching up on correspondence when Lieutenant Adendorff rode up and informed him that the camp at Isandlwana had been taken by the Zulus. Shortly afterwards a message arrived from Bromhead urging him to come up

Regular soldiers and men from colonial units fought side by side in fierce close combat with ferocious Zulu warriors of the uNdi Corps at Rorke's Drift. British dead and seriously wounded numbered less than 30, but Zulu casualties totalled as many as 500. (Richard Scollins)

to the camp. Some of the men offered to moor the ponts in the middle of the river and defend them from the decks. Chard must have been heartened by the plucky offer, but he decided that they would be better deployed defending the garrison with their comrades. On returning to the post, they found that preparations for the defence were underway. Bromhead informed him that a Zulu force was on its way to attack the mission station, which they were to hold at all costs. He agreed with most of the arrangements made, and added a few suggestions for improvements to the barricade, then saw to it that every man knew his place and was prepared for battle.

About two hours into the battle the Zulus launched a particularly fierce assault. Lieutenant Chard was using his revolver to help to keep the enemy at bay when Private Jenkins suddenly ducked the officer's head down as a Zulu slug just missed him. It was due to Lieutenant Chard's good foresight that two piles of mealie bags were built up into a high redoubt as a second line of fire, and from where he could get an elevated view of the perimeter on all sides. It would also be the place where they would make a last stand.

The citation for the award of Victoria Cross to Lieutenant John Chard published in the *London Gazette* of 2 May 1879, states:

> The Lieutenant-General commanding the troops reports that, had it not been for the fine example and excellent behaviour of these two Officers under the most trying circumstances, the defence of Rorke's Drift post would not have been conducted with that intelligence and tenacity which so essentially characterised it. The Lieutenant-General adds that its success must, in a great degree, be attributable to the two young Officers who exercised the Chief Command on the occasion in question.

A colonial trooper said that 'the men spoke highly of Chard', and his cool leadership proved invaluable that day. He was appointed captain and brevet-major dated from the 23 January 1879, thus becoming the first man in history to move from a lieutenancy to a majority in the army in a single day. He, and his fellow defenders received the thanks of the government.

Major Chard remained at Rorke's Drift to supervise the burial of hundreds of dead Zulus in mass graves, and to work on a more permanent stone perimeter. Suffering the hardships of atrocious conditions, he was struck down with fever, and on 17 February he was taken by ambulance wagon to Ladysmith, where he was looked after by a Doctor Park and his wife. After showing signs of improvement he suffered a relapse, and just after the announcement of his Victoria Cross award it was reported in local newspapers that he had died. However, he was nursed back to health, and was able to report for duty in time for the British re-invasion.

He joined Colonel Wood's column at Khambula to inspect the fortifications, and was involved in all the operations with the flying column. His unit followed up Colonel Buller's scouting activities, building bridges and repairing roads, and he was in the British square formation which advanced on Cetshwayo's capital at Ulundi for the final crushing defeat of the Zulus on 4 July.

He was decorated with the Victoria Cross by General Garnet Wolseley during a parade of the troops at St Paul's Camp in Zululand, on 16 July 1879. For his service at the Cape he also received the South Africa Medal with 1879 clasp.

He arrived at Spithead aboard the *Eagle* on 2 October 1879, where the Duke of Cambridge welcomed him and delivered a message from Queen Victoria inviting him to an audience with her at Balmoral, where she presented him with a gold signet ring. He was invited to a second audience with the Queen, and on 21 February 1880, he presented the sovereign with a more detailed account of the action at Rorke's Drift. He was received at Plymouth as a local hero, being presented with a gold chronometer and a superb sword of honour which had been specially manufactured and richly carved. He was presented with an illuminated address by freemasons in Exeter, and was guest of honour at dinner receptions in Taunton and at the Wanderers Club in Chatham. He was held in the highest regard in the West Country for the rest of his life. Queen Victoria was appreciative of his unassuming manner and the modest way in which he told of the events at the defence of Rorke's Drift, and it was said at the time when he submitted his official report, which was modest and to the point, that 'He has spoken of everybody but himself.'

However, John Chard may have been too modest for his own good, and seems to have been a man with no particular ambitions. Some senior officers, including General Wolseley, who was not a supporter of the awarding of gallantry medals, and General Buller, a fellow West Countryman, made less than complimentary remarks about his ability in the field, and some unnecessary personal insults, and Captain Walter Jones of the Royal Engineers, who was a friend, said of him,

> He is a most amiable fellow ... but as a Company Officer he is so hopelessly slow and slack ... With such a start as he got, he stuck to the company doing nothing. In his place I should have gone up to Lord Chelmsford and asked for an appointment. He must have got it, and if not he could have gone home soon after Rorke's Drift, at the height of his popularity and done splendidly at home. I advised him, but he placidly smokes his pipe and does nothing.

His niece, Dorothy, who remembered him from when she was a child, recalled him as a man who never seemed to come to terms with what he had done and never considered his deed to have been as heroic as people thought. Her story of his arrival back in Somerset sums up the type of man he was. Major Chard was met at Taunton by civic dignitaries, and after some speeches he was driven to North Curry, where he was met by crowds waving admiringly. Told by his sister to take off his hat and wave back to them, he reluctantly did so, muttering sheepishly, 'All I did was my duty.'

John Chard never married, but he is known to have had a relationship with a woman called Emily Rowe, who bore a daughter to him at Exeter, believed to have been on 16 February 1882, who was named Violet Mary. Emily Rowe married a man named Lawson Durant, and had a second daughter, Irene, born on 6 January 1884. Emily Durant died in 1939. Violet's birth would have been kept secret because of the stigma of illegitimacy at the time, and because of Chard's fame and association with the Queen. He left an annuity to Emily and Violet for the duration of her lifetime, and the family have preserved two letters written by Chard and addressed to Emily telling her about his trip to Japan. At his funeral it was recorded that an anonymous wreath bearing the inscription 'that day he did his duty', took pride of place beside a tribute from Queen Victoria on the coffin.

In January 1880 he began service at Devonport, before proceeding to Cyprus in December 1881, where he was appointed regimental major on 17 July 1886, and during which time his mother died in 1885. He returned home in March 1887. He was posted to Fulwood Barracks in Preston in May 1887, remaining there until being posted to Singapore on 14 December 1892, where he was commanding Royal Engineer for three years, and was promoted lieutenant-colonel on 18 January 1893. On his return to Britain in January 1896, he took up his final post as Commanding Royal Engineer at the Perth District. In May that year he presented Queen Victoria with Japanese mementoes he had brought back for her. He was promoted to colonel on 8 January 1897.

While in Scotland he was found to have cancer of the mouth. In November 1896, he was too ill to visit Balmoral at the request of Queen Victoria, and underwent an operation in Edinburgh. In March 1897 surgeons had to remove his tongue. He was still able to converse quite well, but his condition became critical, and in August 1897 doctors diagnosed that the cancer was terminal. He was placed on sick leave from 8 August 1897. He spent the last days of his life with his brother in the rectory at Hatch Beauchamp, where many friends, including Queen Victoria, expressed their concern about his condition. On 11 July 1897 he had received the Diamond Jubilee Medal and a book containing a signed portrait of his sovereign. After suffering terrible distress towards the end, he died peacefully in his sleep at Hatch Beauchamp Rectory on 1 November 1897, aged 50. He was buried in the churchyard at Hatch Beauchamp, where a rose-coloured marble cross headstone marks the spot. Queen Victoria sent a wreath bearing an inscription written in her own hand, 'A mark of admi-

The chief Royal Engineer lays a wreath in Hatch Beauchamp Churchyard at the final resting place of John Chard during a service to commemorate the centenary of the defence in 1979, which was attended by some of Chard's descendants.

ration and regard for a brave soldier from his sovereign.' There was a wreath from Colonel Bourne, and the officers of the South Wales Borderers, and there were tributes from all over the world. For many years the Queen's wreath lay beneath a memorial window which was placed in Hatch Beauchamp Church. Memorial plaques have been placed in Jesus Chapel at Rochester Cathedral, Kent, and at Othery Church in Somerset. There is a bronze bust of him in Taunton Shire Hall, Somerset and there are items associated with him at the Royal Engineers Museum, Chatham, and the Territorial Army Centre in Swansea has a 'John Chard VC House'.

The location of Chard's Victoria Cross remained a mystery for many years until 1972, when what was described as his South Africa Medal, and a 'cast copy' of his VC were offered for auction in London. Sir Stanley Baker, who had portrayed Chard in the film *Zulu!*, purchased the set for £2,700. It was offered for auction again in 1996, and one of the most extraordinary stories in the history of the VC began to unfold. Prompted by the mystery surrounding the whereabouts of the original Victoria Cross, the auctioneers decided to send it to the Royal Armouries at Leeds to be examined. The tests revealed it to be identical to all authentic VCs cast from the cascobels of cannon captured by British forces in the East, and therefore proved to be the genuine original medal. It is now in the medal collection owned by Lord Ashcroft.

Charles Robson

Charles John Robson was born on 7 January 1855, at 7 Ebury Mews, Belgravia, London, the son of George Robson, a coachman, and his first wife, Ann (formerly Dieper). He had five older sisters. In 1871 they lived at 16 Bloomsbury Street, Westminster, and his father was working as an ostler.

Charles left his job as a groom, and enlisted into the Corps of Royal Engineers at Bow Street Police Court on 30 April 1873, suggesting that he chose a stretch with Her Majesty's army, as opposed to a stretch at Her Majesty's pleasure. He was described as being five feet five inches tall, and weighing 133 pounds. He had a fresh complexion, grey eyes and brown hair. He had several scars on his neck and between his shoulder blades and his muscular development was average. 12046 Driver Robson was sent to Aldershot, being posted to 'B' troop (Equipment) RE Train. He spent three days in jail at Aldershot in January 1874 for some petty misdemeanour which is unrecorded, and would be the only blemish on his army career, and he was in hospital on several occasions suffering with a variety of ailments. In October 1874 his mother had fallen down some stairs which left her paralysed, and she died a month later.

Charles Robson was Lieutenant Chard's batman. He spent most of his time during the defence shooting down Zulus who were trying to ransack the Royal Engineers' wagon.

Lieutenant John Chard joined the company on 18 April 1876, and Charles was detailed as his batman and groom. He received good conduct pay of one penny a day from 13 September 1876. On 2 December 1878, he and his officer accompanied the 5th company as they boarded the SS *Walmer Castle* bound for active service in South Africa. They arrived in Durban on 4 January 1879, where they were greeted by a torrential downpour in which they had to unload hundreds of tons of stores and equipment. Lieutenant Chard and Driver Robson, a corporal and three sappers, were ordered to go up to Rorke's Drift post to repair the pontoon bridge across the Buffalo River. A small mule train was organised on which the men and their equipment were loaded. Chard rode on horseback with Charles on his spare mount.

On the morning of 22 January the engineers rode to Isandlwana, where they saw Zulus on the distant hills. He and his officer rode back to Rorke's Drift, leaving the other men at the base camp. During the defence he placed himself behind the stone kraal at the eastern end of the defences where he could fire at the Zulus who were trying to ransack the Engineers' wagon. He told Chard that during the fighting 'I was protecting our things.'

Charles remained at Rorke's Drift for several weeks to work on a more permanent fortification of the garrison. On 4 July 1879, he and his officer were in the British square at the Battle of Ulundi, for the final devastating defeat of the Zulus. Following the cessation of hostilities the 5th Company moved to Saint Paul's Mission, where they were occupied in building another fortified position. They embarked aboard the SS *Eagle* and arrived in Portsmouth on 2 October. They were met as heroes, and Charles accompanied his officer on many official engagements, including a trip to Balmoral for an audience with Queen Victoria.

He transferred to the 7th Field Company at Chatham in February 1880. However, when the 7th Company left for Natal in 1881, he decided to leave the army and discharged to the Reserve from the 11th Field Company on 20 June 1881. However, in September 1881, he began a new job at the Chatham barracks as a civilian groom and general servant to Captain C.H. Gordon RE. He accompanied his officer to Cork, and when his officer returned to Chatham in July 1882 they parted company. He was re-called to the Colours on 2 August 1882, and posted to Aldershot as batman to Lieutenant Maude. He received two pence good conduct pay from that date, and on 13 November 1882, he re-engaged to serve a further twelve years. He received his final discharge on 30 April 1894.

Charles met Jane Elizabeth Farrand in Aldershot, and they married at Hale Parish Church in Surrey on 13 May 1883. He and Jane both gave their address as Heath End, Hale, and by 1891 they had moved to 8 Perowne Street, Aldershot, and it was there on 22 June 1891 that their only child, Annie Lilian,

Major Chard seated in foreground, with his batman Charles Robson at the back in uniform and wearing a rosette. This picture was probably taken during Chard's tour of the West Country on his arrival back in England.

was born. The family moved to Orchard Road in Dorking, Surrey, and by 1901 they had moved to Ceres Road in Plumstead, before settling at 43 Swingate Street in Plumstead, where he kept a chicken house, grew a grapevine and enjoyed smoking his variety of pipes. Charles and Jane worked in the Royal Arsenal during the First World War, and in 1917 Annie, then Mrs Peter Ewart, gave them a grandson, Edwin Peter, who remembered his 'kind, solidly-built' grandfather with great respect.

Charles Robson died on 19 July 1933, at St Nicholas Hospital in Plumstead, the cause of death being 'cerebral embolism'. He was 78, and he had been married to Jane for 50 years. He was buried in an unmarked common grave in Plumstead Old Cemetery. A hand-carved wooden marker plaque was placed at the grave site on 22 January 1993, and in 1999 a more permanent memorial plaque was placed at the grave by the Royal Engineers Association.

General Staff

George Mabin

George William Mabin was born on 5 October 1848, the oldest of seven children born to George Jellard Mabin and his first wife Frances (formerly Howe). His father was a mariner, who had become the landlord of The Plough public house in Culver Street, Bristol. On George's seventh birthday, his father composed a special acrostic poem for him. While George senior was at sea in 1855, Frances became the licensee of the Royal Oak in Charles Street, Bristol, and on his return the family moved to 14 Elbroad Street, Bristol, where George earned a living as a sail-maker, before taking over the Elephant and Castle in Merchant Street, Bristol. Frances died in 1865.

They were living at the Bay Horse in Lewin's Mead, Bristol, when George enlisted into the Rifle Brigade (Prince Consort's Own), on 29 May 1868. He was five feet six-and-a-half inches tall, with a fresh complexion, grey eyes and brown hair. He had 'two small blue dots on his left forearm'. 1566 Private Mabin gained a 2nd Class Certificate of Education on 29 November 1869, and was promoted corporal on 3 July 1870. He was appointed military staff clerk

George Mabin was a member of the general staff doing duties as a clerk at Rorke's Drift when he received news that the camp at Isandlwana had been taken by the enemy and a wing of the Zulu army was on its way to attack the small outpost.

on 20 May 1872, and promoted sergeant, being promoted colour-sergeant on 20 May 1875.

He had been posted to Dover on 30 August 1870, where he met Mary Elizabeth Ranger, and they were married at St Mary's Church on 3 January 1872. Three children were born in the next few years: George Gerrard in Manchester in 1873, Florence Gertrude in Dover in 1875, and Samuel Edward in Dover in 1877.

Colour-Sergeant Mabin was appointed to the district officer at the Cape of Good Hope on 6 June 1878, and sailed to South Africa on the SS *Nubian*. His wife apparently went with him, and he was serving at Rorke's Drift on 22 January 1879. In an account given in 1914, he stated

> I was sitting at my office tent door at the station, we did not expect any trouble. Just after three in the afternoon, a man, hatless and bootless, rode up on an exhausted horse; he halted at the tent and I immediately asked him what had occurred. 'Good God, the camp is taken and they are coming here!' We had scarcely finished our preparations when the approaching Zulus were observed coming round the spur of the Oscarberg Mountain. There were eighty-six of us bearing arms, and we prepared to sell our lives as dearly as possible. The first man I ever killed in my life was a big Zulu. As he advanced he took cover behind anything that presented itself. He dropped behind a rock prior to making another rush, when I covered the rock with my rifle, and as he rose to come out again I pulled the trigger, and he leaped at least five feet in the air and dropped dead. About seven in the evening the Zulus attempted to fire the hospital, lighting tufts of grass and attaching these to their assegais and throwing them into the thatched roof of the building which was soon alight. The flames, as a matter of fact, aided us, because by their light we were able to distinguish the Zulu as they formed into bodies for succeeding rushes. I was on the look-out and discovered a movement on the Zululand side of the river. Owing to the light, I could not determine what was happening; whether they be friends or enemies approaching. But in the next ten minutes I found they were mounted men, and to our intense joy it proved to be the General at the head of the remainder of the column, and their approach was the signal for the full flight of the Zulus.

George stated that his only wound was a very slight one on the shin, made by a spent cartridge. He was promoted to sergeant-major on 19 February 1880, being appointed superintendent clerk to the General's Staff at Fort Napier, Pietermaritzburg, where the aptly named Albert Napier was born in 1880.

Sergeant-Major Mabin saw active service during the uprising in the Transvaal in 1881. He was present at the engagement with Boer commando units at

Sergeant-Major Mabin received the Cape of Good Hope Meritorious Service Medal on his retirement from an unblemished military career in 1898.

Laing's Nek on 28 January, at Ingogo on 8 February, and he was standing close to General Colley when he was shot dead during the disastrous engagement at Majuba Hill on 27 February. It was during this campaign that George earned himself the nickname 'The Fighting Clerk.'

He was posted back to England, and in December 1882, William was born at 6 North View, Stapleton Road, Bristol. By 1884 he was garrisoned at The Castle in Cape Town, where five more children were born: Frances Mary Catherine in 1884; Reginald Victor in 1886; Blanche Amy in 1888; Harold Edgar in 1890; Maud Millicent in 1893 and Gladys Elsie in 1897. Sergeant-Major Mabin was discharged at Aldershot on 31 May 1898, after an unblemished military career. He received the Cape of Good Hope Meritorious Service Medal with an annuity.

He returned to South Africa as a civilian in 1900, where he took employment as a clerk for the Governor of the Cape. His wife died in 1906, at their home at 20 Williams Street, Cape Town.

A few years later George married Sarah Annie Stroud, but he was widowed again in 1920. He developed malignant tumours on his thigh and lung, and on 30 October 1938 he underwent an operation at the Groote Schuur Hospital in Cape Town (famous for the world's first heart transplant). However, he did not fully recover and died on 11 November. He was buried alongside his wives in the family plot at Maitland Cemetery in Cape Town. His obituary described him as 'an exemplary husband and father, a soldier, and a veteran of Rorke's Drift.'

The Royal Regiment of Artillery

John Cantwell

John Cantwell was born in May 1845, at St James's parish, Dublin, the son of John Cantwell. He was employed as a servant before enlisting into the 9th Regiment, on 6 November 1868, at the age of 23 years and six months. 1740 Private Cantwell was described as being five feet eight inches tall, with a fresh complexion, hazel eyes and light-brown hair, and had 'marks of cupping over his left scapula.' He gave his next of kin as his sister, Mary, of Melbourne, Australia.

He transferred to the Royal Regiment of Artillery with the regimental number 2076 on 1 April 1872, serving at home until 5 July 1872, when he sailed to the island of St Helena. He gained a 4th Class Certificate of Education on 7 July 1875, and on 16 August 1876 he gained leave to marry Caroline Margaret Dickinson at the Ladder Hill Garrison, Jamestown, St Helena. His new wife was a 22-year-old seamstress, and they had two children. He returned home on 14 September 1876 and joined N Battery, 5th Brigade, as 23182 Gunner Cantwell, on 1 July 1877. He passed a wheelers course on 4 January 1878.

The unit received orders for active service in South Africa and embarked on the troopship *Dublin Castle* on 9 January 1878. They arrived at the port of East London, and marched to King Williamstown, arriving there on 11 February 1878, to find that much of the heavy baggage transported by sea had been broken into. From there they moved to various places in the colony, where they saw active service in the 9th Cape Frontier War.

He was promoted bombardier wheeler on 29 July 1878. Between July and September the Battery marched from the Transkei to Greytown, pausing for a while at Kokstad. By 3 September 1878 they had moved to Natal, and on 2 November 1878 the Battery was given orders to move to Greytown. They arrived at Helpmekaar in December 1878, where they received the order to move up to the Zululand border at Rorke's Drift.

John had reverted back to gunner on 21 January 1879, and he is believed to have been the artillery storeman at Rorke's Drift, probably defending the store building during the battle. When the hospital was being evacuated he saw one of his NCO comrades, Bombardier Lewis, struggling desperately on his hands and knees trying to get from the hospital to the inner entrenchment, with

Zulus scaling the barricade to attack him, so he risked his life to go out and assist him.

He returned to St Helena from South Africa on 15 May 1879, and arrived at the general depot at Woolwich on 4 July that year, which was the day British troops defeated the Zulu army at Ulundi and brought the conflict to a close. On 11 February 1880 he was recommended to receive the silver medal for distinguished conduct in the field for his bravery during the defence, and he was presented with the medal by Queen Victoria at Windsor Castle on 8 March 1880. He also received the South Africa Medal with 1877-78-79 clasp.

His next postings were to Malta from 15 December 1880 until 2 October 1884, and to India from 3 October 1884 until 18 January 1886. As 3460 Gunner Cantwell he served with the 10th Brigade, Royal Artillery, and as 3760 Gunner Cantwell he served with the 9th Brigade. He served at home from 19 January 1886 until 19 July 1887, when he was discharged from the Woolwich depot: 'In consequence of his having been found medically unfit for further service', his character being described as 'very good'.

His intended place of residence was 2 Phillipa Street in Woolwich, and within a month he was appointed by the Secretary of State for War to join the Civil Service, being employed in the engineering department of the Royal Gunpowder Factory at Waltham Abbey, where former-General Noble of the Royal Artillery was the superintendent. He was employed there for over five years. However, his wife's health began to fail and he was recommended to go to South Africa, so he resigned and sailed to the Cape on 5 November 1892, where he lived at 8 Picciones Buildings, Loop Street, Durban. He was employed as a prison officer at the Central Prison in Addington, Durban, from 6 January–6 May 1893, on a salary of £10 a month, until Sir Charles Mitchell appointed him warder at the Central Prison in Pietermaritzburg. He had applied for a transfer back to Durban, when, on 10 August 1898, he was assaulted by one of the inmates, a 'lifer' named A. Dubois, which left him with an enlarged spleen from which he never fully recovered. Having had his pension commuted on 12 December 1895, and no further payments being made to him, he is known to have greatly annoyed his employers for his constant requests for an increase in his pension, which possibly influenced their punishment of Dubois, who only received five days in solitary confinement on half-rations. He then left the prison service and took employment as a lavatory cleaner, but he considered the hours too long, and by 24 March 1900 he had ceased this type of work.

John Cantwell was living at 2nd Avenue, Georgeville, Durban, when he was admitted to the Addington Hospital in Durban, where he died on 14 August 1900, aged 55 (the death certificate states his age as 53). Cause of death was 'hypertrophy of the spleen and valvular cease of the heart.' His daughter, Mrs J.F. Webb, is mentioned on the death certificate, and his effects amounted to 'furniture and one old suit.' He was buried at the Roman Catholic churchyard in Durban.

In 1935, through the Durham Light Infantry Comrades Association, Caroline Cantwell, then aged about 80, presented copies of a 'Roll of Defenders' compiled by Lieutenant Chard after the defence, to the South Wales Borderers Museum at Brecon. A forensic handwriting expert has since suggested that the roll may have actually been compiled by John Cantwell. The whereabouts of his Distinguished Conduct Medal and his South Africa Campaign Medal are not known, but his Long Service, Good Conduct Medal was sold to a private collector at Dix-Noonan-Webb auctioneers, on 28 March 2002.

Abraham Evans

Abraham Evans was born on 7 February 1855 in Twyn-y-ffrwd, near Pontypool, and was baptised on 17 March 1855, at the Park Terrace Methodist Chapel. He was the third of five sons in a family of eight children born to James Evans, a coal miner, and his wife Winifred (formerly Bratt). James was joined at the pit by his three eldest sons, including Abraham. His father died in 1873.

Abraham enlisted into the Royal Regiment of Artillery at Newport. 1643 Gunner Evans was posted to 'K' Battery, 16th Brigade, at Woolwich. However,

The grave of Abraham Evans was renovated and a memorial stone was erected at a rededication service held in 2001.

the unit became 'F' Battery, 24th Brigade on 1 April 1874, and on 1 July 1877 it became known as 'N' Battery, 5th Brigade. Gunner Evans was awarded a penny a day good conduct pay from 7 January 1878. The unit received orders for active service in South Africa and embarked on the troopship *Dublin Castle* on 9 January 1878. They arrived at King Williamstown on 11 February 1878, to find that much of the heavy baggage had been ransacked. The unit saw active service in the 9th Cape Frontier War, which ended in July 1878, and on 2 November the Battery was given orders to move to Greytown. They moved to Helpmekaar, followed by the order to move up to the Zululand border at Rorke's Drift.

Gunner Evans was confined in hospital at Rorke's Drift suffering from dysentery, and during the defence he occupied the north-west corner room of the building with Gunner Howard. The room had access to the veranda and a window from where the two gunners shot at the Zulus who massed at the front of the hospital. When the roof was set on fire and the situation became hopeless, Gunner Evans noticed a lull in the action and seized the opportunity to run out of the front of the hospital and reach the comparative safety of the inner entrenchment.

Abraham and the other sick and wounded men were evacuated to Helpmekaar, where 'N' Battery was camped, having been withdrawn from the field. When he returned to duty Abraham rejoined his battery; in June of that year Prince Louis Napoleon was killed by Zulus while he was out on patrol, and Abraham was on parade as the Prince's body left for transportation to England. Between July and October 1879, 'N' Battery was in the Northern Transvaal, where Gunner Evans saw action against Chief Sekhukhune and the Pedi tribe, at which time he received news that his brother, Paul, had fallen down a pit shaft and been killed.

On 14 November 1880, N/5 was moved to Potchefstroom, where work began to reinforce the old fort on 22 November. On 16 December 1880, the first shots of the First Boer War were fired when Boer commando units laid siege to the town. During the siege Abraham was laid low with typhoid fever, and on 11 March 1881 he was hit in the back by a sniper bullet. The siege ended amicably on 23 March 1881. The Battery was inspected by Queen Victoria at Hay-on-Wye on 3 July 1882, and Abraham was brought to the attention of the Queen as being a defender of Rorke's Drift.

He requested service in Egypt, and as 10148 Gunner Evans he was posted to 'I' Battery, 2nd Brigade, 2nd Division, and embarked aboard the troopship *City of London* on 8 August 1882, arriving in Alexandria on 22 August. By 13 September 1882 he was fighting at Tel-el-Kebir. While stationed at Abbussigeh Camp in Cairo, he sent an eighteen-verse poem to Mary Ann Williams which he had composed, entitled: 'Recitation on Egypt'. The muster roll for 1883 shows Abraham in receipt of two pence a day good conduct pay. Abraham received his final discharge at Woolwich on 19 April 1883. He had earned the South Africa Medal with 1877-8-9 clasp, the Egypt Medal with Tel-el-Kebir clasp, and the Khedives Bronze Star with Egypt 1882 clasp.

Abraham returned to the home of his mother in Harpers Road, Victoria Village, Garndiffaith, and settled back into his former life as a coal miner in Trevethin. He married Mary Ann at the parish church in Trevethin on 5 November 1883, and they lived in Cwmavon Road, Garndiffaith. They moved to The Balance, Varteg, Abersychan, finally settling at Spring Gardens in Varteg. They had eight children: Benjamin James born in 1884; Mary Valentine born in ?; Maggie Hannah born in 1889; Elizabeth Ann born in 1891; Rachel Tye born in 1892; Emma born in 1894; John Leslie born in 1897; and Alice Maud born in 1899. He wrote a letter to the *Free Press of Monmouthshire* which was published on 18 April 1913, and on 20 May 1914 the *Western Mail* published a story about him.

Abraham Evans died at his home in Spring Gardens, Monmouthshire, on 4 May 1915, aged 60. The cause of death was given as 'hepatic disease' (liver disease). He was buried in an unmarked grave at the Chapel Yard, Varteg, Abersychan. Mary Ann died in 1946 and was buried with him. The grave was rediscovered, neglected and overgrown. The site was renovated and a memorial stone was erected at a rededication service held on 17 November 2001. It was reported that 'Royal British Legion and other ex-service standards including those of the South Wales Borderers dipped smartly as a stone was unveiled at the head of the soldier's grave.' However, the new stone was destroyed by vandals and after the 'Gunner Evans Memorial Fund' was set up by various organisations, a replacement memorial was erected in 2002.

Arthur Howard

Arthur Howard was born on 2 May 1851 at Eynsford (pronounced 'Ainsford'), near Swanley in Kent. He was the second son in a family of five children born to William Howard, an agricultural labourer, and his wife Maria (formerly Tucker). All the Howard children were educated at the Eynsford village school.

Arthur began his working life as an agricultural labourer before becoming a groom, but by the beginning of 1871 he was unemployed. Consequently, on 28 April 1871, he enlisted in the Royal Regiment of Artillery at Woolwich Barracks, London. He was described as being five feet six-and-three-quarter inches tall, with a fresh complexion, hazel eyes and brown hair. His chest measurement was 34 inches, and he weighed 140 pounds. His muscular development was good and he had no distinctive marks.

He was posted to the 14th Brigade at Woolwich, where 2077 Gunner Howard transferred to the 15th Brigade, being posted to Newcastle-upon-Tyne on 20 August 1872. He was admitted to hospital for ten days in May 1873, suffering with primary syphilis. He was posted back to Woolwich on 5 May 1874, where he was back in hospital from 22 July until 14 August, being treated for ulcers on the left ankle. He was admitted to hospital with the same complaint on 9 January 1875, and discharged on 15 February 1875. On 17 April of that year he was posted to Newlodge in Ireland. He transferred back to the 14th Brigade on 29 April 1877, and on 1 August 1877 he transferred to the 5th Brigade, where he became the servant and batman to Major Arthur Harness.

The unit received orders for active service in South Africa and embarked on the troopship *Dublin Castle* on 9 January 1878. They arrived at King Williamstown on 11 February 1878, and as previously mentioned found the baggage ransacked; Gunner Howard was annoyed to find that his two sets of servant's clothes had been stolen, along with a clock belonging to Major Harness. The unit saw active service in the 9th Cape Frontier War, and on 2 November the Battery was given orders to move to Greytown. They then moved to Helpmekaar, followed by the order to move up Rorke's Drift, where Arthur was admitted to the hospital on 18 January suffering with fever.

During the defence of Rorke's Drift he occupied the north-west corner room of the hospital building with Gunner Evans, and borrowed Sergeant Maxfield's rifle. The room had access to the veranda and a window from where the two gunners shot at the Zulus who massed at the front of the hospital. When the roof was set on fire and the situation became hopeless, they decided to take a chance and ran out of the front of the building. However, Gunner Howard ran the wrong way, and found himself almost face to face with mad-dened Zulus. He jumped over the breastwork, crawled into the bushes and hid in the shadows. He stayed there throughout the night not daring to move, with Zulus almost trampling on him, but he remained undetected and went into the fort next day. On 7 February 1879, he wrote a letter to his family from Helpmekaar describing the events, which was printed in the *Daily Telegraph* on 25 March 1879, apparently to his dissatisfaction.

Arthur developed a good relationship with Major Harness. In a letter the Major joked: 'Arthur Howard's correspondence is so large that I tell him he must provide separate mail arrangements, and that no government can stand the pressure he puts upon it.' By June 1879 Major Harness and Gunner Howard were camped on the banks of the Upoko River, and they were present at the Battle of Ulundi on 4 July. Harness describes Arthur as 'always anxious to have a clothes-washing, in order, as he calls it, that we may start clean.' In a letter dated 7 September 1879, he hinted to his sister that he wanted Arthur to remain as his servant on his return home

Arthur Howard is with me here. I have not mentioned to him my hope of getting leave, but if successful I intend telling him and getting him a passage home on a troopship if he likes to come. I have not made up my mind which is best; I shall send him to his friends of course on landing in England, I don't suppose you want him roaming about the village and garden.

On 14 October 1879 they boarded the *Edinburgh Castle* and arrived in Plymouth on 14 November 1879. They were posted to Hillsborough Barracks at Nether Hallam in Sheffield, and then to the Cadets Academy on Woolwich Common in 1882. Arthur had met a pantry maid called Frances Bird in Sheffield, and he found accommodation for her at 3 Woolwich Common. They married at the register office in Woolwich on 24 May 1882. They had one child, who was known as Elsie, born in 1883, before Frances died of pneumonia in 1889. Leaving Elsie with his sister in Sheffield, Arthur returned to Woolwich, from where he was discharged at his own request on 30 May 1890 with a pension of eleven pence a day. His character was described as 'exemplary'. He obtained lodgings at 11 Adephi Street, Nether Hallam, Sheffield, and found employment as a bookkeeper's clerk.

By 1901 Arthur and Elsie had moved back to Woolwich, where he obtained employment as an ammunition case examiner at the Royal Arsenal factory, and took lodgings at 1 Parry Place, Plumstead. As his sight and general health gradually deteriorated with age, he retired from his job at the Royal Arsenal and took employment as a night watchman. He eventually retired for good and survived on his pension and savings.

On 14 February 1930 the *Daily Mirror* published a report that it had been announced that he had died in Sydney, Australia, after complaining of an old assegai wound received in the historic Drift fight. Arthur expressed great surprise when he was informed of the report. The report went on to say 'Although he is blind, he is an active man, and takes a keen interest in present day affairs. Arthur added:

> I was at Ulundi too, where we beat the Zulu Armies in forty minutes. I never received a wound of any sort from an assegai, or from anything for that matter. How Sydney Art Gallery can have a picture of me leaving the burning hospital carrying another man over my shoulder is more than I can understand. It certainly cannot be a picture of me. It was as much as I could do to leave the building myself, without carrying anyone else. I think the Australian report must be incorrect in the name.

Arthur Howard died on 15 July 1935 at St Alfege Hospital, Vanbrugh Hill, Greenwich, London, aged 84, the cause of his death being reported as senility. His home address at that time was his lodgings at 7 Harton Street, Deptford,

London SE8. He was buried in an unmarked grave in Brockley Cemetery, Lewisham, London (plot Y, grave 614), which had been purchased by his land-lord, Walter Tanner.

Thomas Lewis

Thomas Lewis was born on 6 October 1854 at 9 Winston's Row, Llanfaes in Brecon. He was the only son of three children born to Isaac Lewis and his wife Annie (formerly Lloyd). Their occupations were described as 'servants in hus-bandry'. The 1861 census shows them as living at 3 Forge Cottages in Brecon, then they moved to Lower Pontwillim, and in 1871 they lived at Priory Mill House in Brecon.

Brecon being a garrison town, it was not surprising when Thomas enlisted into the army on 24 November 1874. However, he chose the Royal Regiment of Artillery as opposed to his local unit the 24th Regiment, and 458 Gunner Lewis was posted to 'N' Battery, 5th Brigade.

The unit received orders for active service in South Africa and embarked on the troopship *Dublin Castle* on 9 January 1878, taking part in the 9th Cape

Thomas Lewis
Date not known but believed to be Circa 1898-1910

Thomas Lewis was in the hospital at Rorke's Drift having been injured in a wagon accident.

Frontier War, and late in 1878 they received orders to move up to Rorke's Drift to prepare for the invasion of Zululand, and Thomas arrived there having been promoted to bombardier. His older sister, Margaret, married Sergeant George Chambers, an Instructor of Musketry with the 1st/24th Regiment. He was also stationed at Rorke's Drift and moved on to Isandlwana with his regiment, where he was killed in action on 22 January 1879.

Thomas was in the hospital at Rorke's Drift having been injured in a wagon accident. His thigh and all down one leg were painfully swollen. During the defence he managed to escape from the hospital through a window, and a letter by Private David Jenkins stated

> Dear Father, please go personally or write a letter to Isaac Lewis, Pendre, Brecon and tell him that … His son Thomas is alive but is still in hospital with the fever. He had a very narrow escape. He crept on his hands and knees and came from the hospital to the fort through all the firing.

Gunner Cantwell saw that Thomas was in great peril from warriors who were climbing over the breastwork to get at them, so he ran out and assisted him.

Thomas remained in South Africa, and on 14 November 1880 N/5 was moved to Potchefstroom, where there was fear of a Boer uprising and work was begun to reinforce the old fort on 22 November. On 16 December 1880 the first shots of the first Boer War were fired at Potchefstroom when Boer commando units began to lay siege to the town. The siege ended amicably on 23 March 1881. On 24 April 1881, he was tried and sentenced to be reduced to gunner, with the loss of good conduct pay, we do not know why. However, on 19 December 1881 his good conduct pay was restored and back-dated for 225 days.

Because his service papers have not survived his date of discharge is not known. In civilian life his first job was a prison officer, but he resigned from the prison service, apparently being unhappy with the treatment of prisoners. He gained employment with the local transport company driving horse-drawn trams in Highgate, London, refusing to use a whip on any of his horses, and when the age of the motor engine began to make its mark his new job description was that of a motorman.

He met a nurse named Annie Price and they married. Annie suffered more than one miscarriage before giving birth to her first child, Thomas, born in 1898 at 6 Eton Grove, Islington. He was followed by Gladys, born in 1899 at 7 Hampden Court, Islington, Rita, born in 1901 at 34 Despard Road, Islington, and Irene, born in 1903 but who died the following year. Florentina was born in 1905, and in the summer of 1910 Annie announced that she was expecting another child.

On 12 August 1910 Thomas suffered severe stomach pains and vomiting, and was admitted to the Richmond Ward of The London Hospital, Whitechapel ten days later; on 23 August he was operated on by Surgeon Hugh Rigby to remove his appendix. On 30 August, after he had suffered great pain, it was decided to remove four stitches from his wound to insert a tube to syringe it internally with carbolic. On the following evening his wound was reopened by the surgeon who found a new pelvic abscess. The hospital notes of 12 September state that Thomas was reported to be 'going on nicely'. However, on the following day Mr Rigby found it necessary to operate on him again. The nursing reports on 26 September state: 'a fair amount of discharge was still being drained from the wound, but the patient felt well in himself.' The last entry in the nursing notes was on 19 October, which stated: 'discharge diminishing by day.'

Thomas had been in hospital for 71 days, and on 1 November he showed signs of recovery. He was sat in a chair in the ward reading a book waiting to be discharged when he collapsed and died. According to his death certificate Thomas had died of a pulmonary embolism (blood clot) aged 56. However, the post mortem report state findings of 'small amounts of fibrin along a sinus which leads to a puss-soaked gauze swab.' The surgeon had left a swab inside the wound following one of the operations, which had caused infection. He was buried on 5 November 1910, in Highgate Cemetery (grave: 37970).

2nd Battalion, 3rd Regiment (The Buffs)

Frederick Millne

Frederick Augustus Millne was born on 18 February 1854 at 2 Suffolk Place, Holly Street, Hackney in London. He was the only child of David George Millne and his wife Mary Ann (formerly Slate). Mary died in 1857, and within a year David married her sister, Frederick's aunt, Louisa Marie, and they had three children. Fred was reasonably well educated and when he left school he became a clerk.

He enlisted into the 2nd Battalion, 3rd Regiment (The Buffs), at Lambeth, on 4 June 1872. 2260 Private Millne was five feet five-and-a-half inches tall, with a chest measurement of 34.5 inches. He had a fair complexion, grey eyes and brown hair. It was noted that he had his own initials tattooed on his left forearm. He gave his age as eighteen years and two months and his religion as Church of England. Promotions came fast, and Fred was promoted corporal on 24 February 1873, lance-sergeant on 1 April 1876, and sergeant on 6 July of the same year. He received a 2nd Class Certificate of Education on 1 March 1876.

In 1876 the 2nd Battalion, 3rd Regiment, received orders for active service in South Africa, and he and his unit set sail from Dublin aboard the troopship *St Lawrence*. The passage was an uncomfortable affair, and on 8 November 1876 the ship struck a reef about 90 miles north of Cape Town. They were forced to abandon ship before it sank, with no loss of life, but nine mountain guns, 50 tons of gunpowder and 1,000 pounds worth of government rations went down with her. Some newspapers listed Sergeant Millne as having been 'lost', so he held the dubious honour of being one of the few men to read his own obituary after the shipwreck.

On the outbreak of the Zulu War The 3rd Buffs were attached to the 1st Column, under Colonel Pearson, 3rd Buffs, which was to cross the river border at the Lower Drift. However, Sergeant Millne probably became attached to Lieutenant Newnham-Davis's unit of mounted infantry which was detached from the Battalion on scouting and reconnaissance duties, and he must have remained at Rorke's Drift when the unit moved on to Isandlwana, maintaining the ponts and waiting for a party of Royal Engineers to arrive.

Frederick Millne was the only soldier of the 3rd Regiment present at the defence of Rorke's Drift. He had been helping to maintain the ferry with the Royal Engineers, and on learning of the Zulu advance he was one of the men who volunteered to moor the ponts in the middle of the river and defend them from the decks. Lieutenant Chard also requested him to post himself in the storehouse, where he was to protect two caskets of rum, with strict orders to shoot any man who tried to touch them.

In his official report Lieutenant Chard stated

I desire here to mention for approval the offer of these pont guards, Daniels and Sergeant Milne, of the 3rd Buffs, who, with their comrades, volunteered to moor the ponts out in the middle of the stream, and there to defend them from the decks, with a few men to assist.

However, as Reverend Smith stated: 'Our defensive force was too small for any to be spared, and these men subsequently did good service within the fort.'

Lieutenant Chard also requested Sergeant Millne to post himself in the storehouse, where he was to protect two caskets of rum, with strict orders to shoot any man who tried to touch them. A trooper of the Natal Carbineers named J.P. Symons later said

The men spoke very highly of Chard, and another man named Millne. He ought to get the Victoria Cross. For when the men were distracted with thirst and parched with dust from the thatch and smoke, they went to breach a cask of rum, but this man stood upon it and threatened to shoot any man who touched it.

The 2nd Battalion, East Kent Regiment, formed part of the British square which inflicted the final crushing defeat of the Zulu Army at Ulundi. For his service Sergeant Millne received the South Africa Medal with 1879 clasp. Fred was promoted to colour-sergeant on 1 October 1879, but he reverted to sergeant at his own request in 1882, being promoted back to colour-sergeant on 11 January 1883. He served in Singapore and Hong Kong, where he won 40,000 dollars on the lottery. He purchased his discharge on 15 December 1883, and gained employment as an instructor with the Shangai Municipal Police.

On returning to England, Fred lived with his aunt-cum-step-mother, Louisa, and her family, at 1 Camden Villas, Sebastopol Road, Edmonton, London. This placed him in an emotional dilemma when he became involved with his own cousin and half-sister, Catherine, who was thirteen years his junior, and they married at Edmonton Parish Church, on 2 April 1889.

He entered into a business partnership with Stephen White as joint proprietors of a grocery store in Dale Road, Matlock. It is listed in Kelly's 1891 directory as 'White and Millne, wholesale and retail family grocers and tea dealers, wine and spirit merchants, and mineral water manufacturers.' They had a daughter named Catherine in 1890, and the 1891 census shows Frederick and his family living at 'The Beehive'. It is uncertain what happened to the business, which only lasted for two years, but it seems that the parting of Frederick and Stephen White was not amicable, and nothing was left of Fred's winnings.

Fred moved to Manchester in 1893, where he gained employment as assistant labour master at the Crumpsall workhouse, before becoming the caretaker at Birley Street Board School in Hulme. The family lodged at the school for a while, where George Frederick was born in 1893. Four girls were also born in Manchester but three of them died very young, the only survivor being Ada Rorke, her second Christian name reflecting the fact that she was born on 22 January 1902.

At the outbreak of the First World War Fred, then aged 60, volunteered for active service with several training battalions of the Lancashire Fusiliers, retaining his old rank of colour-sergeant, and he rose to Regimental Sergeant-Major with the Devonshire Regiment, the unit from which he took his discharge at the age of 65. His son also served in the War. In retirement he became the caretaker at the Princess Road School in Moss Side, where he was described as 'A sturdy gentleman with a small pointed beard.'

Fred died of pneumonia at his home, 5 Lofas Street, Moss Side, on 5 June 1924, aged 71, and he was buried in an unmarked grave at the Southern Cemetery, Manchester (non-Conformist, section H, grave 483). His campaign medal and a commemorative Bible which had belonged to him were sold at a Sotheby's auction in 1990, and on 8 July 2001, a service of commemoration and rededication was held at his grave.

Little is known about Mr Daniells, the civilian ferryman who was one of the men who volunteered to defend the ponts in mid-river with Sergeant Millne, other than he is believed to have died in South Africa.

1st Battalion, 24th (2nd Warwickshire) Regiment

William Beckett

William Beckett was born in Manchester on 27 January 1856, and enlisted there on 14 April 1874. As 135 Private Beckett he was posted to the 2nd Battalion, 24th Regiment, at Brecon, on 17 June 1874, transferring to A Company of the 1st Battalion on 25 November 1874, which was already on active service in South Africa, and he was sent with a draft of the Battalion on 2 August 1877, being stationed at Komga in the Eastern Cape.

He was a patient in the hospital at Rorke's Drift on 22 January, and when the Zulus attacked he was in a room at the far end of the building with a few other invalids which was dangerously exposed to the enemy. He twice managed to escape the Zulus through holes in the walls, but he eventually had to take refuge in a cupboard with Private Waters of the same battalion. When the building was set on fire his situation became perilous so he ran outside.

According to Private Waters, Beckett 'was assegaied right through his stomach, and went into laager next morning. Doctor Reynolds did all he could to save him …' However, Private Beckett had been lying out all night dangerously wounded and exposed to the elements and the doctor 'did not succeed.'

Private William Beckett died of his wounds on 23 January 1879. He was 23 years old. He was buried in the cemetery at Rorke's Drift and his name is inscribed on the monument. For his service he was awarded the South Africa Medal with 1877-8-9 clasps, and his effects were recorded for claim by his next of kin. His South Africa Medal was sold at a Sotheby's auction in 1998, which had been the property of a descendant of the family.

Patrick Desmond

Patrick Desmond was born in Pembrokeshire in about 1857, and enlisted at Fort Hubberstone in Pembrokeshire on 27 March 1875, giving his age as eighteen. The 1881 census records a Patrick Desmond living in Richmond, while there is no Patrick Desmond recorded for Pembrokeshire. If this is the Rorke's Drift man he stated that he was born at Innishannon, County Cork, Ireland.

He enlisted for the army, and as 568 Private Desmond was posted to the 2nd Battalion, 24th Regiment, on 15 April 1875, being transferred to G Company, 1st Battalion, on 15 July 1876, and just over a month later he was part of a unit of reinforcements which sailed to join the battalion for active service in South Africa. While there he was fined, forfeited pay or was imprisoned for drunkenness on numerous occasions from September 1877 to January 1879, and he was also imprisoned by civil power in South Africa from July to October 1878. When he was not in prison he served in the Cape Frontier War.

It was stated in newspapers at the time the unit returned home that 'among the men of the 1st Battalion of the 24th who disembarked were Sergeant Wilson, Lance-Corporal Roy, and Privates Desmond, Payton and Jenkins, who had been to the rear with prisoners.' However, while he was at Rorke's Drift, he was fined for drunkenness on 19 January 1879, and in a letter sent after 13 January, Colour-Sergeant William Edwards of the 1st Battalion, who was killed at Isandlwana, stated that 'a man named Desmond of G Company got 50 lashes for insubordination.' From this it can be presumed that he was in the hospital recovering from the wounds he received during his punishment.

During the defence of Rorke's Drift he was slightly wounded by a slug which passed through the fleshy part of his thumb. His bad behaviour continued after the defence, being fined for drunkenness five times from 22 March–22 August 1879. He was posted with the Battalion to return to England, and arrived at Portsmouth on 2 October 1879. His bad behaviour continued, and he was fined for drunkenness and confined in cells several times in 1880, before being confined in a civil prison for a month. On his release on 15 November 1880 he was struck off and discharged from Pembroke Dock as a worthless character and notorious drunkard. He received the South Africa Medal with 1877-8-9 clasp.

The 1881 census states that a Patrick Desmond, aged 23, and his brother John, aged 18, were living at 1 Marsh Gate Road in Richmond, Surrey, in the home of one Frederick Perkis (probably Perkins). In 1901 he was registered as a pauper inmate at the Union Workhouse of St George's in Hanover Square, London. His campaign medal was requested to be forfeited by order dated 19 June 1906, but there is no record of it having been returned.

William Horrigan

William Horrigan was born in Cork, Ireland, in 1849. He enlisted into the 24th Regiment on 12 November 1863, and as 1861 Private Horrigan was posted to the 1st Battalion. He was just over fourteen and a half years old. He re-engaged at Gibraltar 18 February 1873, and served in the 9th Cape Frontier War, being stationed at East London in August and September 1877.

He may have originally been one of the men of G Company 'who had been to the rear with prisoners' but he was in the hospital at Rorke's Drift during the defence. He and three other patients, Privates Beckett, Adams and Hayden, were in the far end room of the building which had an outer door and no access to the interior. Privates John Williams and Joseph Williams were posted in the room with orders to defend them. When the Zulus attacked the hospital they began to smash at the door trying to force their way in, and Private Horrigan was able to offer some assistance to keep them out while John Williams smashed a hole in the partition with his bayonet as a means of escape. He escaped through the hole but seems to have got disorientated, and ran straight into the clutches of Zulu warriors entering by way of the veranda. He was seen thrown to the ground and stabbed to death. He was buried in the cemetery at Rorke's Drift and his name is inscribed on the monument. His effects were claimed by his next of kin. For his service he received the South Africa Medal with 1877-8-9 clasp.

David Jenkins

David Jenkins was born in about 1847 in Defynnog, Brecknockshire, Wales. He was the son of Thomas David Jenkins, a tailor and draper. The 1861 census states that he was aged fourteen, and was a boarder at 1 Lower Road, Defynnog, being employed as an apprentice currier to a farmer. He had served with the Carmarthenshire Artillery Militia, and gave up his job as a skinner to enlist for the regular army at Brecon, on 19 June 1874. As 295 Private D. Jenkins he was posted to the 1st Battalion, 24th Regiment. He was five feet five-and-a-half inches tall, with blue eyes and dark brown hair. His religion was Wesleyan.

He served on Gibraltar from 16 October–27 November 1874. He was posted to Cape Town on 28 November 1874. He lost privileges and was imprisoned for breaking out of barracks and going absent without leave several times during 1875, and he was hospitalised several times before being posted to King William's Town on 3 January 1876, where he was hospitalised suffering with a venereal disease. He deserted on 21 November 1876 and was hospitalised from 9 December 1876 with a contusion in the foot after being run over by a wagon when in a state of desertion. He rejoined and was placed in confinement on 8 December 1876, being tried and imprisoned for desertion from 8 December 1877 to 15 April 1878, and his former service towards good conduct pay and pension was forfeited. He was posted to Cape Town on 18 April 1877 where he was hospitalised for a week, and was posted back to King William's Town on 8 August 1877. He served in the Cape Frontier War, being in confinement from 6–9 August 1878, and was imprisoned from 19 August–1 November 1878 for leaving his post while on picquet duty in Natal.

He was present at the defence of Rorke's Drift, where, about two hours into the battle the Zulus launched a particularly fierce assault. Lieutenant Chard was using his revolver to help to keep the enemy at bay when Private Jenkins suddenly ducked the officer's head down as a Zulu slug just missed him. He wrote a letter to his father at the Tanner's Arms, Davynock, on 26 January 1879, which was published in the *Merthyr Express* on 22 March 1879.

> Just a few lines to let you know that I am one of the ten that escaped out of the five companies. The remainder were cut to pieces, – in fact cut in bits – with those savages. Oh I never saw such a sight. Please to pray to God to continue to save my life …

He arrived back in Portsmouth on 2 October 1879 and was posted to Gosport, being hospitalised on 18 October. He was tried and imprisoned for drunkenness before being posted to Colchester on 26 November 1880. He transferred to the 1st Class Army Reserve, Brecon District, on 11 June 1882, his character being described as fair. He was re-called to the colours at Brecon on 1 August 1882 and was posted to Salford on 29 August 1882. He was appointed lance-corporal 1 November 1882 to 7 February 1883, received good conduct pay of a penny a day from 24 January 1883, and obtained a 2nd class certificate of army education. He transferred to Brecon on 8 February 1883 to complete his service, and transferred to the Cardiff District, 11 August 1883 to 24 May 1884. He discharged from the 1st Class Army Reserve Brecon on 10 June 1888.

He married Annie Downey in Battersea, London, on 14 June 1880, giving his address as 7 Howey Street. They had seven boys. Thomas M. was born in 1882, William in 1883, David D. in 1885, Harry W. in 1888, Stanley T. in 1891, Frederick J. in 1894 and John J. in 1896. From 1884 to 1903 the family lived at 52 Bryn Melyn Street, St Marks, Swansea, before moving to 13, where David worked for the Swansea Corporation and Harbour Trust as a clerk and store-keeper. He died at 62 Bryn Melyn Street, Swansea, on 20 August 1912, aged 66, and was buried in Cwmgelli Municipal Cemetery in Swansea (section D grave 945). His wife died in 1939 and is buried with him. There is a memorial stone at the grave.

James Jenkins

James Edmund Jenkins was born on 29 October 1848 at 18 Broad Street, Littledean, near Cinderford, Gloucestershire. He was the third child in a family of six to Griffith Jenkins and his wife Fanny (formerly Limbrick). James, who apparently preferred to be called Edmund, was educated at the local Dame School, Littledean, from about 1855, later attending Littledean Parochial Primary School until he passed his Labour Exam at the age of ten. He started work as a dram boy just before his eleventh birthday in the local iron ore mine, and by 1861 he was labouring in a coal mine.

He enlisted at Monmouth on 18 July 1876, and as 841 Private Jenkins he was posted to the 1st Battalion, 24th Regiment. He was sent with a draft of the Battalion for active service in South Africa, which arrived on 2 August 1877, serving in the Cape Frontier War. He may have originally been one of the men of G Company 'who had been to the rear with prisoners' but he was in the hospital at Rorke's Drift on 22 January 1879, presumably suffering with fever, as Surgeon Reynolds stated 'the only men actually killed in the hospital were three … The names were Sergeant Maxfield, Private Jenkins, both unable to assist in their escape, being debilitated by fever, and Private Adams.' Reverend Smith stated that as the patients were trying to escape from the Zulus through holes in the partitions 'One poor fellow (Jenkins), venturing through one of these was also seized and dragged away …'

He was buried in the cemetery at Rorke's Drift and his name is inscribed on the monument. His effects were claimed by his next of kin. For his service he received the South Africa Medal with 1877-8-9 clasp. There is a memorial at Brecon Cathedral, and his name was added to the family headstone in Littledean. The inscription read 'Also of Edmund, Their son, Who Was Killed In

Battale At Isanduls, Zululand, South Africa, Jan 22nd 1879, Aged 30 Years.' The area was cleared to make way for a play area for the Sunday school children, and the headstone is now against the wall.

Edward Nicholas

Edward Nicholas was born in 1857. He enlisted in Newport on 30 July 1875, stating his age as eighteen, and as 625 Private Nicholas he was posted to the 1st Battalion, 24th Regiment. He was sent with a draft of reinforcements from the Battalion on 2 August 1877 for active service in South Africa, taking part in the Cape Frontier War.

He may have originally been one of the men of G Company 'who had been to the rear with prisoners' but was present at the defence of Rorke's Drift, where he was killed in action by a bullet through the head. He was buried in the cemetery at Rorke's Drift and his name is inscribed on the monument. His effects were recorded for claim by his next of kin. For his service he received the South Africa Medal with 1877-8-9 clasp, which is now regimental property. His name is variably spelt wrong on regimental records with errors such as E. Nicholls and W. Nicholas.

Thomas Parry

Thomas Parry was born on 2 July 1853, at Swainshill Bank, Stretton Sugwas, Herefordshire. He was the son of Thomas Parry, a gardener, and his wife Elizabeth (formerly Nicholls, nee Lewis). He had an older sister named Ellen. He enlisted as 572 Private Parry and was posted to the 1st Battalion, 24th Regiment on 4 April 1875. He transferred to the 2nd Battalion on 22 May 1875, and served in Aldershot and Dover. He was confined to cells for three days in October 1876 and forfeited pay. He was on furlough from 15 February to 14 March 1877, during which time he transferred to D Company of the 1st Battalion, and was sent to South Africa with reinforcements, taking part in the Cape Frontier War.

He is mentioned in an account of Rorke's Drift by John Williams VC, and he wrote a letter to his parents from Helpmekaar on 14 February 1879.

> Then they made their way down to Rorke's Drift where I was with A Company of the 2/24th. We gave them such a warming there they won't forget for some time to come. They kept coming at us all night, but gave it up as a bad job.

The following appeared in the *Merthyr Express* on 12 April 1879:

> This week Mr Thomas Parry, gardener at the Castle Hotel, who had a son in the 24th Foot at Natal, and had given him up as dead, was overjoyed at the receipt of a letter from the young man reporting himself alive and well, and explaining his providential escape. He was groom to Colonel Pulleine, whose horse had got lame, and he took young Parry's horse instead, directing Parry to come along slowly with his own charger. By this exchange Private Parry was delayed on the road so long that he did not reach the camp at all, but was on the march with the lame horse when he met the fugitives, returned to Rorke's Drift, and formed one of the gallant band which repulsed the night attack of the enemy on the evening of the fatal day at Isandula. We hope he will be spared to return to his native country unwounded.

A report also appeared in the *Herefordshire Times* on the same day. He was promoted to corporal on 1 June 1879, but he was confined and reduced to private on 11 August 1879. For his service he received the South Africa Medal with 1877-8-9 clasp.

He was posted to England, being reported absent from 4–7 November 1879, for which he was imprisoned from 25 November–23 December 1879. He transferred to the 1st Class Army Reserve at Cardiff on 31 May 1880, then to Brecon on 25 May 1884. He rejoined the Colours and was posted to the 2nd Battalion, Royal Sussex Regiment depot at Chichester on 14 March 1885. He was posted to Egypt on 12 May 1885, serving at Alsiout and Abbassaieh, before returning to England on 5 January 1886, and was transferred back to the Reserve. He was posted to the 35th Regimental District at Chichester on 20 January 1886, from where he was discharged with good character on 2 April 1887.

On the outbreak of the First World War he tried to re-enlist into the Army Service Corps at Aldershot on 11 September 1915, giving his age as 46. However, on 6 December he was discharged as unfit due to his true age being 60. His address was 19 Corporation Road, Pendown, Merthyr Tydfil, Glamorganshire, his trade was a groom, and he was stated to have had 'Ellen' tattooed on his left forearm. He died of chronic bronchitis at 44 Thomas Street, Merthyr Tydfil, on 13 September 1922, aged 69, his home address being 10 Mill Street, Quakers Yard, Merthyr Tydfil. He was buried in Cefn Cemetery, Merthyr Tydfil (grave J/17) consecrated section.

Thomas Payton

Thomas Payton was aged 23 when he enlisted in Manchester on 12 July 1874, and as 372 Private Payton was posted to the 24th Regiment on 11 October 1874, and joined the 1st Battalion in South Africa. He was stationed in East London in 1877, and received numerous fines for drunkenness throughout 1877. He served in the Cape Frontier War and in the Zulu War. For his service he received the South Africa Medal with 1877-8-9 clasp.

He returned to England with his battalion on 2 October 1879, being transferred to the 1st Class Army Reserve at Gosport on 2 January 1880. His intended place of residence was 7 Planet Street, off Cross Street, Stafford, the town where he is believed to have died.

William Roy

William Roy was born in November 1854 at Portmoak, Scotlandwell, near Kinross, his religion being Church of England. He was the youngest of five sons of James Roy, a ploughman of Orwell near Kinross, and his wife Elisabeth (formerly Buchan), who came from Kent. Their eldest son, also named William, had died in infancy before the second William was born. By 1861 they had moved to Gospetay, Strathmiglo, Fife, where their only daughter was born, and by the mid-1860s they lived at 316 Hawkhill, Dundee.

William left his job as a baker at the Grassmarket in Edinburgh to enlisted into the 32nd Regiment on 8 August 1870, at Edinburgh Castle. He was described as five feet five-and-a-half inches tall, with a fresh complexion, red hair and brown eyes. He weighed 120 pounds, with a chest of 33 inches and good muscular development. 1933 Private Roy arrived in South Africa with his unit on 16 June 1871. He was admitted to hospital at Fort Napier in Pietermaritzburg with a head wound he suffered in a fall when drunk. He then arrived at Mauritius on 18 November 1871 and served for two years and nine months. He contracted malaria and was admitted to hospital for treatment on eight occasions between 12 March 1872 and 9 May 1874. He returned to South Africa on 27 August 1874, where he was admitted to hospital several times for treatment of tonsillitis and primary syphilis. During his service with the 32nd Regiment he twice deserted for periods of fourteen months and four months. He transferred to the 1st Battalion, 24th Regiment on 4 December 1877, regimental number 1522, and served in the Cape Frontier War and the Zulu War.

In a letter home he stated that he was a patient in the hospital at Rorke's Drift suffering with a sore throat, and while he was defending a window at the back of the building he was unaware that the Zulus had broken in at the front.

Private William Roy was a
Scottish-born soldier who part
in the defence of Rorke's Drift,
for which he was awarded the
Distinguished Conduct Medal.

'My rifle got disabled so I fixed my bayonet and charged out of the house.
There were thirty Zulus chasing us but the men in the fort shot them before
they could harm us.' Major Chard particularly mentions Private Roy in both
his official account and the one he submitted to Queen Victoria a year later.
For his conduct in the battle he was mentioned in dispatches and was awarded
the Distinguished Conduct Medal, which he received from Queen Victoria at
Windsor Castle on 9 December 1879. He also received the South Africa Medal
with 1877-8-9 clasp.

He transferred to the 2nd Battalion on 13 August 1879, being promoted
lance-corporal on 22 September 1879, and Corporal on 24 November 1879.
However, a medical examination held at Haslar Hospital in Gosport on 2
October 1879 found him to be suffering from 'opacity of the cornea result-
ing in impairment of vision – the result of syphilis.' He was declared unfit for
further service and discharged on 7 December 1880. His discharge papers state
that his conduct was 'irregular' and his character was 'indifferent and intemperate'. However, his latterly habits were regular and his conduct good and
temperate.

An injury assessment board held at the Royal Hospital, Chelsea, confirmed
his condition, although it was considered that he could contribute to his own
keep, and he was awarded a pension of seven pence a day for a year. The docu-

Private Roy standing far right of picture with the colour-party of the 1st Battalion, 24th Regiment, after presenting the Colours before Queen Victoria at Osborne House on 28 July 1880.

ment states that he was five feet nine-and-a-half inches tall, suggesting that he had grown four inches since he signed on. Being promoted corporal and having gained a 3rd Class Certificate of Education and one good conduct badge, it would seem that he had just started to perform his duties as a good soldier when his eyesight failed him.

His intended place of residence was the Post Office in Gosport, but the 1881 census records that he was living with his parents at 316 Hawkhill, Liff and Benbie, Dundee, being described as a 26-year-old labourer. On 27 October 1882 he married Cecilia Butcher, a domestic servant, of 11 Southerly Street, Dundee, at Brook Street, Broughty Ferry, Monitieth, Dundee. She was the youngest daughter of William Butcher (deceased), the local railway station master, and his wife, Mary (formerly Nicol). William is described as a railway worker.

On the invitation of an older brother, John, who had emigrated to Australia, William boarded the bounty ship SS *Roslyn Castle* at Plymouth and set sail for Sydney, where he arrived on 1 March 1883. Cecilia followed after him aboard the SS *Pericles* as a single woman in her maiden name of Butcher, arriving in Sydney on Christmas Eve 1883. However, by 1887 William was: 'in very sad circumstances, almost blind and helpless', and he was described as 'an invalided inmate of a New South Wales benevolent institution.' On 27 October 1887 a

Grand Military Concert under the patronage of Lord Carrington, Governor and Commander-in-Chief, and attended by the Lord Mayor, was held at the Sydney Exhibition Centre, which raised £120 for his benefit.

William Roy had been living in an asylum when he died on 30 May 1890, of paralysis and arterial decay 'after years of painful illness', at the home of his brother, John, at 182 Hunter Street, Parramatta, near Sydney, aged 35. He was buried in the Mays Hill Baptist Cemetery, Parramatta, 'two of his old comrades from Sydney being among the little band of mourners.'

Henry Turner

Henry Turner was born at Ball Bridge, County Dublin, Ireland, in 1851. He enlisted at Aldershot on 27 March 1874, being described as aged 24, six feet one inch tall, with a fresh complexion, light hazel eyes and brown hair. His trade was given as a bricklayer, later described as a mason, and his religion was Church of England. He was medically examined on the following day, when his birth place was recorded on the medical history sheet as Killeatty, County Wexford, Ireland, and he was found to have a scar on his right cheek from a decaying tooth.

One of the defenders of the hospital cuts down Zulu warriors as they try to force their way into the building to get at the patients.

As 104 Private Turner he was posted to the 2nd Battalion, 24th Regiment on 30 March 1874, before transferring to the 1st Battalion on 26 November. He was granted a penny a day good conduct pay from 30 March 1876, and gained a 1st Class Certificate of Education. He served for nine months on the island of St Helena. When on picquet duty in 1876 he was struck over the left ear by a black bottle, the scar being evident. Since that time he suffered with epilepsy at long intervals, the first attack being at Simonstown, Cape Colony in 1876.

He served in the Cape Frontier War and the Zulu War. He was a patient in the hospital during the defence of Rorke's Drift. For his service he was awarded the South Africa Medal with 1877-8-9 clasp.

He suffered an attack of epilepsy on 17 June 1879, and was admitted into hospital at Pietermaritzburg on 9 July 1879, when a medical board declared him unfit for further service. He suffered an epileptic fit on the ship bringing him home to England, and he had a further attack before being examined at Netley Hospital on 29 January 1880, where it was considered that his disability was permanent and that he would not be able to support himself. He was discharged as unfit for further service on 9 February 1880, and his character was described as good and temperate. An injury assessment board held at the Royal Hospital in Chelsea on 25 May 1880 confirmed that he was suffering from epilepsy and that he had no memory. He was awarded a pension of a shilling a day, which was amended to a permanent award of six pence a day on 11 July 1882.

He was passed into the care of the Surrey County Borough, where he was admitted to Guy's Hospital, London. It is possible this is where he spent the rest of his life due to his disability, as it is unlikely that he was able to work. He died at Guy's Hospital and was buried in the cemetery in the hospital grounds.

John Waters

John Waters was born on 24 December 1839 in Carnaby Street, London, and he was christened on 16 February 1840. He was the second child of four to William Waters, a coach builder, and his wife Ann (formerly Smith). By the time of the 1851 census, the family had moved to 16 Silver Street, Golden Square, Westminster. In 1861 his father was a ship's mate working on the vessel *Industry* moored near Exeter, while John remained in London working as a clerk.

On 7 March 1858 he enlisted at Westminster, and as 447 Private Waters was posted to the 1st Battalion, 24th Regiment, at Chatham. He was described as being five feet five inches tall, with a fresh complexion, hazel eyes and brown hair. His place of birth was given as Lichfield, Staffordshire. The 1861 census shows Private John Waters in barracks at 1st Depot Battalion, Chatham. He was awarded good conduct pay of one penny a day on 3 May 1864, and this was increased to two pence a year later. From 31 March–3 August 1865 the Battalion was stationed at Curragh Camp in Ireland, and from August 1865 to February 1866 at Begger's Bush in Dublin, returning in February to receive their new colours at Curragh Camp, where they remained until August 1866. During August and September 1866 they were garrisoned in Belfast and Londonderry. They sailed for Malta in February 1865, where they were garrisoned in Fort Verdala until February 1868. While in Malta he re-engaged to complete 21 years service on 9 September 1867. In February 1868 the Battalion moved to Floriana Barracks in Malta, and from 23 September 1869 to 29 February 1872 they were garrisoned at Fort Ricasoli. John was promoted to corporal on 10 October 1871, and on 5 March 1872 the Battalion was posted to Gibraltar. In September 1874 he was charged with 'neglect of duty', being tried and confined from 16–26 September of that year, with loss of one penny of his good conduct pay.

On 28 November 1874 the 1st Battalion was posted to South Africa for active service in the Cape Frontier War, and from 1 April–30 June 1877 he was stationed at the Wynberg Musketry Camp, Cape Colony. When hostilities with the Zulus began and the 1st Battalion crossed into enemy territory, John was left behind at Rorke's Drift as a special orderly to Surgeon Reynolds in the hospital, and was present at the defence of Rorke's Drift. John's own account of events was published on 13 June 1879 in *The Cambrian*.

> I stopped there, firing at the enemy through holes made by other men and the others did the same, but we were not able to prevent the enemy coming right up to the hospital. Some of them came in and set fire to it. Whilst I was there I took refuge in a cupboard. As they were going out, I killed many of them, and as I could not stay there long, the place being so suffocating, I put on a black cloak which I had found in the cupboard, and ran out in the long grass and lay down. The Zulus must have thought I was one of their dead comrades, as they were all around me, and some trod on me. I got up at daybreak, having expected every minute my life would be taken, and then saw my comrades on top of the mealie sacks, and I said 'Thank God, I have got my life'. I had been shot early in the engagement in the shoulder and the knee, and here's the bullet, which was taken out next morning by Dr Reynolds.

Major Chard reported that John had told him that, having escaped the burning hospital, he found himself lying in a position with Zulus all around him. It was too late to retreat so he slowly made his way to the cookhouse and, standing up in the chimney, blackened his hands and face with soot, he remained there until morning when he emerged from his hiding place. On coming out into the

The scene at Rorke's Drift soon after the battle, looking at the post from the south-east. The remains of the destroyed hospital building have been removed, but the storehouse stripped of its thatch is still visible. The cemetery wall and the white monument are visible to the left of the picture.

open he was nearly shot when one of the men on the wall raised his rifle to fire, but Waters cried out in time to save himself. Private Waters had been severely wounded, 'a bullet having entered the arm six inches from the shoulder joint and lodging.' The ball was cut out twelve hours later by Surgeon Reynolds, and he kept it as a souvenir.

He arrived at Pietermaritzburg on 14 July 1879, where he was found to be unfit for further service. He returned to England and the *Stroud News and Gloucestershire Advertiser* for 13 June 1879, carried a report which stated

> The bullet with which Waters was wounded passed into his shoulder, and made its exit at his elbow, and the missile is now saved and prized by him as a memorable memento of the struggle in which he took part ... The wounded men arriving home from the affair at Rorke's Drift assert that the Zulu did not throw their assegais, but waited until they had chance of getting within stabbing distance, and then used them with deadly effect.

John was officially discharged from the army at Netley on 27 October 1879. He had earned four good conduct badges, was entered in the regimental defaulter's book six times, twice being court martialled, and his conduct during his service was described as: 'very good'. He received the South Africa Medal with 1877-8-9 clasp. The medal was originally inscribed G. Waters, which was later changed to J. Waters. His pension was eighteen pence a day for the first six months, then it was reduced to eight pence. From 31 January 1882 he received a permanent pension of ten pence a day. The address he gave for his intended place of residence was 12 Courtfield Gardens, London, the home of a wealthy landowner, where his sister, Mary Ann, lived and worked as a house servant.

Within weeks of his discharge he became a messenger for the War Office, while lodging with the family of one of his co-workers, John Delve, at 8 Britten Street, London. By 1881 he had a home of his own at 8 Little Windmill Street, St James. He married Bridget McNally on 2 October 1881 at St Peter's Church in the parish of St James. Bridget's address was given as 5 Cambridge Street, and by 1882 they had moved to 84 Burnthwaite Road, Fulham, and John remained in the employment of the War Office. On 17 November 1883, after only two years of marriage, John died of pneumonia at his home, aged 43. He was buried in Fulham Cemetery on 24 November (section E16, grave 11).

Edward Wilson

Edward Wilson was born on 28 October 1855, at Peshawur in India, the son of Colour-Sergeant Thomas Wilson and his wife Annelin. He had purchased his discharge from the 3rd East Surrey Militia when he joined the regular army at Kingston-upon-Thames in Surrey on 27 January 1874. He was five and a half feet tall, with a fresh complexion, hazel eyes, and brown hair, and he had two moles on his neck. His religion was Church of England. As 56 Private Wilson he was posted to the 1st Battalion, 24th Regiment at Brecon on 31 January 1874.

He served in the Cape Frontier War and the Zulu War. He was mentioned in newspaper reports has having returned home on 2 October 1879. For his service he was awarded the South Africa Medal with 1877-8-9 clasp.

Edward died of hypotrophy of the heart at the Cambridge Military Hospital on 19 February 1891, aged 36, and was buried in the Aldershot Military Cemetery.

B Company, 2nd Battalion, 24th Regiment

Gonville Bromhead

Gonville Bromhead came from a distinguished military family, whose home was at Thurlby Hall in Lincolnshire. He was born on 29 August 1845 at Versailles in France, the third of four sons to Edmund de Gonville Bromhead, 3rd Baronet, a retired Major and landowner, and Judith Christine Cahill, the daughter of James Wood of Woodville, County Sligo, Ireland.

His great-grandfather, Boardman Bromhead, served as ensign under James Wolfe at Quebec in 1759, and is believed to have been the man who assured the

Gonville Bromhead came from a distinguished military family, some of whom had fought alongside Wolfe and Wellington. He was awarded the Victoria Cross for his fine example and excellent behaviour during the defence of Rorke's Drift.

dying General, 'They run.' He gained the rank of general, and had four brothers in the army, one of whom was killed at Falkirk in 1746. He married into the family of the founders of Gonville and Caius College, Cambridge, hence his great-grandson's unusual Christian name. He himself gave his name as 'Gunny Brumhead', and a descendant remembered him as Uncle Gunny.

His grandfather, the 2nd Baronet, was a lieutenant-general who had distinguished himself with General Burgoyne in the American War of Independence, and had been captured at Saratoga in 1777. His father fought at Waterloo as a lieutenant in the 54th (Dorset) Regiment, where he lost an eye, and led the 'Forlorn Hope' at the Battle of Cambrai. His uncle commanded the 77th (Middlesex) Regiment at El Bodon, where he led them in a successful uphill assault against French cavalry. His eldest brother had fought in the Crimea and died while serving as a captain with the 76th (West Riding) Regiment in Burma. In 1879 the second son, and 4th Baronet, Benjamin Parnell, was serving with the 22nd Bengal Native Infantry at Kandahar in the Afghan War, and later served in the Sudan. His younger brother, Charles, was serving with the 24th Regiment, and had become a favourite of Garnet Wolseley while on active service in the Ashanti campaign of 1874.

The Bromhead family worshipped at the medieval church of St Germain, and were educated at the Thomas Magnus Grammar School, Newark-on-

A scene from the 1964 film, *Zulu!*, which introduced Sir Michael Caine in his first major acting role, playing the part of Lieutenant Bromhead.

Trent. Gonville excelled at various sports, in particular as a good left hand medium bowler for the cricket eleven. He was one of a very small number of ex-pupils to have a school 'house' named after him.

On 20 April 1867 he entered the 24th Regiment as Ensign by purchase, and was trained at Croydon, where he gained popularity among his fellow officers as a helpful senior to new recruits. At nearly six feet tall and with a powerful frame, he became a champion at boxing, wrestling and singlestick. He made a good impression, and was promoted by selection to the rank of lieutenant on 28 October 1871. Unfortunately he was developing a hearing problem which threatened the progress of his military career. However, in 1878 he was the officer in command of B Company, 2nd Battalion, 24th Regiment, when the unit received orders for active service in South Africa, and they embarked aboard the troopship *Himalaya* at Portsmouth on 1 February 1878, and set sail for the Cape of Good Hope. He took part in the 9th Cape Frontier War, and during the Zulu War he was present at the defence of Rorke's Drift.

At about three o'clock on the afternoon of 22 January 1879, Lieutenant Bromhead and Commissariat Officer Walter Dunne were relaxing with their pipes in the camp area at Rorke's Drift, when several men came in at intervals to report that the base camp at Isandlwana had been taken by the Zulus and that a large force of warriors was on its way to attack the garrison. Bromhead sent a man down to the river to warn Lieutenant Chard, and after a consultation with other officers he set to work in helping to supervise the building of the defences.

As the Zulu attack began to develop, a mass of warriors moved around the post to make determined rushes at the breastwork at the front of the hospital, and some Zulus managed to get over the wall into the compound. Lieutenant Bromhead, keeping an ever-watchful eye, saw this danger and with great coolness he got a handful of men together and led six bayonet charges to counter the enemy and force them back out. Lieutenant Bromhead and Private Hitch were fighting shoulder to shoulder and the officer was using his revolver to great effect, when a warrior managed to get behind him and was about to attack him from the rear, but Hitch came to his assistance before the warrior made his deadly strike. Soon afterwards, Hitch was hit in the shoulder by an enemy bullet and fell to the ground at the mercy of a Zulu who was running towards him to finish him off, but Bromhead returned the favour and shot the warrior down.

For his gallant conduct at the defence of Rorke's Drift, Bromhead was mentioned in dispatches and was awarded the Victoria Cross, which was announced in the *London Gazette* on 2 May 1879. He received the medal from Sir Garnet Wolseley while he was still on active service at Pine Tree Camp, Utrecht, Transvaal, on 22 August 1879. He also received the South Africa Medal with 1877-8-9 clasp. He was promoted captain and brevet-major from 23 January 1879, and was mentioned in dispatches on 1 March and 15 March 1879. He and Major Chard had the rare distinction of being thanked by the British Parliament. Men of B Company who took part in the defence of Rorke's Drift received an illuminated address from the Mayor of Durban just before they sailed to Gibraltar in January 1880.

The official citation for the VC stated:

> The Lieutenant-General commanding the troops reports that, had it not been for the fine example and excellent behaviour of these two Officers [Lieutenants Chard and Bromhead] under the most trying circumstances, the defence of Rorke's Drift post would not have been conducted with that intelligence and tenacity which so essentially characterised it. The Lieutenant-General adds that its success must, in a great degree, be attributable to the two young Officers who exercised the Chief Command on the occasion in question.

He served Gibraltar in 1880, and while home on leave in June that year he was invited to Windsor Castle for an audience with Queen Victoria, who gave him a signed photograph. He was guest of honour at several functions, and on 25 June he was invited to Lincoln Masonic Hall, where the Mayor presented

Gonville Bromhead standing far right of picture with the 1862 Magnus School cricket team. He was a stocky young man who also excelled at boxing, wrestling and singlestick.

him with a jewelled sword and an illuminated address. The tenants of Thurlby Hall presented him with a commemorative revolver. In August 1880 he was posted to Secunderabad in India, and returned to England in the summer of that year. On 1 July 1881 the 24th Regiment were re-designated the South Wales Borderers. From 1 October to 5 December 1882 he attended the Hythe School of Musketry and gained a 1st Class Extra certificate. On 2 January 1883 he sailed from Portsmouth on the *Serapis* to join the 2nd Battalion, South Wales Borderers, at Secunderabad. He was promoted major on 4 April 1883. He took part in the expedition to Upper Burma from 27 October 1886 to 24 May 1888, for which he received the Burma Medal with 1885-9 and 1887-9 clasps.

Major Bromhead never married, his main passion in life being salmon fishing. He died of enteric (typhoid) fever, at Camp Dabhaura, Allahabad, India on 9 February 1891, aged 46. He left his medals to his brother, Charles, and they are now with the Regimental Museum in Brecon. His name is inscribed on the colour pole of the 24th Regiment.

William Allan

His parents being of Scottish descent, the birthplace of William Allan, registered in the September quarter of 1844, is Berwick-upon-Tweed. However, his father, Thomas, was an itinerant agricultural labourer, and his six children were born in different towns on the Northumberland coast. The 1851 census states that his first child, William, was born at Ryton, near Newcastle-upon-Tyne. His mother's name was Ellen, and he adopted the middle name 'Wilson', which was

William Allan had been a soldier for 20 years when he fought at Rorke's Drift. He was wounded in the arm by a Zulu slug while protecting the patients as they were trying to escape from the burning hospital, and subsequently received the Victoria Cross for his action.

probably his mother's maiden name. In 1861 the family were living at Gloster Hill, Northumberland.

William was fifteen when he enlisted at York on 27 October 1859, and as 1240 Private Allan was posted to the 2nd Battalion, 24th Regiment at Aldershot. He was slightly built, at five feet four inches tall, but he was a tough Geordie character, and was confined in cells on several occasions in the early 1860s before he settled into army life. He served on Mauritius and following thirteen years service in the East, he returned to the depot at Brecon on 21 April 1874.

He married Sarah Ann Reeves at the Brecon Registry Office on 16 August 1876, his new wife being twelve years younger than him. Her father, Richard, had been a staff-sergeant in the Monmouthshire Militia. Their first two daughters, Helena and Elizabeth, were born in Brecon in 1877 and 1878 respectively. William was promoted to lance-corporal on 18 May 1876, corporal on 6 July 1877, and having gained a 2nd Class Certificate of Education, he became an assistant schoolmaster. In 1878 he was awarded a prize for 'good shooting and judgement of distance.' Corporal Allan was posted to his battalion on 26 January 1878, and on 2 February sailed with his unit from Portsmouth on the troopship *Himalaya* for active service in South Africa. He took part in the Cape Frontier War, being promoted lance-sergeant on 22 May 1878, but was reduced to corporal at Pietermaritzburg on 21 October 1878.

During the defence of Rorke's Drift, Corporal Allan was posted with some other sharp-shooters at the south barricade. As the patients were being evacuated from the burning hospital, it was due to Corporal Allan and Private Hitch that communication was kept up with the building, as they placed themselves in a dangerously exposed position in the centre of the compound to keep back warriors who were climbing over the barricade to get at them. William was helping the last of the invalids to the wooden boxes when a Zulu bullet went right through his arm. Surgeon Reynolds dressed his wound and he went back to his duties, but being too injured to fight, he spent the rest of the night distributing ammunition to his comrades at the barricade.

Disabled by the injuries he received at Rorke's Drift, he was taken to Helpmekaar, and on 4 February he wrote a letter informing his wife, 'I am getting the better of my wound more rapidly than could be expected ... My arm is mending quickly.' He was transported back to England on the *Tamar* and taken to Netley Military Hospital. The Zulu slug had left William's arm partly disabled, but with such a strong constitution he was well enough to attend a victory celebration banquet at Portland Hall, Portsea, on 25 October 1879, organised by the people of Portsmouth for the servicemen who had fought in the Zulu campaign. By 8 November he was serving as provisional staff-sergeant with the 3rd/24th Regiment Militia, and on 9 December 1879 he went to Windsor Castle to receive the Victoria Cross from Queen Victoria. He also received the South Africa Medal with 1877-8-9 clasp. On 11 June 1880, William was appointed sergeant at the Colchester depot.

He returned to Brecon for the birth of his first son, Llewellyn Glendower, in 1880. Grace was born in 1883 and Gladys in 1884. On 13 November 1880, one of Sergeant Allan's fellow defenders of Rorke's Drift, William Partridge, 24th Regiment, married his wife's sister, Mary Letitia, known as 'Polly', at the Brecon Registry Office, and Sarah's brother, Richard Reeves, was also serving with the 24th Regiment in 1881. In 1886 he became sergeant, instructor of musketry, to C Company, 4th Volunteer Battalion, South Wales Borderers, stationed at Monmouth, and made the family home at 85 Monnow Road, Monmouth, Gwent, where he became a well-known and respected member of the community. Sarah opened a grocery shop next door at number 87. A child named Jessie was born in 1886, but she died less than two years later. Olive was born in 1888.

In March 1890, with Sarah about to give birth, a serious influenza epidemic hit the town, and it was thought that William was a victim. However, he was seriously ill with dropsy for seven days, and when further complications developed he deteriorated and died of 'aortic valvular disease of the heart' at his home on 12 March 1890, aged 46. He was buried with his baby daughter at Monmouth Cemetery, with military honours provided by the South Wales

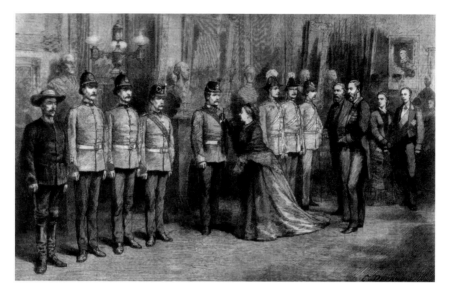

Corporal Allan receives the VC from the sovereign, while Private Roy waits in line, second left of picture. Windsor Castle, 8 December 1879.

Borderers, and a stone cross was erected at his grave by the 4th Volunteer Battalion (section B, grave 25). The new baby was named Sibyl.

Sergeant Allan's sudden death left his wife and children unprovided for, so the Mayor of Monmouth set up a benefit appeal to help them. Allen's VC is with the South Wales Borderers Museum, along with an inscribed pocket watch which was given to the museum by his grandson. It had been presented to Sergeant Allan by the Mayor of Brecon while he was serving at the barracks as an instructor.

James Ashton

Anthony McHale was born in Ireland, although his WO97 papers state he was born at St Mary's Parish, Liverpool, in June 1841. His enlistment papers record him as Church of England, but he was actually Church of Ireland (Protestant). Colour-Sergeant Bourne described him as 'a lusty Irishman', but as a point of interest, the 1841 census for Liverpool records a James Ashton, aged nine months, who was the son of John and Alice Ashton, living at Cavendish Street, St Mary's, and the parish register of St Peter's Church of England Church at St Mary's records the baptism of a James Ashton on 17 January 1842 to John and Alice Ashton, a carter, living in Cavendish Street.

He left his job as a domestic groom to enlist at York on 2 March 1859, and as 1939 Private James (John) Ashton he was posted to the 2nd Battalion, 24th Regiment. He was five feet five-and-a-half inches tall, with a fresh complexion, hazel eyes and dark brown hair. He gave his age as seventeen. He was posted to Mauritius on 23 May 1860, spending a week in prison there in 1862, before being posted to India on 6 October 1865. His conduct pay was increased to two pence a day on 16 February 1868, and he re-engaged at Secunderabad on 13 April 1869, to complete 21 years service. He forfeited his good conduct pay and he was deprived of two days pay for being absent on 8 March 1872, but one penny a day good conduct pay was restored two days later. He returned from India and his Home Service began on 4 January 1873. His good conduct pay was forfeited and restored several times, and he was imprisoned by his commanding officer for seven days in April 1874 for fraudulent enlistment when he admitted his true name and place of birth.

He received orders for active service in South Africa, and sailed to the Cape in February 1878. He fought in the Cape Frontier War and was one of the oldest soldiers at Rorke's Drift. On 23 January 1879, when the Zulus had withdrawn, Private Ashton reported to Lieutenant Bromhead with a Zulu prisoner and was told to 'get the hell out of here – and I did.' Lieutenant Smith-Dorrien had erected a gallows at Rorke's Drift, and stated, 'On returning to Rorke's Drift after the battle, I saw two Zulus hanging from my gallows.' For his service he received the South Africa Medal with 1877-8-9 clasp. He was on colonial leave from 6 March 1879, so his copy of the commemorative address was forwarded to 25 Brigade Depot at Brecon.

His good conduct pay was restored to two pence on 24 November 1880, and he returned for Home Service on 6 March 1881. He was discharged from the army at Brecon on 12 April 1881, his conduct being very good; he was in possession of two good conduct badges and was awarded a pension of ten pence a day. His intended place of residence was Knockmore, County Mayo, Ireland, where he died and is buried.

Thomas Barry

Thomas Barry enlisted at Newport, Monmouthshire, on 5 April 1877, and as 1381 Private Barry was posted to the 2nd Battalion, 24th Regiment on 11 May 1877. He sailed for active service in South Africa on 1 February 1878, taking part in the Cape Frontier War and the Zulu War.

He transferred to A Company on 1 March 1879. His name appears on the Company list at Rorke's Drift on 8 March 1879, when he was confined for ten days for making replies when ordered for duty. For his service in South Africa he received the South Africa Medal with 1877-8-9 clasp.

He sailed with the unit to Gibraltar, where he served from 12 February–10 August 1880, during which time he was fined for drunkenness on 28 May, 2

July and 7 July 1880. He was posted to India on 11 August 1880, and returned to England on 26 April 1883. He received his pay at Gosport, Hampshire until 20 June 1883, and he was discharged to the Reserve on 21 June 1883. His intended residence was c/o the Post Office, Merthyr Tydfil, Monmouthshire. A travel warrant with the destination of Newport was issued to him, and his intended place of residence was c/o the Post Office, Merthyr Tydfil.

William Bennett

William Bennett enlisted at Brecon on 21 November 1876, and as 918 Private Bennett he was posted to the 2nd Battalion, 24th Regiment. He received orders for active service in South Africa, and sailed to the Cape in February 1878. He took part in the Cape Frontier War, later being confined to cells for eight days, and during the Zulu War he was present at the defence of Rorke's Drift. He deserted at Pinetown on 21 December 1879. For his service he was entitled to the South Africa Medal with 1877-8-9 clasp, but due to his desertion the medal was never issued and was returned to the mint.

A death notice for a Trooper W.E. Bennett, 4th South African Horse, appeared in a Great War Roll of Honour published in the *Natal Mercury Pictorial* of 30 June 1916, which is almost certainly the Rorke's Drift man. He had previously served in the Natal Mounted Rifles under Colonel Sparks. Trooper Bennett succumbed to an attack of enteric fever in East Africa. He was the son of Meyrick Bennett of Messrs Randles Brothers and Hudson, of Durban, and he was the firm's managing partner in Johannesburg. The article stated that he played football for Berea FC, South Africa, and included a picture.

William Bessell

William Henry Bessell was born on 12 April 1856 at 1 Edgar Place, Stepney, London. He was the third child of five to James Bessell, who was a brick-layer like his father before him, and his mother was Caroline Anna (formerly Slow). William was baptised with his two older siblings at St Peter's Church in Stepney on 6 May 1858.

By 1860 they had moved to 4 Chester Street, Bethnal Green, London, and several family losses followed. The 1861 census shows that William's eldest brother, James, was 'a convicted boy under sentence of detention' aboard the notorious prison vessel HMS *Cornwall*. Life on this ship was very precarious and the fate of James is unknown. By 1864 they had moved to 55 Lessada Street, Bethnal Green, where his eldest sister died of fever aged eleven, and his father died in 1867, after the family had moved to 1 Green Street, Bethnal Green. They moved to 4 Punderson Gardens, Bethnal Green, where his mother gave birth to a step-sister, and on re-marrying she gave birth to a step-brother.

The 1871 census shows that William was in the Staines Industrial School for Juvenile Offenders, and probably in consequence of being on the wrong side of the law again, he enlisted at Bow Street Police Court in London on 27 February 1877. His trade was recorded as a porter and his description was given as five feet five-and-a-quarter inches tall, with a fresh complexion, brown hair and hazel eyes. He had a brown patch on left arm. As 1287 Private Bessell he was posted to the 2nd Battalion, 24th Regiment at Brecon, and he was posted to Dover and Chatham, where he was admitted to hospital from 15 to 30 January 1878, suffering from gonorrhoea.

He received orders for active service in South Africa and sailed to the Cape in February 1878. According to Private Wood, during the defence of Rorke's Drift

> the firing got very slack – just now and again from their 'Brown Besses'. They were evidently getting tired of their job. 'Now chaps,' said Corporal Bissell, 'What do you say we fill a pipe and have a smoke?' 'Right ho', we replied. 'Keep a sharp look out and we can have a few draws each.' The pipe was filled and oh how nice it was.

Following the arrival of the relief column on the morning of 23 January, William Bessell was promoted to corporal to replace some of the men who had been killed in action.

William had been making a monthly remittance of £1 to his Aunt Mary (Porter), of 252 Green Street, Bethnal Green, and in March 1879, the remittance was changed to £2 per month and was then paid to his mother, Mrs Stoneham. He was in receipt of good conduct pay from 11 September 1879, however, he was tried and imprisoned on 25 November 1879, reduced to the rank of private and forfeited his good conduct pay. He was confined until 16 February 1880, when he was posted with the regiment to Gibraltar, before being posted to India in August 1880, and arrived in Secunderabad on 17 September. On 14 December 1880 he was hospitalised several times with various ailments, and on 17 February 1881 his good conduct pay was restored. Having reached his expiry date for army service on 1 May 1883, he embarked on the SS *Armenia* with the other 'time served men' for the return journey to England, and was discharged to the 1st Class Army Reserves.

He gave his intended place of residence as 252 Green Street, Bethnal Green, the home of his aunt Mary. He received his final discharge from the 1st Class Army Reserves on 26 February 1889. His mother died in 1891, at a time when William began to descend into alcoholism. He was living at Grays Inn Buildings in Holborn in 1901, with Jane F. Bessell, stated on the census to be his wife, along with two young boys named William and Albert, although there is no record of a marriage on the registers in Great Britain, so she was probably his common-law wife.

William had been employed as a bricklayer, but his depression deepened and the drinking bouts became more frequent. The family moved to 27 Sonning Buildings, Mount Street, Bethnal Green, and he took employment as a bar and cellar man, which did nothing to discourage his drinking habit. He was admitted to the Bethnal Green Workhouse on 17 July 1903, and on the following day he was transferred to 'Justice Ward' of the Bethnal Green Infirmary, where he died, aged 46. The cause of death was recorded as 'delirium tremens and pneumonia.'

John Bly

John Bly attested for the British Army in about November 1872, and as 2427 Private Bly he was posted to the 2nd Battalion, 24th Regiment on 1 January 1873. He sailed with the regiment for active service in South Africa in February 1878, where he took part in the 9th Cape Frontier War and the Zulu War, being present at the defence of Rorke's Drift. For his service he received the South Africa Medal with 1877-8-9 clasp. He was sent to Netley Military Hospital on 1 February 1880, and was transferred to the Army Reserve.

Frank Bourne

Frank Bourne was born on 27 April 1853 at 2 Brookhouse, Balcombe, near Crawley in Sussex, the youngest of eight children born to James Bourn, an agricultural labourer, and his wife Harriett (formerly Galton). It may have been due to working out in the wet and frosty fields in the winter of 1872 that prompted him to travel to Reigate on 18 December to enlist in the army, and as 2459 Private Bourne he was posted to the 2nd Battalion, 24th Regiment. His father attempted to prevent him, but he was persuaded not to do so. He had a dark complexion, grey eyes and brown hair. According to Frank

the 'A' Company of any regiment in those days was always called the Grenadiers' Company and was supposed to have the biggest men. I think the Sergeant-Major must have been a wee bit humorous for he posted me to our 'A' Company, although I stood only five feet six inches and was painfully thin.

He settled into army life very well, and was promoted corporal on 11 April 1874.

He received orders for active service in South Africa, and sailed to the Cape with his unit in February 1878, where he was promoted three times within as many weeks; lance-sergeant on 7 April 1878, sergeant on 15 April 1878, and colour-sergeant in 'B' Company on 27 April 1878, while serving in the Cape Frontier War.

Colour-Sergeant Frank Bourne was the senior NCO at Rorke's Drift. A recommendation that he should be awarded the Distinguished Conduct Medal was submitted to Queen Victoria, and she authorised it personally. He later said 'for the men who fought that night. I was moving about amongst them all the time and not for one moment did they flinch, their courage and their bravery cannot be expressed in words; for me they were an example all my soldiering days.' For his service he received the South Africa Medal with 1877-8-9 clasp. He served on Gibraltar in 1880, and in India and Burma.

He married Eliza Mary Fincham in Bombay on 27 September 1882, and they had five children. Percy was born in 1883, Sydney was born in 1887, Beatrice was born in 1889, while Mary and Constance were born during his service in Kent. Percy attended the Blue Coat School in Liverpool, and became a commander in the Royal Navy.

Frank Bourne settled into army life very well. He was known as 'The Kid' by his men as he reached the rank of colour-sergeant on his 25th birthday, having been promoted three times in as many weeks. He was awarded the Distinguished Conduct Medal for his gallantry during the defence.

A Blue Plaque was placed at Frank Bourne's former home at 16 King's Hall Road in Beckenham in 2001.

Frank became quartermaster and honorary lieutenant on 21 May 1890, and on 1 May 1893 he was appointed acting lieutenant and quartermaster at the Hythe School of Musketry, Kent. He retired on 18 December 1907. In 1915 – soon after the outbreak of the First World War – he was re-employed as quartermaster and honorary major, serving as quartermaster and acting adjutant at the Irish Command School of Musketry in Dublin from 24 January 1916. He retired as honorary lieutenant-colonel on 3 June 1918, being awarded the Order of the British Empire (OBE) in recognition of his services. For many years he was active in assisting Lord Roberts VC in promoting marksmanship within the Society of Miniature Rifle Clubs in London.

On 4 July 1910, at Beckenham in Kent, he completed a roll of defenders. Lieutenant Chard had himself compiled a Roll of Defenders on 3 February 1879, and when this was published in 1937, Colonel Bourne was prompted to produce an amended roll. He kept in touch with many of the survivors, who came to be known as 'Rorke's Drift Men'. He wrote a letter to the *Daily Mail* on 24 August 1932, naming the survivors of the defence. From 7–14 July 1934 he attended the Northern Command Tattoo at Ravensworth Castle in Gateshead, when the South Wales Borderers re-created the action at Rorke's Drift, and he appeared in the arena with four surviving comrades from the garrison.

On 20 December 1936 he broadcast his reminiscences on the BBC Radio programme ' I Was There', and as a result of this he received over 350 letters, to which he personally replied to every one. Unfortunately the programme was not recorded, but on 30 December 1936 the BBC publication *The Listener* carried an article based on the radio broadcast, a transcript of which has survived.

There are two things which I think have made Rorke's Drift stand out so vividly all these years. The first, that it took place on the same day as the terrible massacre at Isandlwana, and the second, that Natal was saved from being overrun by a savage and victorious foe. If there are any service, or ex-servicemen listening, may I say this to you; that if your company had found itself in the same position as we were, you would have done the same as we did, fought it out and won!

Frank Bourne was a very modest man, who considered himself lucky to have been present at Rorke's Drift, and the anniversary of the battle was commemorated by a dinner held at his home. His wife died in 1931, and Colonel Bourne died at his home on 9 May 1945, aged 90. He was buried with military honours at Elmer's End Cemetery in Beckenham. A commemorative blue plaque was placed at his former home in 2001, and his medals are with the South Wales Borderers Museum.

Charles Bromwich

Charles Bromwich was born in June 1840 at Milverton, Warwickshire, the oldest child of Joseph Bromwich, a journeyman painter, and his second wife Maria (formerly Kayte). Joseph had a son with his first wife before her death. Three girls were also born at Milverton, and when they moved to Saltisford Rock, Joseph and three other boys were born, and by 1861 the family had moved to Hadley's Yard, St Mary's, Warwick where four boys and a girl were born. Joseph senior died in 1875.

Charles had served in the 2nd Warwickshire Militia from 11 October 1858, before enlisting into the regular army at Plymouth on 22 March 1859, and as 981 Private C. Bromwich was posted to the 2nd Battalion, 24th Regiment. He served on Mauritius, and re-engaged to serve 21 years at Preston on 20 August 1869 before serving in the East Indies.

He received orders for active service in South Africa and sailed to the Cape in February 1878. He took part in the Cape Frontier War, being sent to the general depot at Pietermaritzburg on 31 October 1878. During the Zulu War both he and his brother Joseph were present at the defence of Rorke's Drift. For his service he received the South Africa Medal with 1877-8-9 clasp.

He transferred to the 91st Highlanders at Cape Town on 30 November 1879. He became attached to the Royal Welch Fusiliers on 19 May 1880 for the purpose of discharge, which occurred on 9 June 1880. His intended place of residence was the home of his widowed mother, Maria, at 12 Brook Street, Saltisford, Warwick. He died in Warwick on 27 May 1893, aged 52.

Joseph Bromwich

Joseph Bromwich, the brother of Charles, was born on 18 November 1856 at Saltisford Rock, St Mary's, Warwick. Joseph left his job as a porter and joined the 28th Infantry Brigade on 29 August 1877. He was described as five feet five-and-a-half inches tall, with a fair complexion, brown eyes and dark brown hair. He had a 33-inch chest measurement, and his religion was Church of England. 1028 Private Bromwich transferred to the 2nd Battalion, 24th Regiment on 31 January 1878 and was given the new service number 1524.

He received orders for active service in South Africa and sailed to the Cape in February 1878 where he took part in the Cape Frontier War. He and his brother Charles were present at the defence of Rorke's Drift. Joseph was trans-ferred to 'A' company on 29 January 1879, to replace men of that unit who had been wiped out at Isandlwana. For his service he received the South Africa Medal with 1877-8-9 clasp.

He served on Gibraltar, and while serving in India he was granted good con-duct pay, gained a 4th Class Certificate of Education, and by 1882 had earned two good conduct badges. In April 1882 he was admitted to hospital with chronic hepatitis and an abscess on the liver, and in May of that year he was shipped back to Netley hospital where he was found to be suffering from a chronically damaged liver with a liability for it to recur in a hot climate. His condition was judged to be the result of climate and military service, and not to have been aggravated by intemperance or misconduct. The medical board considered the condition to be permanent and would for some twelve months impair Joseph's ability to earn a living. He was declared medically unfit for further service and invalided out of the army on 25 July 1882, with a pension of seven pence a day for twelve months, which was later changed to a permanent pension.

Joseph returned to the home of his widowed mother at 12 Brook Street, Saltisford, Warwick. He met Betsy Fellows Davis and they married at the parish church on 22 April 1883. By 1891 Joseph and Betsy had moved to 183 Darwin Street, in the parish of St Albans, Aston, Birmingham, where they established a boot and shoe repairing shop. They eventually moved to 14 Asylum Road, St Stephen's, Selly Oak, Birmingham, where Joseph took employment as a shoe repairer. The 1901 census shows them as having a fifteen-year-old daughter named Elina, who had been born in Birmingham. They then moved to 5 Duke Street, Bilston in Staffordshire, the place where Betsy had been born, and Joseph continued to work as a boot and shoe repairer.

Betsy died in 1914, and by the end of the year Joseph's health was in decline; in 1915 he was diagnosed with cancer of the tongue. Early in 1916 he was admitted to the workhouse infirmary at Heath Town, Wolverhampton, where he spent his last days. He died on 25 February 1916, aged 60. He was buried in a private family ceremony, in an unmarked grave in Bilston Cemetery, Wolverhampton (section D, plot 55).

Thomas Buckley

Thomas Buckley was born on 23 March 1859, and he attested for the army in Liverpool on 15 February 1877. 1184 Private Buckley was posted to the 2nd Battalion, 24th Regiment at Brecon a week later. He sailed for active service in South Africa in February 1878. For his service he received the South Africa Medal with 1877-8-9 clasp. He made a monthly remittance of £1 to a Mr Buckley, presumably his father, in March 1879.

He served on Gibraltar in 1880, and was promoted corporal in India on 1 August 1883, but he was reduced to private on 6 October 1883. He returned home from Burma on 12 January 1889. He received the Indian General Service Medal with Burma 1885-87 and Burma 1887-89 clasps.

He discharged from the British Army in 1899, when he must have been about 40, and went back to South Africa to fight in the Boer War with the Imperial Light Horse, and is believed to have served with the Royal Flying Corps in the First World War. Tom presumably lived in straightened circumstances as he resided at the Thomas Lloyd Hostel in Liverpool, and having lost or sold his medals a set of replacements were issued to him on 5 July 1934, possibly to wear at the Northern Command Tattoo. However, he did not attend, probably due to illness, as he died on 31 December 1934 and was buried by the Royal British Legion in an unmarked grave at Anfield Cemetery, Liverpool (section 19/ grave 923).

Thomas Burke

Thomas Burke was born in Liverpool on 29 November 1858, the son of Michael and Catherine Burke (formerly Gullery), and was baptised at St Mary's (Roman Catholic) Church, Highfield Street, Liverpool six days later. He was employed as a labourer, and, like Patrick Kears and John Thomas, he had served with the 2nd Royal Lancashire Militia (Duke of Lancaster's Own Rifles), which formed the 3rd and 4th Battalions, King's (Liverpool) Regiment, when he enlisted at Liverpool, on 14 February 1877, aged eighteen years and four months. He was five feet four-and-a-half inches tall, with a fair complexion, blue eyes and brown hair. He attested at Brecon on 16 February 1877 and 1220 Private Burke was posted to the 2nd Battalion, 24th Regiment on 11 May 1877.

A well-known picture believed to have been taken at Pinetown in Natal soon after the Zulu War, of most of the men of B Company who defended Rorke's Drift.

He sailed to the Cape in February 1878. He was granted one penny a day good conduct pay on 6 October, and for his service he received the South Africa Medal with 1877-8-9 clasps. He did not receive the Address from the Mayor of Durban.

He served on Gibraltar in 1880, and in India until 27 May 1883. He reached the rank of corporal on 1 November 1881, and his good conduct pay was increased to two pence a day on 16 February 1883. On returning home he transferred to the Army Reserves at Warrington on 21 June 1883, transferring to Brecon on 25 May 1884, and to Liverpool on 15 October 1884. His character was described as very good.

On 19 October 1884 he re-joined as 871 Corporal Burke in the 1st King's (Liverpool) Regiment. He served in India in 1885, and on 8 July he was tried for being drunk on duty, being confined for five days and reduced to the ranks. He was also fined £1 and forfeited his good conduct pay. He served in Burma from 1885 to 1887, being promoted lance-corporal on 22 March 1886, and having his good conduct pay of two pence a day restored. He returned to India, gaining a 2nd Class Certificate of Education on 14 June 1887, and was promoted to corporal on 21 June 1887. He re-engaged at Fyzabad on 20 August 1888 to complete 21 years service. He rose to the rank of sergeant on 6 February 1890, and was entitled to three pence a day good conduct pay from 16 June 1890.

He suffered from two forms of venereal disease for which he received treatment in 1885 and 1886, and suffered from dyspepsia (severe indigestion) caused by the climate and intemperance (excessive alcohol). He was admitted to hospital several times, the last occasion being on 21 May 1891. He was charged with drunkenness when on duty on 4 June 1891, being sentenced to be reduced to corporal and to forfeit one penny a day good conduct pay. He returned to duty as sergeant on 16 June 1891.

On 27 February 1892 a medical board in Aden declared that he was suffering from debility, and having been recommended for a change of climate he returned home on 6 April 1892. For his service he received the Indian General Service Medal with Burma 1885-87 clasp. He was posted to the Regimental Depot at Liverpool on 11 June 1892, but was admitted to hospital in Warrington on 29 June after suffering an attack of dyspepsia. He became entitled to four pence a day good conduct pay from 16 February 1895. He discharged at his own request on 10 May 1897. His character was described as fair and his habits intemperate. It was recorded in a Liverpool newspaper that a Michael Burke, father of Thomas, died in the workhouse on 16 March 1897, which may have influenced Sergeant Burke's decision to leave the army soon afterwards.

He became the landlord of the Crown Vaults public house in Park Road, Liverpool, and in spite of the nature of his illnesses, he married Honora Lambert and had three children, making the family home at Wellesley Road in Toxteth, Liverpool 8. Robert was born in 1903, but he died aged only nine months, and Thomas Aloysius, who was born in 1906, died aged only 39. Thomas Burke died on 23 April 1925 and was buried in Ford Roman Catholic Cemetery, Litherland, Liverpool, where his two sons are buried with him, along with his wife, who died in 1950, beneath an impressive stone obelisk topped by a wheel of eternity. His age inscribed on the monument is 64, but this does not tally with his enlistment papers, or some other sources, and he was probably 67. He may have lied about his age because his wife was much younger than him. A rededication service was held at his graveside by the 1879 Group in 2002 to honour his name and the part he played in the heroic defence of Rorke's Drift.

James Bushe

James Bushe was born in St John's Parish, Dublin around 1852, and had been employed as a tailor when he enlisted for the 24th Regiment at Dublin on 14 September 1870. He was just over five feet five inches tall, with a fresh complexion, grey eyes and black hair. His religion was Church of England. As 2350 Private Bushe he was posted to the 2nd Battalion, and joined the unit at Chatham on 28 September 1870.

His army life began well, and after serving in India for two years he was promoted to corporal on 20 November 1875, gaining a 3rd Class Certificate of Education, and he was granted two pence a day good conduct pay from 15 September 1876. However, he was confined for drunkenness on 13 May 1877, tried by Court Martial four days later, and sentenced to be reduced to private and to forfeit a penny a day of his good conduct pay. He was appointed lance-corporal on 20 September 1877, but a month later he reverted to private again. He forfeited his good conduct pay, but it was restored on the same day.

He received orders for active service in South Africa, and was wounded at the defence of Rorke's Drift. Lieutenant Chard later said

> I was glad to seize an opportunity to wash my face in a muddy puddle, in company with Private Bush 24th, whose face was covered with blood from a wound on the nose caused by a bullet which had passed through and killed Private Cole 24th. With the politeness of a soldier, he lent me his towel, or, rather, a very dirty half of one, before using it himself, and I was very glad to accept it.

James was promoted to lance-corporal soon after the defence, and to corporal on 28 November 1879. For his service he received the South Africa Medal with 1877-8-9 clasp.

Seven holders of the VC pictured in 1898, five of whom were defenders of Rorke's Drift, 23 January 1898. Rear left to right: Private R. Jones, Private A. Hook and Private W. Jones. Sitting left to right: Private D. Bell, Lieutenant Colonel E.S. Browne, Private F. Hitch and Private J. Williams. The 'odd men out' are Bell and Browne.

He served on Gibraltar in 1880, and having been appointed lance-sergeant on 24 November 1880 he re-engaged to complete 21 years service at Secunderabad in India in the following month. His service continued in the South Wales Borderers with the new regimental number 2360, and he reverted to private at his own request on 30 October 1881. He was granted three pence a day good conduct pay on 16 September 1882. He served in Burma, during which time he reached the rank of corporal again on 27 April 1887, was granted a fourth good conduct badge and achieved a 2nd Class Certificate of Education. Having returned home, he discharged from the army as time-served on 10 October 1891. His character and conduct were described as good and his habits as regular. He received the India General Service Medal with 1887-9 clasp.

William Camp

William Henry Camp was born at Camberwell, Surrey in about 1854. He left his job as a clerk to enter 25 Brigade at Liverpool on 8 February 1877, and as 1181 Private Camp he was posted to the 2nd Battalion, 24th Regiment at Brecon. He was described as being just over five feet eight inches tall, with a sallow complexion, hazel eyes and dark brown hair. He gained a 2nd Class Certificate of Education and was granted a penny a day good conduct pay.

He sailed to the Cape on 2 February 1878. For his service in the Cape Frontier and Zulu Wars he received the South Africa Medal with 1877-8-9 clasp.

He served on Gibraltar in 1880 and was admitted to hospital at Secunderabad in India on 17 September 1880, suffering with rheumatism, dyspepsia and melancholia. He returned to England, and a medical examination at Netley on 25 November 1881 found that he was suffering from melancholia caused by an hereditary predisposition and aggravated by masturbation. The condition was considered to be of a permanent nature rendering him unable to contribute to his own support. He was declared insane and was discharged on 27 December 1881 as unfit for further service. His character was described as very good, and he was in possession of one good conduct badge. An injury Assessment Board meeting held at the Royal Hospital in Chelsea on 27 February 1882 confirmed all the previous findings and William was awarded a pension of seventeen pence a day for fifteen months. His intended place of residence was the Union Workhouse at Camberwell.

Thomas Chester

Thomas Chester was born at Knowle near Warwick on 3 August 1851 and was christened there on 7 December 1851. He was the first child of Thomas Chester and his wife Charlotte (formerly Chilwell), and his father was living at the Leek Wooton Vicarage near Warwick, where he worked as a groom and coachman. In 1882 they moved to the village of Catthorpe in Leicestershire, the place of Thomas senior's birth, where Charlotte gave birth to three children. The family then moved to 14 Hermitage Street in Cheltenham, where four more children were born, including twin boys. By 1871 they had moved to 2 Harmony Cottages, Leckhampton, Gloucestershire and Thomas had taken lodgings at 9, Shottery, Old Stratford and was earning a living as a gardener.

Thomas enlisted for the army at Bow Street Police Courts on 20 February 1877, being described as five feet ten-and-a-quarter inches tall, with a fair complexion, blue eyes and brown hair, and he had good muscular development. He gave his next of kin as T. Chester (father), c/o The Conservative Club, Albion Hill, Cheltenham, Gloucester. His religion was stated as Church of England. As 1241 Private Chester he was posted to the 2nd Battalion, 24th Regiment at Brecon where he attained a 4th Class Certificate of Education. He sailed to the Cape in February 1878 and received the South Africa Medal with 1877-8-9 clasp for his service in the Cape Frontier and Zulu War.

He served on Gibraltar in 1880 and on 8 May 1881 he was hospitalised at Secunderabad in India suffering with 'glands', which was the only occasion on which Thomas suffered any kind of illness. He was awarded two pence a day good conduct pay on 20 February 1883. He left India on 1 May 1883 aboard the SS *Armenia* with the rest of the time-served men, and returned to England. On 21 June he was discharged to the 1st Class Army Reserves, Bristol District, 28th Gloucestershire Regiment. His conduct on discharge was described as very good and temperate.

He gave his intended place of residence as St Mark's, Cheltenham and he found accommodation at 16 Grosvenor Terrace, a lodging house in Cheltenham, gaining employment as a porter. He married Ellen Cave at All Saints Church, Cheltenham on 9 December 1883. On 14 May 1884, just five months after the wedding, Thomas was transferred out of the Gloucestershire area at his own request and moved to the Brecon District Reserves (South Wales Borderers), leaving Ellen alone and pregnant at 2 Sherborne Place, Cheltenham; it would appear that the couple separated.

Thomas was discharged from the Reserves in Brecon on 19 February 1889, having served a total of six years with the colours and six years with the Reserves. He moved to 10 Wood Street, Tylorstown-with-Ferndale, Ystradyfodwg, Glamorgan where he took lodgings and obtained employment as a coal trimmer underground at the number 5 pit at the Ferndale Colliery. By 1901 he was living at 7 Long Row, Ystradyfodwg.

Thomas was killed in a pit accident in 1908. The inquest found that

> Thomas Chester was killed on 12 February 1908. He was a coal trimmer aged 55. Deceased was breaking up a lump of coal which had fallen on the empty road leading to No. 1 pit screens, when he was knocked down by a wagon which was being lowered towards the screens. Deceased had stood to one side to allow two wagons to pass, but was not aware that others were to follow.

Thomas was buried at St Gwynnos Anglican Churchyard at Llanwonno, attended by friends, neighbours and fellow miners. His grave remains unmarked. His South Africa Medal was donated to the Regimental Museum at Brecon by a family relative.

Thomas Clayton

Thomas Clayton was born on 16 May 1855 at Draper's Lane, Leominster, Gloucestershire, the first child of ten born to Thomas Clayton, a railway worker, and his wife Emily (formerly Davenport). Thomas and his sister Sarah were baptised together on 26 February 1860. By 1861 they had moved to the railway house at Kingsland Crossing, where Emily became the gate keeper for the railway crossing and Thomas senior was working as a railway plate-layer. The

Helpmekaar was the closest depot to Rorke's Drift, and many British soldiers who lost their lives during the Zulu War are buried in the military cemetery established there. Thomas Clayton was interred in the cemetery close to the rear wall.

family moved to the village of Kingsland and Thomas junior obtained lodgings at 'Thornlands' in Kingsland, gaining employment as a general servant.

Thomas enlisted into the Monmouthshire Militia in 1873 and then into the regular army via the Militia Returns for 8 February 1876. As 735 Private Clayton he was posted to the 2nd Battalion, 24th Regiment, stationed in Dover. He received orders for active service in South Africa and sailed to the Cape with his unit in February 1878. He took part in the Cape Frontier War and was present at the defence of Rorke's Drift.

Sadly, Private Clayton was amongst the number of men afflicted by various ailments caused by bad conditions and was transferred to the hospital at Helpmekaar where he died on 5 April 1879, just one month from his 24th birthday. He was buried in the Military Cemetery at Helpmekaar, the cause of death being given as fever. His name appeared on the casualty lists published in the *London Gazette* on 23 May 1879.

Thomas Cole

Thomas Cole was born in about 1855. He enlisted at Monmouth on 23 March 1876, and as 801 Private Cole he was posted to the 2nd Battalion, 24th Regiment at Brecon on 20 June 1876. With such a surname it was inevitable that he would be given the nickname 'Old King Cole' by the men of B Company. He received orders for active service in South Africa and sailed to the Cape in February 1878. He took part in the 9th Cape Frontier War and during the Zulu War he was killed in action at Rorke's Drift, when a Zulu slug went through his head.

He was one of six men who were ordered to barricade themselves in the hospital to defend the patients as best they could. Private Hook later said

> I had charge with a man that we called Old King Cole of a small room with only one patient in it. Cole kept with me for some time after the fight began, then he said he was not going to stay. He went outside and was instantly killed by the Zulus.

As previously mentioned Lieutenant Chard was leant a towel by Private Bush (see above) who had been injured by the bullet which killed Cole.

Thomas was buried in the cemetery at Rorke's Drift and his name is inscribed on the monument. He was entitled to the South Africa Medal with 1877-8-9 clasp, but there is no record of a claim for his effects.

Thomas Collins

Thomas Collins was born on 13 September 1861, at Pelcomb, Camrose near Haverfordwest in Pembrokeshire, the seventh child of eight born to Thomas Collins, a farm labourer, and his wife Dorothy (formerly Lewis). Thomas junior was already working as a farm labourer at the age of twelve, and when the family moved to the Tenby area he remained in the Haverfordwest, where he lived in St Martin's. His three eldest siblings had died young and his mother and father died within a year of each other.

Thomas drifted across to Monmouthshire, where he enlisted in the Monmouthshire Militia before joining the regular army on 22 May 1877. He was aged fifteen years and eight months, but his age on enlistment was stated to be 'apparently 22'. He was described as five feet six-and-a-half inches tall, with grey eyes and light-brown hair. He had a chest measurement of 38 inches and had a wart on his back. His religion was Church of England. As 1396 Private Collins he was posted to the 2nd Battalion, 24th Regiment at Brecon, joining the regiment at Chatham.

He sailed to the Cape in February 1878. He took part in the Cape Frontier War, and at seventeen he was possibly the youngest man to take part in the defence of Rorke's Drift. For his service he received the South Africa Medal with 1877-8-9 clasp.

The surviving building at Rorke's Drift pictured soon after the battle. It has been stripped of its thatch, and a more permanent stone wall has been constructed. It measured 80 feet by 20 feet and was originally Jim Rorke's barn before being utilised as the mission station's chapel.

While serving at Gibraltar on 8 June 1880 he was confined and charged with being drunk on piquet duty, and sentenced to 42 days imprisonment with hard labour. In the meantime most of his surviving siblings emigrated to Nebraska in the United States. He then saw service in India and extended his service to twelve years on 27 August 1882. In 1884 he served in Madras, then Wellington, then back to Madras.

He re-engaged at Rhaniket in Bengal on 19 August 1889 for such term as would complete 21 years service. Having twice been admitted to hospital with rheumatism the medical officer recommended a change of climate, and Thomas was shipped back to England to be admitted to Netley Hospital on 22 April 1891. A medical board found him to be suffering from severe rheumatism attributable to climate, and he was invalided out of the army on 16 June 1891. He gave his intended place of residence as 'c/o, the Star Inn, Pontypool'. He settled in Newport, where he lived at 19 Arlington Street, and obtained work as a labourer.

There was an obvious hereditary weakness in the constitution of his family. Thomas's health deteriorated and he had been admitted to the Newport Borough Asylum by 1901, where he remained for the rest of his life. He died on 17 April 1908, aged 47, the cause of death being recorded as pthesis pulmonalis, the same illness which had struck two of his siblings. He was buried in the cemetery within the grounds of the asylum.

Anthony Connors

Anthony Connors was born at Westminster in London in 1852. He joined the army in the summer of 1870, and as 2310 Private A Connors he joined the 2nd Battalion, 24th Regiment in India on 28 December 1871. He was five feet six-and-a-half inches tall, with a fresh complexion, grey eyes and brown hair. He was sentenced by civil power to serve 168 days imprisonment with hard labour at Millbank Prison in London. He returned to his regiment and sailed to South Africa on 17 July 1878. He took part in the Cape Frontier War and during the Zulu War he remained at Rorke's Drift after the battle, where he was accidentally shot by a comrade while they were on duty slaughtering cattle. For his service he received the South Africa Medal with 1877-8-9 clasp.

He was sent to Netley Hospital from Gibraltar on 18 July 1880, and an injury assessment board held at the Chelsea Hospital on 18 August 1880 confirmed that he had received a gunshot wound in the left thigh which would seriously affect his powers regarding employment. He was awarded a pension of seven pence a day for six months and was discharged from the army on 14 September 1880, his character being described as fair. His intended place of residence was London.

Timothy Connors

Timothy Connors was born at Killeady, County Cork, Ireland, in about 1842. He left his job as a labourer to enlist at Bandon, County Cork, on 15 March 1860. He was just under five feet five inches tall, with a fair complexion, light-blue eyes and dark-brown hair, and as 1323 Private T. Connors he was posted to the 2nd Battalion, 24th Regiment. He was admitted to hospital for treatment of a social disease on 6 March 1862, and having re-engaged at Rangoon on 26 July 1867, he was later tried by Court Martial, but his offence and punishment was not recorded. He was admitted to hospital in Secunderabad for treatment of hepatitis on 11 November 1870, and after being examined by a special invalidity committee he was recommended to be sent to England for a change of climate, being admitted to Netley Hospital. He was admitted to the hospital at the barracks in Warley, Birmingham in March 1873.

He received orders for active service in South Africa and sailed with the battalion to the Cape in February 1878. He took part in the Cape Frontier War and during the Zulu War he was present at the defence of Rorke's Drift. For his service he received the South Africa Medal with 1877-8-9 clasp.

He received the Long Service and Good Conduct Medal at Gibraltar on 1 April 1880 and was shipped to England from India, being discharged at the Colchester depot on 19 April 1882. His intended place of residence was Quogh, near Bandon in County Cork, and he was registered as an out-pensioner from the Chelsea Hospital.

George Davies

George Davies was born in 1853. He joined the army at Wrexham on 15 October 1874, aged 21 years, and as 470 Private Davies he was posted to the 2nd Battalion, 24th Regiment. He sailed to the Cape with his battalion in February 1878, fighting in the Cape Frontier War and Zulu War. For his service in the campaign he was awarded the South Africa Medal with 1877-8-9 clasp. His name has not been traced on the muster rolls after 4 March 1881.

William Davis

William Henry Davis was born at St Bartholomew's, Camden Town, London during the June quarter of 1853. He enlisted at Bow Street Police Court on 26 February 1877, being described as five feet four inches tall, with a dark complexion, hazel eyes and dark brown hair. His religion was Church of England.

Cetshwayo after his capture on board HMS *Natal* en-route for England.

As 1363 Private Davies he was posted to the 2nd Battalion, 24th Regiment in the following month.

He received orders for active service in South Africa and sailed to the Cape with the battalion in February 1878. While at Rorke's Drift he was granted a penny a day good conduct pay on 27 February 1879, which he forfeited in the following June. For his service he received the South Africa Medal with 1877-8-9 clasp.

While serving at Gibraltar he was confined in cells on 1 July 1880, charged with breaking out of the barracks and doing away with necessaries. He was tried by Court Martial and sentenced to 42 days imprisonment with hard labour, being released on 12 August 1880 to sail with the battalion to India. On his return from the sub-continent on 27 May 1883 he transferred to the Army Reserves HQ, London District in the following month, his character at that time being described as bad – latterly good. He had received a 4th Class Certificate of Education. He discharged on 10 April 1889. He died in London.

Thomas Daw

Thomas Daw was born on 8 July 1858 at his grandmother's house in Higher Street, Merriott, Somerset. He was the third child of four born to Thomas

Daw, a farm labourer, and his second wife Priscilla, known as Ann (formerly Druce). Thomas senior had a daughter from his first marriage. They moved to 29 Piddletown, Haselbury Plucknett in Somerset, where Thomas Daw senior died in 1870, and by the time of the 1871 census Tom and his two brothers were working as agricultural labourers.

Thomas enlisted at Crewkerne in Somerset on 5 February 1877, where his description was given as five feet four-and-a-half inches tall, with a florid complexion, brown hair and grey eyes. His muscular development was good and he had a 36-inch chest. His religion was Church of England. As 1178 Private Daw he was posted to the 2nd Battalion, 24th Regiment at Brecon.

He sailed to the Cape in February 1878. He served in the Cape Frontier War, being hospitalised in June 1878 suffering with dyspepsia, and was hospitalised in Natal in August suffering with blisters caused by the long march across country. After Rorke's Drift he was granted a penny a day good conduct pay from 6 February 1879 and was transferred to 'H' company on 3 April 1879. For his service he received the South Africa Medal with 1877-8-9 clasp.

He served on Gibraltar in 1880, and on arriving in India in September 1880 he was hospitalised on several occasions with ailments such as dysentery, dyspepsia and venereal diseases. He was granted two pence a day good conduct pay from 6 February 1883, and on returning to England he was discharged at Gosport and posted to the 1st Class Army Reserves, Taunton District on 31 May 1883. His character was described as clean, good and temperate.

Thomas obtained work as a wagon driver for the local wool factory. He married Emily Westcott at Wellington Parish Church on 26 May 1887, and in the following October Emily gave birth to Ernest Herbert at Five Houses in Tone, Wellington, Somerset. Ada Priscilla was born in 1889, and Harold Percival was born in 1897. Sadly, Emily died after giving birth to a stillborn child in 1906.

After seeing his sons return safely from service in the First World War, Thomas Daw died peacefully at his home on 23 May 1924, aged 65. The cause of death was given as 'carcinoma of the pancreas'. He was buried in unmarked grave number 2963 at Wellington Cemetery. His birth and marriage certificates state his name as Daw, but he was buried as Thomas Dawe.

George Deacon

George Deacon Power was born on 23 August 1852 at 76 Hampden Street, St Mary's, Paddington, London. He was the fourth son of six children born to William John Power, who worked for the Great Western Railway, and his wife Mary Ann (formerly Deacon). Following George's birth the family moved to Bromley Road, Paddington, and the 1871 census states that the family had moved to 22 Beringden Street, Kensington.

George left his job as a clerk to join the army at Chatham on 10 November 1877, and using his mother's maiden name he joined as George Deacon. The age on his service papers was given as eighteen but he was in fact 25, and as 1467 Private Deacon, he was posted to the 2nd Battalion, 24th Regiment. He sailed to the Cape with the battalion in February 1878. He took part in the Cape Frontier War, being confined for six days in March 1878. At Rorke's Drift, according to Private Hitch

> Deakin [Deacon], a comrade, said to me as I was leaning back against the bis-
> cuit boxes, 'Fred, when it comes to the last shall I shoot you?' I declined. 'No,
> they have very nearly done for me and they can finish me right out when it
> comes to the last.'

George realised that army life was not for him and he deserted at Pietermaritzburg on 9 September 1879. He was entitled to the South Africa Medal with 1877-8-9 clasp.

By 1884 he had set himself up in business as a provision's merchant in the Poplar district of London. He married Helena Teresa Sincock, a well-travelled and educated daughter of a civil engineer, on 26 November 1884 at the parish church in Poplar. In 1887 Helena gave birth to twin daughters in Hackney, Middlesex, Helena Mercedes and Mary Elizabeth, and John George Homer was born in 1888. They then moved to 14 Wherstead Road, Ipswich, where William Donald Bain was born in 1890, Edward Richard was born in 1892, and Cecil Frederick was born in 1895.

George became a police officer on the Great Eastern Railway, becom-ing Police Inspector by 1891, and having moved to 184 Portway, West Ham by the turn of the century, he became a Chief Inspector of Railway Police. Helena died in 1926 and George moved to the home of his daughter Helena at Gantshill Crescent, Ilford. He died at the Romford Hospital on 16 February 1934, aged 81, and the cause of death was recorded as myocardial degeneration. He was buried with his wife in the City of London Cemetery on Aldersbrook Road, Little Ilford. Regimental representatives were present at his funeral, including Lieutenant-Colonel Frank Bourne, and his death was reported in the April 1934 issue of the *South Wales Borderers Journal*. George did not receive his campaign medal due to his desertion, but he claimed it in 1920. It was sold at a auction on 16 September 1991.

Michael Deane

Michael Deane attested for 25 Brigade on 10 March 1877, and as 1357 Private Deane was posted to the 2nd Battalion, 24th Regiment, at Brecon on 26 January 1878, the unit having received orders for active service in South Africa. He was entitled to the South Africa Medal with 1877-8-9 clasp, but he deserted while serving at Gibraltar on 22 July 1880.

James Dick

James William Dick was born at Island Magee, County Antrim, Ireland in about 1847. He enlisted in Belfast on 3 February 1865, to serve ten years, being described as five feet seven inches tall, with a fresh complexion, grey eyes and curly brown hair, and as 1697 Private Dick he was posted to the 2nd Battalion, 24th Regiment. He gave his next of kin as his mother, Mrs J. Dick of Island Magee. He served in India from 1865 to 1873, during which time he was granted good conduct pay of a penny a day in 1868, which had risen to two pence by the time he re-engaged at Secunderabad on 18 November 1871. He was granted three pence a day good conduct pay on 6 February 1877.

He sailed to the Cape with his battalion in February 1878, taking part in the Cape Frontier War and Zulu War. He had forfeited a penny of his good conduct pay, which was restored to him soon after the defence of Rorke's Drift.

He served on Gibraltar in 1880, and in India from 1880–1889, during which time he was awarded the Long Service and Good Conduct Medal with a gratuity of £5 on 1 January 1884, and his good conduct pay had risen to five pence a day by 6 February 1888. He claimed his discharge as time-served in Secunderabad on 20 February 1889, his conduct being described as exemplary.

William Dicks

William Dicks was born at Islington, London, in 1847. He enlisted for eleven years service at Westminster Police Court on 25 November 1864, being described as five feet six inches tall, with a fresh complexion, brown eyes and brown hair. As 1634 Private Dicks he was posted to the 1st Battalion, 24th Regiment, transferring to the 2nd Battalion on 1 February 1865. His next of kin was his sister, Mrs A. Framplar of 42 Havelock Street, Islington, London.

He served in India from 1865–1873, and he was granted and forfeited good conduct pay on several occasions, being sentenced to six days in prison by his commanding officer in 1874. His good conduct pay was at two pence a day and

The men who defended the storehouse concentrated mainly on stopping the warriors from getting near enough to set light to the thatched roof, as they had succeeded in doing to the roof of the hospital.

he had reached the rank of corporal when he received orders for active service in South Africa, and he sailed to the Cape with his battalion in February 1878. While taking part in the Cape Frontier War he was appointed lance-sergeant on 13 May 1878, but having moved to Natal, he was tried and sentenced to be reduced to private 16 September 1878, and spent the next two days in prison. During the Zulu War he was present at the defence of Rorke's Drift. For his service he was awarded the South Africa Medal with 1877-8-9 clasp.

He served on Gibraltar in 1880, and in India from 1880 until 22 January 1886, during which time he re-engaged at Secunderabad on 6 August 1882 to complete 21 years service. He discharged at Gosport on 9 February 1886, and his conduct was described as very good. He died in Chelsea, London on 19 October 1925.

Thomas Driscoll

Thomas Driscoll attested for the army on 5 December 1876, and as 971 Private Driscoll was posted to the 2nd Battalion, 24th Regiment, on 22 January 1877, a date which would have some significance exactly two years later. He sailed to the Cape with his battalion in February 1878. He transferred to A Company on 29 January 1879, and for his service he received the South Africa Medal with 1877-8-9 clasp.

He later served on Gibraltar and in India. He attended The Old Comrades Club of the 24th Foot reunion at the Victoria Barracks in Portsmouth on 30/31 March 1929. Thomas Driscoll died at Ebbw Vale, Monmouthshire, on 16 June 1931.

William Dunbar

William Dunbar stated that he had run away from home at the age of thirteen. He enlisted at Newport on 20 June 1877, and as 1421 Private Dunbar was posted to the 2nd Battalion, 24th Regiment, at Brecon on 13 December 1877.

He received orders for active service in South Africa, and was appointed lance-corporal on 1 February 1878, the day he embarked to sail to the Cape. He took part in the Cape Frontier War, being promoted corporal on 15 March 1878, but soon after arriving in Natal he was confined in cells, tried by court martial on 22 July 1878, and received 28 days imprisonment with hard labour and reduced to private.

At the defence of Rorke's Drift he was evidently one of the sharpshooters posted behind the wagons in the south rampart, as Lieutenant Chard stated that during the first Zulu attack 'a Chief on horseback was dropped by Private

Dunbar, 24th.' According to Private Hook 'Private Dunbar, shot no fewer than nine Zulus, one of them being a Chief.' For his service he received the South Africa Medal with 1877-8-9 clasp.

He served on Gibraltar in 1880, and in India, from where he returned home on 9 October 1883. His intended place of residence was Newport. It is believed that he returned to South Africa and lived the life of a miner and prospector and eventually became an overseer there. He was interviewed by a reporter from the *Natal Mercury* at the Centenary Home for aged men in Durban in 1938, and he was known then as Charles Dunbar. He died at Hillcrest, Pinetown, Natal on 29 January 1940, aged 82, one of the last surviving Rorke's Drift men, and he was buried at Stellawood Cemetery in Durban.

George Edwards

George Edward Orchard was born on 25 August 1855 at 5 Charles Street, Bristol, the eldest son of three born to George Orchard, a master tailor, and his second wife Anna (formerly Goodman). George Orchard senior died in 1871, and George junior seemed to be jinxed when it came to employment. He

George Edward Orchard joined the army as George Edwards. He and his wife Rena had eleven children.

was apprenticed to a shoemaker in John Street, Bristol, but his employer died, and he took a job at a boot factory near Stone Bridge in Bristol, which closed down. He headed for Wales, where he gained employment as a labourer in the building trade, but the business failed and closed down.

Perhaps not surprisingly, George went to the army recruiting office in Newport and enlisted on 23 November 1876, as George Edwards. His description was given as just over five feet four inches tall, with a fresh complexion, blue eyes and brown hair, and his religion was Church of England. As 922 Private Edwards he was posted to the 2nd Battalion, 24th Regiment. He served in Dover and Chatham, and from 15 June–28 July 1877 he was attached to the Grenadier Guards in London, completing a course in training and drill.

He sailed to the Cape with his unit in February 1878. He took part in the Cape Frontier War, and on 17 July 1878 he made a remittance of £2 to Anna Orchard. No other details of Anna being his mother were given to the paymaster owing to the fact that he had enlisted as George Edwards. George was up in front of his commanding officer in August 1878 charged with an offence which was unrecorded, but earned him eight days loss of pay and he was confined to cells from 23–30 August. He was fined seven shillings for drunkenness on 1 December 1878.

Of Rorke's Drift he remembered that

> when Lord Chelmsford rode in on the morning of the 23rd, I was sitting on a biscuit box drinking a cup of cocoa. For some reason he stopped to speak to me and asked me my opinion about the defence we had put up. There was only one answer I could make to him 'It was an act of providence.'

He wrote a letter to his father in St Luke's Road, Bedminster, and on 29 March 1879 the *Bristol Observer* carried a report under the title 'A Bedminster Man at Rorke's Drift', in which he stated:

> Our company was fighting hard from three o'clock in the afternoon until 6 o'clock the next morning, when we beat them off. These Zulus are a strong, savage, determined race of people, and we have not enough British troops out here for the war, so it will take a long time before it is over unless we get more troops as the enemy come in such large numbers.

It was also reported that 'Pte Orchard and another comrade simultaneously fired at and wounded in the knee, the brother of the King of the Zulus, and he was taken prisoner in consequence.' He was also stated to have been present when the Prince Imperial was killed. For his service he received the South Africa Medal with 1877-78-79 clasp.

The final resting place of George Orchard in Paulton Cemetery in Somerset. He was one of the last known survivors of the Rorke's Drift garrison when he died in 1940, aged 84.

He served on Gibraltar, where he was fined a day's pay in March 1880, and again in April of that year. He was in confinement for seven days in May, and for three days in June. He sailed to India, where he was awarded a penny a day good conduct pay from 9 June 1882. He arrived at Gosport on 27 January 1883, and was admitted to Netley Hospital until 6 February 1883. He was then posted to the 1st South Wales Borderers in Manchester to await discharge. He forfeited his good conduct pay while stationed at Manchester, and he was discharged to the 1st Class Army Reserves on 1 April 1883. He received his final discharge at Brecon on 23 November 1888.

He gave his intended place of residence as Withy Mill, Paulton, Somerset, and it is thought that he found employment at Ashman's Boot Factory in Paulton. He married Rena Elizabeth Swift at the Clutton Registry Office on 14 April 1884, and they lived at New Pit, Paulton. They had eleven children. Mabel Elizabeth was born in 1884, Sarah Hannah in 1885, William George in 1887 and Albert Edward in 1888, who died at the age of three months. Mary Ellen was born in 1890, Edith Emily in 1892, Charles Frederick in 1894, Dennis Bertram John in 1897, Olive Rena in 1899, Herbert Ernest in 1903 and Florence Gertrude in 1907.

George was a member of the Royal Defence Corps, and he and Rena attended the Methodist Church. He attended the Northern Command Tattoo in 1934, and he gave an interview to the *Somerset Guardian* not long before he died, which appeared under the title: 'Helped to Defend Rorke's Drift. Paulton Veterans Recollections.' George died on 14 February 1940, aged 84, the cause of death being given as myocardia (heart failure), and he was buried at the Paulton Parish Cemetery with full military honours (section 25, row P, plot 25).

John Fagan

John Fagan attested for the army on 13 December 1876, and as 969 Private Fagan was posted to the 2nd Battalion, 24th Regiment at Brecon. He received orders for active service in South Africa and sailed to the Cape in February 1878, taking part in the Cape Frontier War. He was confined by civil power in Natal, tried on 7 November 1878, and sentenced to five days imprisonment. he was killed in action at Rorke's Drift. He was providing cover fire for the men who were evacuating the hospital when he was hit in the chest by a Zulu bullet, but he managed to keep hold of his rifle and remained at his post. Private Savage was interviewed by a newspaper which reported that 'In the night time, when under fire, Savage heard a fellow soldier of the name of Fagan cry out for water, and managed to crawl along to help his disabled comrade-in-arms, who died before daylight next morning.' He was buried in the cemetery at Rorke's Drift and his name is inscribed on the monument. For his service he was entitled to the South Africa Medal with 1877-8-9 clasp, and his effects were listed as claim by his next of kin.

John French

John Barker French was born on 6 August 1841 at 2 Dukes Lane, Kensington, London. He was the first child of four to William George French, a coachman, and his wife Mary Ann (formerly Barker). John was christened at St Mary Abbott's Church in Kensington on 3 October 1841. As the family increased they moved to a larger home at 2 Adam and Eve Yard, Kensington. John was working as a groom when he contracted erysipelas, a skin disease associated with dermatitis, which is passed from infected animals and can also affect the joints.

Consequently, John left his job at the stables and enlisted into the army at Westminster in London on 16 December 1858. His description was five feet four inches tall, with blue eyes and brown hair. He had a 30 3/4-inch chest measurement, with a 'wiry' build. As 582 Private French he was posted to the 2nd Battalion, 24th Regiment. He was admitted to hospital on 12 May 1859 for treatment of his skin disease, which was to cause him problems throughout his army life. He sailed from Cork to Mauritius on 10 March 1860, where he reached the rank of sergeant on 13 November 1861. However, he was tried by court martial on 18 August 1862, being sentenced to five days imprisonment and reduced to private. He received several promotions and demotions, never rising above the rank of corporal. He served in Burma from 6 October 1865, and he was sent to the hospital in Port Blair, India, in June 1866, when his skin complaint flared up again. He returned to Burma, after which the regiment was posted to India on 16 February 1869. He was invalided to Bombay on 17 February 1870 with his skin problem, and then sent to Netley Hospital on 8 April 1870. He was promoted to corporal on 16 July 1870.

While stationed at the Warley depot in Birmingham he met Mary Pricilla Johnstone of 2 Dukes Lane, Kensington, and they married at Kensington Parish Church on 13 April 1873. They had five children. Elizabeth was born in 1874, William James Alexander in 1876, Louisa Beatrice in 1877, Thomas George in 1880, and Ernest John in 1882. While stationed at Aldershot John was in hospital suffering with another bout of erysipelas, which appeared to be lasting longer each time it erupted.

He received orders for active service in South Africa, and his family accompanied him as he sailed to the Cape in February 1878. He was promoted to sergeant on the day after the defence of Rorke's Drift and was transferred to G Company. However, on 24 June he was registered in the defaulters book and reduced to private.

He served on Gibraltar in 1880, returning to Brecon on 3 November 1880 where he was promoted to corporal on 9 February 1881. However, he was tried by court martial and reduced to private in the following August. He discharged on 3 January 1882, having completed nearly 22 years service, his conduct and character being described as good. His intended place of residence was 8 William Street, Kensington, Middlesex, the home of his mother, and, despite his condition, he gained employment as a stableman. His wife died after giving birth to a stillborn child in 1884.

He and his mother moved the family to live at Kintbury Cottage, Vine Terrace, Kensington, where John died suddenly on 27 June 1895, aged 54, the cause of death being recorded as compression of the brain from sanguineous apoplexy (natural). He was buried in a common grave at Hanwell Cemetery, London (section 92, grave 47).

Henry Gallagher

Henry Edward Gallagher was the second child of Henry Gallagher, a merchant's clerk, and his wife Mary (formerly Kennedy), born at Killenaule,

Lance-Sergeant Henry Gallagher
with his wife, Caroline, whom he had
married in Dover in 1877. He was
promoted sergeant later that year aged
only 22.

Thurles, County Tipperary in Ireland. He was baptised on 28 October 1855. His parents died while he was young, and it is believed that the church claimed the Gallagher's smallholding as payment for raising and educating the children. Henry became a clerk and travelled to England in March 1874.

He enlisted into the army on 14 March 1874. He was just over five feet six inches tall, with a fresh complexion, amber eyes and dark brown hair, and his religion was Roman Catholic. As 81 Private Gallagher he was posted to the 2nd Battalion, 24th Regiment at Brecon. He was promoted to corporal on 11 March 1875. He was posted to Dover where he gained a 2nd Class Certificate of Education in 1875, and he attended the Hythe School of Musketry in 1876. He was promoted to sergeant on 9 October 1877, aged only 22.

Henry married Caroline Maria Stanley at the Dover Registry Office on 7 April 1877. They had six children. Caroline Lilian Gertrude was born in 1881, Henry Edward in 1883, William Alfred in 1885, Violet Elizabeth in 1888, Daisy Dorothea in 1890 and Lawrence Stanley in 1895. Henry, William and Lawrence would later enlist in the army.

He sailed to the Cape in February 1878, taking part in the Cape Frontier War. At Rorke's Drift, due to the continuous firing of his rifle, the heat made the breech of his weapon expand, which caused the powder to flash back. From that day he had a permanent black mark burnt into his right cheek and the side

A floral tribute from the South Wales Borderers takes pride of place at the grave of Henry Gallagher at Christ Church Cemetery in Portsdown Hill, soon after his funeral. The cortege was accompanied by men of his old regiment, including Fred Hitch's son, Charles, who laid a wreath on behalf of the surviving Rorke's Drift men who were too frail to make the journey.

of his nose. For his service he received the South Africa Medal with 1877-8-9 clasp.

He served on Gibraltar in 1880, where he extended his service to twelve years. When the regiment sailed for India he returned to Brecon, where he was promoted to colour-sergeant on 26 January 1881, and when the unit became the South Wales Borderers on 1 July 1881 he was given the new regimental number 1590. He was posted to India in December 1882, and to Burma at the beginning of 1886. He was promoted sergeant-major on 9 January 1889, and served at Aden, where an ulcerated foot caused him to be hospitalised for the only time in his army career. He served in Malabar in India from 27 October 1893–9 January 1895, and on returning to England he was stationed at Hilsea, then Gosport. He served at Cairo in 1895, returning to England on 18 March 1897. While serving in Cairo his medals went missing and he had to get replacements.

Henry was discharged at Gosport, having completed over 23 years, and his conduct throughout his army career remained unblemished. His intended place of residence was Borstal House, 48 London Avenue, North End, Portsmouth. However, after only 24 hours as a civilian he was appointed barrack warden at Coleworth Barracks in Hilsea, a position he retained until 1911. He was described on discharge as being an exemplary soldier, with regular and temperate habits, and Army Orders for January 1911 announced that Sergeant-Major Gallagher had been awarded the Meritorious Service Medal.

Henry's retirement was spent at 'Wistaria' 16 Augustine Road, Drayton, Hampshire, where Fred Hitch sometimes visited him. Sergeant-Major Gallagher died of a massive heart attack at his home on 17 December 1931, aged 75, and he was laid to rest in Christ Church Cemetery, Portsdown Hill, Hampshire with semi-military honours. A new memorial stone was installed at the grave, and a rededication service was organised in 2005.

Edward Gee

Edward Gee attested for the army in November 1872 and as 2429 Private Gee he was posted to the 1st Battalion, 24th Regiment, transferring to the 2nd Battalion on 1 January 1873. He received orders for active service in South Africa and sailed to the Cape in February 1878. He took part in the Cape Frontier War, and during the Zulu War he was present at the defence of Rorke's Drift. For his service he received the South Africa Medal with 1877-8-9 clasp. He was sent to Netley Hospital on 1 February 1880, and transferred to the Army Reserve.

James Hagan

James Egan was born at Neenagh, County Tipperary, Ireland, in 1857. Having previously served in the Royal Monmouth Militia, he enlisted at Monmouth on 23 March 1876, being just over five feet six inches tall, with a freckled complexion, grey eyes and light-brown hair. His religion was Roman Catholic. As 798 Private Hagan he was posted to the 2nd Battalion, 24th Regiment at Brecon. He obtained a 4th Class Certificate of Education on 18 January 1877.

He sailed for the Cape in February 1878, taking part in the Cape Frontier War and the Zulu War. For his service he received the South Africa Medal with 1877-8-9 clasp. He was granted a penny a day good conduct pay in South Africa in July 1879, which he forfeited while serving in Gibraltar in June 1880, and it was restored while he was in India in June 1881. He returned to England on 24 November 1881, and transferred to the Army Reserves, 2nd Welch Regiment District, on 24 March 1882. He married Catherine Julia Barry at St Dubritius Chapel, Treforest, near Pontprydd, Glamorgan, on 8 July 1882, and they had five children. He was re-called to army service in the 2nd Battalion, South Wales Borderers, on 3 August 1882, when he resumed his one penny a day good conduct pay, but he forfeited it a month later. He re-transferred to the Army Reserves, Cheshire Regiment District, on 8 February 1883, finally discharging at Brecon on 23 March 1888. His character was described as good.

He died on 27 May 1916, aged 55, and he was buried in the Gyntaf Cemetery, Pontypridd. A new headstone was erected at his grave in a dedication service held on 20 September 2009.

William Halley

William Halley was born in Ireland in 1859. He attested for 25 Brigade on 3 March 1876, and as 1282 Private Halley he was posted to the 1st Battalion, 24th Regiment, transferring to the 2nd Battalion on 13 December 1877. He received orders for active service in South Africa and sailed to the Cape with his unit in February 1878. He took part in the Cape Frontier War and was promoted lance-corporal on 17 July 1878. He was promoted corporal on the day after Rorke's Drift and was appointed master shoemaker on 29 January 1879. While he was still at Rorke's Drift he was reduced to private on 2 August 1879. For his service he received the South Africa Medal with 1877-8-9 clasp.

He was promoted to lance-corporal on his arrival on Gibraltar on 21 February 1880, but was reduced to private while in India on 10 January 1882. He died while serving at Thayetmayo in Burma on 30 April 1887. His campaign medal was returned to the Mint on 23 November 1897.

John Harris

John Harris was born at Crickhowell, Breconshire in 1858. Having previously served in the Royal South Wales Borderers Militia, he enlisted for the regular army at Brecon on 15 January 1877, and as 1062 Private Harris he was posted to the 2nd Battalion, 24th Regiment. He was described as five feet six inches tall, with a sallow complexion, grey eyes and light-brown hair. His religion was Wesleyan. He was admitted to hospital in Brecon on 8 February 1877 suffering from anaemia, being admitted to hospital in Dover on 10 April 1877 suffering with the same complaint.

When the 2nd Battalion received orders for active service in South Africa it would seem that he had been granted permission 'for return home', and did not initially sail with his unit. However, he joined them on 1 July 1878, and apparently took part in the latter stages of the Cape Frontier War. He claimed compensation for loss of kit at Rorke's Drift and for his service he received the South Africa Medal with 1877-8-9 clasp.

He was admitted to the sick bay on board the ship transporting the regiment to Gibraltar on 26 January 1880, and was admitted to hospital on their arrival. He was awarded a penny a day good conduct pay on 25 March 1880. He was brought before a medical board in Gibraltar and invalided on 12 July 1880. On his return to England on 24 July 1880, he was admitted to Netley Hospital suffering from chronic osteo-arthritis. He was discharged as unfit for further service on 14 September 1880, his character being described as good, his habits temperate, and he was in possession of one good conduct badge. An Injury Assessment Board held at the Royal Hospital, Chelsea on 14 August 1880 confirmed that he was suffering from osteo-arthritis due to lying for months on damp ground, provoked and aggravated by climate and service. It was stated that he could eventually earn a living, and he was awarded a pension of seven pence a day for three years. His intended place of residence was Wandsworth, Surrey.

Patrick Hayes

Patrick Hayes was born at Newmarket, County Clare, Ireland on 9 September 1854. He enlisted at Ennis in County Clare on 8 September 1868, and as 2067 Private Hayes was posted to the 2nd Battalion, 24th Regiment. As a boy of fourteen he was just over four feet eight inches tall, with a fresh complexion, grey eyes and light-brown hair. He was appointed drummer on 8 December 1869 and embarked for service in India on 29 December 1869. Having reverted to private, he returned home on 3 January 1873, and was appointed drummer on 1 April 1873.

He received orders for active service in South Africa and sailed to the Cape in February 1878. For his service he received the South Africa Medal with 1877-8-9 clasp.

He re-engaged on 22 November 1879 and gained a 2nd Class Certificate of Education. He served on Gibraltar in 1880 and in India, where he reached the rank of corporal on 22 September 1885, and after reverting to private he was appointed bandsman on 7 October 1887 while serving in Burma. Having returned to India on 10 November 1888, he was permitted to continue in the service beyond 21 years on 29 October 1889. He returned home on 16 February 1892, being awarded a third good conduct badge on 9 September 1892. He discharged on 30 November 1892, being awarded a pension for life on the following day.

He became a civilian worker at the barracks in Brecon until he was over 60, and on his retirement he lived in Riverhall Street, Wandsworth, London. He died in Lambeth, London, on 2 October 1940, aged 86, and Colonel Frank Bourne attended his funeral.

Frederick Hitch

Frederick Hitch was born on 29 November 1856 at 7 Chase Side in Southgate, Edmonton, Middlesex (now Greater London), and was christened at the local Weld Chapel. He was the sixth son and ninth child of eleven to John and Sarah Hitch (formerly Champness), and his father was a shoemaker (journeyman). The 1871 census shows that, while the family had moved to 153 Chase Road, Fred lived at Eastpole Farm, 202 Chase Side where he worked as a farm labourer.

He enlisted at Westminster Police Court on 7 March 1877, and as 1362 Private Hitch was posted to the 2nd Battalion, 24th Regiment, at Dover, on 11 May 1877.

On the afternoon of 22 January he was making tea for the company at a temporary cookhouse behind the post when news of the Isandlwana disaster was received. As the defences were being built he was ordered to climb onto the roof of the store to watch out for the enemy, who soon appeared to appeared to the south-west, and he estimated their number to be about 4,000. Some warriors occupied caves on the Oscarberg Hill to the south and Private Hitch was the target of the first shot in the battle. Hitch returned fire, and also took a pot shot at a Zulu who appeared at the top of the Oscarberg. This man made a signal with his arm and the Zulu attack began.

Frederick Hitch still strapped-up after being wounded in action when a Zulu slug tore open his shoulder during the defence of Rorke's Drift. For his valour that day he was awarded the Victoria Cross.

As a mass of warriors advanced towards the north-west corner of the defences, Hitch scrambled down from the roof and fixed his bayonet as he ran across the compound. He took up a position in support of the men holding that section, where the Zulus showed fanatical bravery as they tried to get over the breast-work, and several al warriors succeeded. Hitch shot one, but as he tried to reload a second Zulu grabbed the muzzle of his rifle and tried to disarm him. He managed to load the weapon as they struggled for possession and blasted the Zulu at point blank range. As Lieutenant Bromhead was using his revolver to good effect, Hitch saw a warrior creeping up behind the officer with his assegai ready to strike. He needed to act quickly, but realising that his rifle was empty, he put the muzzle of the gun against the Zulu as if about to fire. The bluff worked, and the Zulu scrambled out before he delivered the fatal thrust.

Later, Private Hitch took up a position in the centre of the compound with Corporal Allan. The two men gallantly kept the enemy at bay while helping the patients out of a hospital window to the inner entrenchment. During the next fierce attack Hitch was again exposed to enemy fire, and he was hit by a slug which shattered his right shoulder as it passed through his body. He fell seriously wounded as a warrior moved in for the kill. Lieutenant Bromhead saw the danger and shot the Zulu with his revolver. The officer helped him to take off his tunic and put his wounded arm into his waistbelt to secure it. He was suffering terrible pain, but he continued to make himself useful by handing out ammunition to his comrades, until he collapsed from fatigue and loss of blood. He spent the rest of the battle in the storehouse in the care of Surgeon Reynolds.

Private Hitch was mentioned in dispatches, and his award of Victoria Cross was announced in the *London Gazette* on 2 May 1879. On returning to England he went to Netley Hospital, and on 12 August 1879 Queen Victoria visited him and presented him with the VC in person. He also received the South Africa Medal with 1877-8-9 clasp. He had 39 pieces of broken bone taken from his shoulder, and a medical board decided that his arm was permanently disabled. He was discharged unfit for further service on 25 August 1879. He left two accounts of the action at Rorke's Drift.

Fred Hitch returned to civilian life in London, where he gained employment with the Corps of Commissionaires, and lived at 44 Bedford Street, St Martin-in-the-Field. On 5 July 1881, he married Emily Meurisse, who was of German descent, at St Matthew's Church, Bayswater. They made their home in Westminster and had six children. Their three sons all passed-out as drum majors at the Duke of York School. Frederick later joined the Metropolitan Police, and Charles served with the 60th Rifles and the South Wales Borderers.

The 1891 census shows Fred living with his family at 9 Highbury Road in the parish of St James's, Fulham, London, and while he was working at the Royal United Services Institute in Whitehall Cecil Rhodes visited and

Alphonse de Neuville's 'Saving the Colours'. It depicts Lieutenants Teignmouth Melville and Neville Coghill, 1st/24th Regiment, during their ill-fated dash to save the colour of their battalion.

A sketch of the Rorke's Drift post by Trooper Henry Lugg of the Natal Mounted Police, which was used by Alphonse de Neuville as background information for his famous picture. It is accompanied by a list of interesting notes, the numbers being visible on the sketch. *2. Fort to retire to in case of necessity. 3. Wash house where the Kaffirs [Zulus] made themselves at home by smoking, boiling coffee and otherwise enjoying themselves. 10. Please imagine [Zulus] lying in heaps, also a tree and vultures.* (B. Lugg)

A medic attends to a wounded man as exhausted soldiers of the 24th Regiment defend the ramparts at the south of the defences. The Zulu warriors who attacked Rorke's Drift expected to face little resistance. However, the British fought for their lives with great gallantry, and held the Zulu assaults back so stubbornly that the warriors lost heart and retreated back across the river border.

Opposite: Alphonse de Neuville's painting of the defence of Rorke's Drift catches the scene much as it must have looked during the height of the battle, when the Zulus launched a particularly fierce attack at about seven in the evening. To the right of the picture Reverend Smith and an injured soldier hand out cartridges to Lieutenant Chard's section of the defences, while in the centre of the picture Surgeon Reynolds looks after a wounded man. To the left the invalided patients can be seen being evacuated from the hospital as the thatched roof of the building blazes out of control above their heads. 50,000 people paid to see the painting when it was exhibited in London in 1880.

A scene from within the hospital as William Jones holds back Zulu warriors with the *arme blanche* while Robert Jones attempts to dress Sergeant Maxfield to try to get him away. Maxfield was difficult to handle because he was delirious with fever and they eventually had to leave him to a terrible fate.

A kraal near Umlazi. The animal skin signified that the inDuna were present.

a Pte in the
2nd 24 Rgt
Zulu Campaign
S. Africa 1879.

A sketch of a Victorian soldier wearing the red tunic with green facings of the 24th
Regiment, which in 1881 was re-designated the South Wales Borderers, and is now a
unit of the Royal Welsh, still in the forefront of military operations to this day. Most
of the rank-and-file soldiers at Rorke's Drift were from the coal mining and cotton
manufacturing communities in and around the city slums. In addition to this there were
a number of men present who had gained a great deal of experience serving in various
campaigns around the world in defence of the Empire. This combination, and their
staunch loyalty to their regiment made them a formidable fighting unit. (John Anderson)

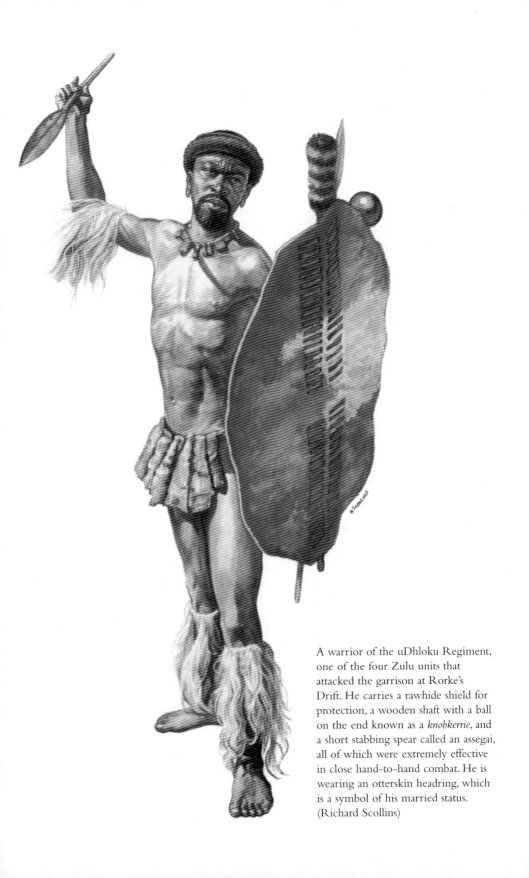

A warrior of the uDhloku Regiment, one of the four Zulu units that attacked the garrison at Rorke's Drift. He carries a rawhide shield for protection, a wooden shaft with a ball on the end known as a *knobkerrie*, and a short stabbing spear called an assegai, all of which were extremely effective in close hand-to-hand combat. He is wearing an otterskin headring, which is a symbol of his married status. (Richard Scollins)

CHURCH ARMY MISSION

STATION ROAD

On SATURDAY, Apr 19, 1913

MR CALEB WOOD

Late of the 25th Brigade 2nd Batt. 24th Regiment, B Company
will give his experience of the

ZULU WAR

AND THE

DEFENCE OF RORKE'S DRIFT

BAYONET and PHYSICAL EXERCISES

Will be displayed by the

ILKESTON ST. MARY'S C.L.B.

Fantasia entitled "A Military Church Parade"
[J. Ord Hume.] by the Church Army Silver Band

Rev. W.F. BUTTERTON

PRESIDING

Tickets 1/-, 6d, and 3d, Doors open at 6.30 pm. To commence at 7 pm.

PROCEEDS FOR MISSION AND LAND FUND

Rorke's Drift man Caleb Wood. After retirement he was a member of the Church Army Mission, and on 19 April 1913 he was invited to give a talk on his experiences to help raise money for the Church Land Fund. The talk was followed by a display of bayonet practice and physical exercises, which was accompanied by a fantasia of music entitled 'A Military Church Parade' played by the Church Army Silver Band, of which he was a member. He was also a local volunteer fire fighter. (Erewash Museum)

Left: The impressive stained glass memorial window at the Church of St Germain in Lincolnshire, which includes panels dedicated to Lieutenant Gonville Bromhead, who was the senior officer of the 24th Regiment during the defence of Rorke's Drift.

Below: The Havard Chapel at Brecon Cathedral, which was the regimental chapel of the South Wales Borderers, displaying a proud history in battle honours and colours, including the Queen's Colour of the 24th Regiment which was rescued after the disastrous engagement at Isandlwana. (J. Smith)

Left: Abraham Evans was a patient in the hospital during the defence of Rorke's Drift. He is wearing the South Africa Medal with 1877–8–9 clasp, the Egypt Medal with Tel-el-Kebir clasp and the Khedives Bronze Star with Egypt 1882 clasp. (Tom Roberts)

Below: A set of commemorative stamps issued at the time of the centenary of the Zulu War in 1979, depicting action from the three most famous battles of the campaign at Isandlwana, the defence of Rorke's Drift, and the Battle of Ulundi. The fourth plate depicts the Victoria Cross and the John Chard Decoration for bravery instituted by the South African authorities.

Left: Lieutenant Gonville Bromhead commanded B Company, 2nd/24th Regiment at the defence of Rorke's Drift.

Below: The monument at Rorke's Drift as it looks today. It has become an essential focal point for enactment groups and enthusiasts on historical tours of the Zulu War battlefields. (Ian Priddon)

Below: Rorke's Drift as it looks in 2010. The building on high ground at the centre of the picture is on the site of the original hospital and is now a museum. The Oscarberg Hill can be seen rising up behind the building to the right. (Lenny Hodges)

ACTING ASSISTANT COMMISSARY
JAMES LANGLEY DALTON, V.C.

MR. DALTON WON THE VICTORIA CROSS AT
RORKE'S DRIFT. 22ⁿᵈ JAN. 1879
WHERE HE ORGANIZED THE DEFENCES AND
EXHIBITED OUTSTANDING GALLANTRY IN THE SIEGE.

Above left: The South Africa Medal with 1877-8-9 clasp which was awarded to most of the soldiers who defended the mission station at Rorke's Drift. There was no individual Zulu War medal, as this particular medal was issued with clasps to represent several campaigns in which British soldiers had been involved in South Africa.

Above right: Dalton's medals. The South Africa medal is a replacement for the original, which was lost.

Above left: The final resting place of Frank Bourne at Elmer's End Cemetery in Kent. He was awarded the Distinguished Conduct Medal for his gallantry during the defence of the garrison, and he was the last known surviving Rorke's Drift man when he died at the age of 90 in 1945.

Above right: The grave of Colonel John Chard VC in the churchyard of St John the Baptist, Hatch Beauchamp near Taunton.

Opposite: Charles Mason (Frederick Herbert Brown) was issued with two South Africa Medals by mistake, the edges being engraved with both upright and sloping lettering.

The new headstone of Rorke's Drift man John Jeremiah Lyons (seen here) and Alfred Saxty, along with a plaque on the grave of a third defender, John Murphy, were placed at St Woolos Cemetery in Newport in 1996. (Andy Lee)

In Memory of
CHARLES JOHN
ROBSON
DRIVER
ROYAL ENGINEERS
A DEFENDER OF RORKES DRIFT
ZULU WAR 1879
DIED 19th JULY 1933.
THE RESPECTED ZULU
WARRIORS ARE ALSO
REMEMBERED

Above: The hand-carved wooden marker plaque which was placed at the grave of John Robson by the Royal Engineers Association in 1993, which was followed by a family service held at the graveside. (Lee Stevenson)

Left: A poignant moment as a lone bugler stands to attention at the final resting place of Rorke's Drift man Robert Tongue, during a re-dedication service held at Ruddington Cemetery in 2004, which was attended by several descendants of Rorke's Drift men. (Kris Wheatley)

Members of the Royal British Legion and the 1879 Group during a service of re-dedication and remembrance at the grave of Frederick Millne at Southern Cemetery in Manchester in 2001. Sergeant Millne was the only soldier of the 3rd Regiment present at the defence. (John Lester)

Fred Hitch became a London cabbie after retiring from the army. Here, some of the 24 taxi drivers are pictured as they prepare to pull his cab, which is covered with floral tributes, to Chiswick Cemetery in 1913.

congratulated him on his bravery. By the time of the 1901 census the family had moved to 1 Epirus Mews, St John's Parish, Fulham. His VC was stolen from his coat, the family had to pay for a replacement, and Fred had to sign a declaration to return the medal if the original was found. He was presented with the replacement by Lord Roberts in 1908, and later the family located the original VC at an auction and had to buy it back for £85. He wore his VC at the coronation of King Edward VII.

He was living in Duke Street, Chiswick when he bought a taxi cab and two horses and set up a small transport business in south London. He later worked as a taxi driver for the General Motor Cab Company in Chiswick. By 1912 he was living on his own in rented accommodation at 62 Cranbrook Road, Chiswick. During Christmas 1912 the drivers at his depot went on strike and he spent much of his time on picket duty in bitterly cold weather, which seems to have damaged his health, and on 6 January 1913, he complained of bad pains in his side. His landlady tried to comfort him but he died later in the day, aged 56. An inquest found that he had died of pleura-pneumonia and heart failure.

His funeral was an impressive affair, attended by John Fielding VC, Frank Bourne DCM, his friend Joseph Farmer, a Boer War VC, and over a thousand London cab drivers. He was buried with military honours provided by the South Wales Borderers, at St Nicholas Churchyard, Chiswick Old Cemetery. His monument was paid for by public subscription, one of the donations coming from the family of Major Chard. His Victoria Cross is with the Regimental Museum in Brecon.

Henry Hook

Alfred Henry Hook was born in Churcham, Huntley, near Gloucester on 6 August 1850, the eldest of six children born to Henry and Ellen Hook (formerly Higgs). His father was a rural labourer, and the family home was a house called 'Birdwood', known locally as 'Hook's Farm'. By 1860 they had moved to Westbury-on-Severn, and by 1863 to Blaisdon. While living at Aston Ingham, Newent, Herefordshire, Henry married Comfort Jones on 26 December 1870, and they had three children. Raymond was born in 1871, Henrietta in 1873 and Julia in 1876.

He had enlisted into the Royal Monmouth Militia at Monmouth on 7 May 1869, and served with the unit until May 1874. He joined the regular army on 13 March 1877, and as 1373 Private Hook was posted to the 2nd Battalion, 24th Regiment at Monmouth, signing up for six years.

At Rorke's Drift he was making tea for the hospital patients when he was one of six men ordered to barricade themselves inside the hospital to protect the bedridden sick. He and Private Thomas 'Old King' Cole were in charge of a room which contained a native. There was a door leading to an interior ward where eight patients were situated. Private Hook was shooting at the Zulus

Henry Hook was described in the film *Zulu!* as a malingerer, thief, coward and insubordinate, and was portrayed so until he fights like a lion during the evacuation of the hospital patients. However, the fact that he received good conduct allowance not long before the defence, and was made orderly to a senior officer soon afterwards, suggests quite the opposite, and he is believed to have been teetotal, notwithstanding the scene in the film where he drinks alcohol from a broken bottle. He was certainly a well-respected man for the rest of his life.

Private Hook was in a far corner room of the hospital which contained a native patient, shooting down warriors as they tried to get near the building and smash their way in. Eventually, the flames from the burning roof became too fierce and he was forced to retire to an inner room, leaving the native to his fate.

from a window and brought several crashing to the ground, and as a warrior was moving from cover to cover to sneak nearer, he shot him through the head. The Zulus eventually assaulted the hospital, setting fire to the thatch roof. Private Cole was killed and Hook was forced to keep the Zulus out for some time single-handedly. As the enemy were smashing their way in and the flames became fierce, he was forced to retire to the inner room leaving the native to his fate.

He was now in charge of nine men, and was joined by Private John Williams. They worked together, Hook keeping the enemy at bay while Williams smashed at the far wall with a pickaxe to break into the room beyond. An assegai thrust hit the front of his helmet causing a wound to his forehead. Private Williams got all the patients out except one soldier, a heavy man named John Connolly who had an injured knee. When Hook saw his chance he rushed from the doorway and grabbed Connolly, dragging him through the hole before the Zulus rushed in. They had to repeat their action again before they could make their own escape to the inner entrenchment.

Private Hook was mentioned in dispatches, and his award of Victoria Cross was announced in the *London Gazette* on 2 May 1879. On 29 January he transferred to 'G' Company as orderly to Major Black. He remained stationed at Rorke's Drift and on 3 August 1879 Lord Wolseley decorated him with the VC

There is a look of anxiety on the face of the patient as he is dragged through a hole in the hospital wall by his comrades. Private Hook twice saved Private Connolly from the clutches of the Zulus by doing this, but Connolly failed to mention his rescuer in his own account of the action.

at the place where he had earned it. He also received the South Africa Medal with 1877-8-9 clasp.

Possibly due to being informed that his father was in ill-health, he returned from Gibraltar to discharge from the army at Brecon on 25 June 1880. His wife was apparently led to believe that Henry had been killed in action, which seems to have caused problems as Henry appears on the 1881 census as a domestic groom, working in Glendower Street, Monmouth, while Comfort and their three children lived at Mount Pleasant, Newent, Gloucester.

Henry moved to London later that year where he lived in lodgings at Sydenham Hill, and gained employment as a general cleaner. He applied for a job at the British Museum, and after being recommended by Major Bromhead and Lord Chelmsford he was taken on as an 'inside duster' from 26 December 1881. He was later appointed umbrella caretaker in the reading room at the museum, a position he held until his retirement. He became a member of the Loyal St James Lodge of Oddfellows, London, served as a corporal in the Bloomsbury Rifle Volunteers and was sergeant, 19th Middlesex RVC, from April 1896–January 1905. He was Sergeant Instructor of Musketry, 1st Volunteer Battalion, Royal Fusiliers, serving the unit for 20 years. A silver-plated memorial trophy bearing his name was presented to the British Museum Rifle Association, to be awarded for services to the Association. In the mid-1890s he moved to 4 Cumberland Street, Pimlico. He met Ada Taylor at a concert, and on 10 April 1897 they married at St Andrew's Church, Islington, although Henry's divorce was not finalised until 25 August 1897. They had two daughters, Victoria Catherine was born in 1899 and Letitia Jean in 1902. In 1901 they were living at 25 Lesley Street, Lower Holloway, Islington.

For some years Henry had suffered from headaches, which were possibly caused by his wound, and by 1904 his condition had become serious. He was advised to return to his native county in the hope that the air would help combat his condition. He tendered his resignation, which took effect from 31 December 1904, and the museum trustees granted him a pension of more than £40 a year. He was placed in the care of the Phoenix Lodge of Oddfellows at Gloucester, who recommended a suitable doctor, and his family resided at 2 Osborn Villas, Rosebury Avenue, Gloucester. He died of pulmonary consumption on 12 March 1905, aged 54. His funeral was attended by thousands of people, and 23 regiments were represented. He was buried with military honours at St Andrew's Churchyard, Churcham. Fred Hitch attended the funeral with his son, who was one of the bearers. On 28 September 1906 his widow and daughters were present when a memorial cross was unveiled at his grave, and there is a memorial brass plate at Brecon Cathedral. His medals are in the South Wales Borderers Regimental Museum. His grave was renovated in 2008.

John Jobbins

John Samuel Jobbins was born on 18 July 1856 at Queen Street in Newport, Monmouthshire, the second child in the family of six to William Jobbins and his wife Harriett (formerly Greenaway), who had married in St George's, Bristol. They moved to Malthouse Lane, Trevethin in 1864, and by the age of fifteen John was working as a puddler at the local iron works.

He enlisted in the Monmouthshire Militia on 8 January 1876, being described as having a 37-inch chest. He enlisted for the regular army in Pontypool on 11 January 1877, described as five feet six inches tall, with fair complexion, hazel eyes and brown hair. As 1061 Private Jobbins he was posted to the 2nd Battalion, 24th Regiment. He received orders for active service in

South Africa, and sailed to the Cape with the battalion in February 1878, taking part in the Cape Frontier War. In mid-1878 his father was unemployed, so he began making remittances of £2 to his mother.

He wrote many times to his parents letting them know how he was and one such letter he wrote on 6 February 1879 was published in the *Hereford Times and Monmouthshire Beacon* on 29 March 1879.

> Before it was daylight in the morning, what was left of our poor soldiers had to retire upon the stores where I was with about 120 men of our company and volunteers. The day before, four men on horseback, who had escaped from the camp, arrived at the stores and told us what had happened. This was about 3 o'clock in the afternoon of the 22nd January. We at once let our tents fall to the ground, and got inside the stores and made a small fort with the sacks of grain. Just as we finished our little fort we could see thousands of Zulus coming down on our little body of men.
>
> At the end of the fort was a large house which had been used as a hospital, the owners of which were Swedes, who fled as soon as the Zulus were in sight. There were a lot of sick men in the hospital at the time, one poor Sergeant [Maxfield] was insane, and he was burned alive, or killed and then

John Jobbins was 22 when he took part in the defence of Rorke's Drift. He settled in Pontypool and went on to have eight children.

burnt. Well we fought hard from about 3.30pm till the following morning when they retired, they killed about 12 of our men, but we killed at least 450 of them. They were charging over the sacks but we repulsed them. All that night a minister in the fort was praying they would go away. God helped us and gave us the victory. In the morning we could see in the distance a large body of men. We did not at first recognise them, but after a bit we could see the welcome redcoats retiring on us from the unfortunate camp. We then gave a hearty cheer, as we felt safe when we were all together.

For his service he received the South Africa Medal with 1877-78-79 clasp.

He served on Gibraltar in 1880 and in India, returning to England from Secunderabad in January 1883, where he was discharged to the 1st Class Army Reserves. During his six years with the colours he had received two good conduct badges.

He gave his intended place of residence as Osborne Road, Pontypool, Monmouthshire, the home of his parents. By 1884 he had found work as a labourer in Llantarnum, Cwmbran. It was here that he married Elizabeth Wilmott on 13 October 1884 at the parish church, and by 1886 they had made their home at 24 Chapel Lane, Pontypool, where John found work at the local steelworks, and then as an underground worker at the local pit. They had eight children. Elizabeth was born in 1886, James in 1889, William in 1891, Harriett Maud in 1894, Sylvia Leah in 1895, Mary Ann in 1897, John Samuel in 1900 and Evan in 1902. By 1900 John was working as a colliery roadman and moved to lodgings at 32 Railway Parade in Pontypool, while Elizabeth and the children moved to Rose Cottage, 6 Pear Tree Road, Abersychan, before the house at 31 Railway Parade became vacant and John took over the tenancy for his wife and children. He lost his original campaign medal and had to have a replacement made.

He attended The Old Comrades Club of the 24th Regiment reunion at the Victoria Barracks in Portsmouth on 30/31 March 1929, was present at the ceremony for the laying up of the colours at Brecon Cathedral in 1934, and in the same year he attended the Northern Command Tattoo in Gateshead. John died of old age at his home on 22 September 1934, aged 78, and was buried at St Cadoc's Parish Church, Trevethin, Pontypool (plot Y grave 37).

Evan Jones

Evan Cosgrove was born on 10 April 1853 at Nantyglo, Aberystruth, Monmouthshire, the first child of five to John Cosgrove, who was a blast-furnace filler at the steel works, and his wife Tabitha (formerly Evans). Evan was sometimes known as Patrick. John eventually moved his family to 19 Armoury

Row, Man-moel, Ebbw Vale, where he obtained employment as a hot bank haulier. By 1871, Evan and his three younger brothers had found work as rollers in the steelworks, and the family moved to 31 Armoury Row.

Evan joined the Monmouthshire Engineers Militia at Abergavenny on 17 February 1875, before enlisting into the regular army at Brecon on 19 July 1877, using the name Evan Jones and giving a false age. He was described as five feet four inches tall, with a fresh complexion, grey eyes and light brown hair. His chest measurement was 39 inches and he weighed 140 pounds. 1428 Private E. Jones was posted to the 2nd Battalion, 24th Regiment at Brecon. For his service in the Cape Frontier and Zulu Wars he received the South Africa Medal with 1877-8-9 clasp.

He was appointed drummer while serving at Gibraltar on 30 July 1880, and attained a 4th Class Certificate of Education while in India on 8 March 1882. He chose to revert to private on 31 October 1884. He was posted to Burma in 1886, where he was again appointed drummer on 17 December 1887, and returned to India in 1888. He re-engaged at Ranikhet in 1889 as bandsman with the Gloucestershire Regiment. He transferred back to the South Wales Borderers with effect from 30 December 1892, and while he was in India he was a member of the Governor's Band at Bombay. He was posted to Aden

Evan Cosgrove enlisted with the surname Jones, and after being present at the defence of Rorke's Drift, he served on Gibraltar, in India and Burma, during the Boer War and in the First World War, in a military career lasting from 1875–1920.

Evan Cosgrove (Jones), being introduced to the Prince of Wales, later King George VI, during the Royal Welsh Show in 1923.

in 1893, and in October of that year he was posted back to India. He arrived at Gosport on 26 November 1893, by which time he had been overseas for fifteen years. He was appointed lance-corporal and reverted to drummer on several occasions during 1894–95. He was admitted to hospital with a fractured hand on 11 March 1896, and while in hospital he was appointed to the 4th Militia Battalion of the South Wales Borderers, for duty on the permanent staff. He was promoted lance-corporal on 1 September 1897, and was awarded five pence a day good conduct pay on 21 July 1898. He was living at 16 Mount Street, Welshpool, in 1898, and retaining the surname Jones, he married Alice Evans (formerly Pugh), at Forden Registry office on 15 October 1898. Alice was a widow with four children, Alice, born in 1885, Richard, born in 1887, William, born 21 June 1890, and Agnes, born in 1895.

He discharged on 17 October 1899. However, the Boer War began, and he attested at Welshpool on 17 March 1900 for short service of one year in the Royal Northern Reserve Battalion. He was stationed at Pembroke Dock and was discharged again on 16 March 1901, when the regiment was disbanded. From around 1902–1915 Evan served with the Montgomeryshire Yeomanry, and when the First World War began he re-attested for the 2nd/7th Welsh Fusiliers, at Aberystwyth on 15 April 1915. He passed as fit for territorial force Home Service at the age of 62. The *Montgomery County Times* ran a story about his career under the title 'A Welshpool Veteran. Over 40 Years Service and Still in the Army.'

He was promoted corporal on 24 August 1916, and acting lance-sergeant on 7 August 1917, and when hostilities ended he was discharged on 15 February 1919. However, he re-enlisted soon after his discharge as a private in the Northumberland Fusiliers. It is believed that he was posted to Germany and served as part of the army of occupation in 1919 and 1920. He received his final discharge on 10 February 1920, while in his 67th year.

He died on 29 July 1931, aged 78, at his home at 18 Union Street, Welshpool, the cause of death being given as 'carcinoma of rectum' (bowel cancer). He was buried with military honours in St Mary's Churchyard, Welshpool where a cross marks his final resting place. His rare combination of medals are now the property of the National Museum of Wales.

John Jones (970)

John Jones was born at Caredraw, near Merthyr Tydfil, Glamorganshire, and he attested for 25 Brigade on 13 December 1876. As 970 Private Jones he was posted to the 2nd Battalion, 24th Regiment, on 22 January 1877, a date which had great significance to him two years later. He received orders for active service in South Africa, and sailed with the unit to the Cape in February 1878. He took part in the Cape Frontier War, and during the Zulu War he was present at the defence of Rorke's Drift. For his service he received the South Africa Medal with 1877-8-9 clasp. He served on Gibraltar in 1880, and in India, from where he returned on 29 January 1883.

John Jones (1179)

John Jones was born at Merthyr Tydfil, Glamorganshire, in 1853. He served in the Cardiff Militia and enlisted for the regular army at Tredegar, Monmouthshire on 2 February 1877. As 1179 Private Jones he was posted to the 2nd Battalion, 24th Regiment at Brecon. He was described as five feet five-and-a-half inches tall, with a dark complexion, blue eyes and light-brown hair. His religion was Church of England. He was charged with drunkenness and placed in confinement on 22 July 1877, being tried and fined two days later.

He received orders for active service in South Africa and sailed to the Cape with his battalion in February 1878. For his service he received the South Africa Medal with 1877-8-9 clasp. He served on Gibraltar in 1880, and in India. He obtained a 4th Class Certificate of Education, and on returning to England he discharged to the Army Reserves on 28 June 1883, giving his next of kin as D Morgan, cousin, High Street, Merthyr Tydfil, Glamorgan. His character was described as very bad and his habits were intemperate. He received his final discharge at Brecon on 6 February 1889.

Robert Jones

Robert Jones was born at 5 Ty Newydd, Clytha, Monmouthshire on 19 August 1857, the fourth of five sons in a family of seven children born to Robert Jones, 'a farmer of thirty-three acres', and his wife Hannah (formerly Fryer). He was christened at Penrhos in Monmouth. He became a rural worker like his father, the 1871 census stating that at the age of fourteen he was employed at and living in the Drybridge Farm, St Mary's Parish, Monmouth.

His father is said to have greatly disapproved when he joined the army at Monmouth on 10 January 1876, and as 716 Private R. Jones he was posted to the 2nd Battalion, 24th Regiment. He was described as being five feet seven inches tall, with a fresh complexion, grey eyes and brown hair. He sailed to the Cape in February 1878.

Robert Jones was awarded the Victoria Cross for his action in helping to evacuate the patients from the burning hospital at Rorke's Drift. He was wounded in four places during his service in South Africa, and never really recovered from the ordeal. He shot himself in the head at the age of 41.

At Rorke's Drift He was one of six men posted inside the hospital with orders to defend the building and protect the bedridden patients. Having used all his ammunition when the Zulus assaulted the hospital, he and a patient were forced to retire into an adjoining room, where Private William Jones was defending six patients from Zulus who were crowding at the doorway trying to force their way in. He too had used all his bullets. The two soldiers crossed bayonets and cut the warriors down, until the doorway was almost blocked by their dead bodies. Robert Jones received three stab wounds to his body during this struggle, but they managed to get six patients out of a window into the compound. Sergeant Maxfield was delirious from fever, and although they had dressed him they were unable to get him to move. When Robert returned to try to get him away, he found him being stabbed by Zulus as he lay on his bed. The roof was a mass of swirling flames and the rooms full of choking smoke fumes, so he made his own escape, and spent the rest of the fight in the inner entrenchment.

For his conduct Private Robert Jones was mentioned in dispatches, and his award of Victoria Cross was announced in the *London Gazette* on 2 May 1879. He received the medal from Lord Wolseley while still on active service at Utrecht in the Transvaal, on 11 September 1879. He also received the South Africa Medal with 1877-8-9 clasp. His service in the campaign left him with one bullet and four assegai wounds, and he left an account of the part he played in the action.

He served on Gibraltar in 1880, and in India, from where he returned to Britain on 25 November 1881. He transferred to the Army Reserve, was recalled for service on 2 August 1882, and transferred back to the Army Reserve on 7 February 1883. He finally discharged from the army on 26 January 1888.

He married Elizabeth Hopkins at Llantilio, Monmouthshire on 7 January 1885 and they had five children. Alice was born in 1886, Emily in 1887, Robert in 1892, Mary in 1895, and Nellie in 1897. Alice was born in Monmouth, while the others were born in Hereford. In 1891 Robert was living at The Lodge in Dorstone, Hereford, while his wife and two girls were 'visiting friends' at Ewyas Harold, Hereford.

They went to live in the village of Peterchurch, Herefordshire, and Robert gained employment for Major De La Hay, a retired officer, at the nearby Crossways House. The family home was at Rose Cottage on Rose Farm, and they also acquired some land in the village of St Margaret's. Robert had been wounded close to his eyes and sometimes suffered severe pains in his head. In August 1898 he collapsed, and although he recovered his wife noticed a change in his character. On 6 September he was seen to be acting strangely before he went to work, and when he arrived he asked to borrow the Major's gun and two cartridges and went into the garden, presumably to shoot birds. The gun was heard to go off, and he was found dead with the back of his head blown away. An inquest found that he had committed suicide whilst of unsound mind. He was 41. Two days later he was given a modest military funeral and members of his old regiment attended the burial in St Peter's Churchyard. Robert Jones was known to be a good father and was a talented amateur poet. A poem of his is preserved at the Regimental Museum. His is the only Victoria Cross of the seven gained by the 24th Regiment at Rorke's Drift which remains in private hands, as part of the collection owned by Lord Ashcroft.

William Jones

Two individuals named William Jones were born in Bristol during the September quarter of 1839, and his family descendants believe him to be the one born on 16 August at 5 Lucas Street, Castle Precinct. He was the son of a stonemason named William Jones, and his wife Mary Ann (late Martin, formerly Lancastle). The Wesleyan Methodist Chapel at Coleford in the Forest of Dean, Gloucestershire records the baptism of William and James Jones on 22 March 1840, and the 1851 census records a family living in East Dean, near Ross-on-Wye, which may be them. William served an apprenticeship as a shoe-

William Jones had been in the army for 20 years when he received orders for active service in South Africa, where his wife died soon after he arrived there. He was awarded the Victoria Cross for his bravery within the hospital at Rorke's Drift.

maker before entering the army, and there are records of a shoemaker named Jones who lived in Cowell Street in Evesham, Worcestershire, who may have been William.

He enlisted at Birmingham on 21 December 1858; as 593 Private W. Jones he was posted to the 2nd Battalion, 24th Regiment. He was described as being five feet five inches tall, with a sallow complexion, dark brown eyes and brown hair. While serving at Mauritius he was promoted corporal on 1 September 1859, but was reduced to private on 5 September 1860. He re-engaged at Rangoon on 10 January 1868 to complete 21 years service, and he also served in India.

He married Elizabeth Goddard at the Wesleyan Methodist Chapel in Farnham on 25 May 1875. He was posted to Dover, where a child named William was born on 15 November 1876, who was sent to live with his grandparents in Farnham.

He received orders for active service in South Africa and sailed with his battalion to the Cape in February 1878, taking part in the Cape Frontier War. His wife went with him, but she died of tuberculosis on 11 October 1878. During the Zulu War he was present at the defence of Rorke's Drift.

He was posted in the doorway of a room in the hospital building which contained six patients, and had to keep warriors out single-handedly until he was joined by Private Robert Jones. Later, Privates Henry Hook and John Williams broke through a wall and entered the room with more patients, and together they fought back the Zulus while the patients were helped out through a small window. He made his own escape from the burning building, and spent the rest of the night with his comrades in the inner entrenchment. For his service he was mentioned in dispatches, and his award of Victoria Cross was announced in the *London Gazette* on 2 May 1879. He also received the South Africa Medal with 1877-8-9 clasp. He was decorated by Queen Victoria at Windsor Castle on 13 January 1880. He was examined by a medical board at Pietermaritzburg on 3 September 1879, which found that he was suffering from chronic rheumatism. He was sent to Netley Hospital, and on 2 February 1880 he was discharged as 'unfit for further service due to chronic rheumatism of the joints.' He was in possession of three good conduct badges

His intended place of residence was 174 Lupin Street, Birmingham, and by 1881 he was named as a warehouseman visiting Charles and Elizabeth Goddard at Court 3, 6 Love Lane, Duddeston, Aston, Birmingham. A child named Albert Ulundi (Frodsham) was born there on 12 May 1881, and Elizabeth (Frodsham) was born on 19 June 1883 at 7 Holt Street, Duddeston, Aston, Birmingham. Albert's unusual name suggests that he may have been fathered by William, and he and Elizabeth are the only two children who had their names changed to Jones. By 1891 the family home was 8 Luxton Street, Duddleston, Aston. Charles had moved out and William was recorded as a boarder.

A commemorative plaque was placed at the church in Philips's Park Cemetery, Manchester, in 1985. William is buried in a community grave at the cemetery.

He moved to Rutland Street, Chorlton-on-Medlock, Manchester and by 1901 lived at 7 Ash Street, Miles Platting. He toured with Buffalo Bill's Wild West Show when it came to Lancashire, and he appeared at Hamilton's Pansterorama in Rochdale to recite his account of the defence. He could not get regular employment because of his health, and he was forced to pawn his VC to provide for his family. It is now with the regimental museum. William was aged 61 when he married Elizabeth at St Augustine's Church in Newton Heath, Manchester, on 16 July 1901. In 1912 they were living at 72 Sanderson Street, Collyhurst, Manchester, when William was found wandering the streets in an 'impoverished' condition and his wife had to collect him from Bridge Street Workhouse in Salford. He died at his daughter's home, 6 Brompton Street, Ardwick, Manchester, on 15 April 1913, aged 73, and was buried with military honours at Philips Park Cemetery, Manchester. A ceremony was held there in 2007 to commemorate the unveiling of a headstone for the grave.

Peter Judge

Peter Judge is believed to have attested for the army in late 1872; as 2437 Private Judge he was posted to the 2nd Battalion, 24th Regiment in January 1873. He was awarded a good shooting prize. He received orders for active service in South Africa, and sailed to the Cape with his unit in February 1878. After

Rorke's Drift he made a monthly remittance of £1 to a Mrs Judge beginning
in March 1879. For his service he was awarded the South Africa Medal with
1877-8-9 clasp. He served on Gibraltar in 1880, and on his return to England
from India on 29 January 1883, he transferred to the Army Reserves.

Patrick Kears

Francis Kears was born in Ireland in about 1859. He was the eldest child of
Francis Kears, believed to have been a blacksmith, and his wife, Margaret, who
left Ireland to try to make a better life for themselves. In 1872 they lived at 99
Charter Street, Manchester, and Francis senior had been earning a living as a
hawker when he died that year. Patrick's mother was pregnant at the time of his
father's death, and she is believed to have had a daughter in Blackburn. By the
mid-1870s they lived at 41 Fontenoy Street, Liverpool, and Patrick found work
as a labourer. Unfortunately, Margaret had taken to drink.

Frank served with the 2nd Royal Lancashire Militia, and he enlisted for 25
Brigade at Liverpool on 6 December 1876. He gave his name as Patrick and his
place of birth as Liverpool, and he was described as being just under five feet
five inches tall, with a fresh complexion, blue eyes and brown hair. His religion
was Roman Catholic and he had a star on his left hand. As 972 Private Kears he
was posted to the 2nd Battalion, 24th Regiment.

He received orders for active service in South Africa, and sailed to the
Cape in February 1878. For his service in the Cape Frontier and Zulu Wars
he received the South Africa Medal with 1877-8-9 clasp. He was admitted to
hospital with enteric fever in Pietermaritzburg on 17 June 1879, and he was
re-admitted on 20 July suffering with debility. He was examined by a medical
board on 23 July and was recommended for a change of climate. He was sent to
Netley Hospital on 3 October, and at Brecon in April 1880 he was admitted to
hospital suffering from bronchitis.

He married Annie Lewis on 16 November 1880 at St Mary's Chapel, St
John the Evangelist, Brecon. They had five children. Honor was born in 1882,
Amy Ethel in 1884, Ellen Florence in 1885, and Francis junior in 1888, who
died after four days. Margaret was born in 1889. Patrick was discharged to the
1st Class Army Reserves on 1 February 1883, his conduct being described as
very good, and his habits good. Following his discharge the family moved to 3
Davies Street, Brynmawr, Crickhowell, where Patrick obtained employment as
a railway porter. At certain times the family moved to 99 King's Street, and then
to 6 Hitchman's Court, both addresses being in Brynmawr.

He was charged and tried for having been absent without leave from the
Army Reserves; the result of the hearing was an acquittal, and he was dis-

charged from the 1st Class Army Reserve at Brecon on 8 December 1888. The 1901 census shows Annie Kears still residing in Brynmawr, but there was no sign of Patrick. The marriage certificate of one of his daughters states that her father was a sailor, suggesting that Patrick had gone to sea. A Patrick Kears died at the Rosscommon County Home, Ireland on 16 March 1932, aged 75, and it is believed that this is the former 972 Private Patrick Kears.

James Keefe

James William Keefe was born on 28 May 1857 at St Giles and St George, London. He was the only child of James Keefe, a general labourer, and his wife Ellen (formerly Vickers). His mother died of tuberculosis in 1868, and James was placed in the care of his aunt and uncle in Aldersgate, St Botolph, London.

James enlisted as a boy soldier at the Marlborough Police Courts on 3 March 1871. His army records show his age as 'apparently' fourteen years and ten months, but James had given himself an extra year. He was four feet seven-and-a-half inches tall, with a fresh complexion, grey eyes and brown hair. It is also noted that he had a scar on his forehead. His next of kin was his aunt

Drummer James Keefe and his wife, Margaret. James joined the army as a thirteen-year-old boy, and he was the company bugler during the defence of Rorke's Drift.

A. Baines, Holdgate Street, London. As 2381 Boy Keefe, he was posted to the 2nd Battalion, 24th Regiment. By May 1871 he was fifteen and was given the rank of 'lad', and having attained the age of seventeen on 4 May 1873, he was promoted to private and was appointed drummer on 21 October 1873. He was awarded and forfeited good conduct pay and badges on several occasions.

He received orders for active service in South Africa and sailed to the Cape with his battalion in February 1878. He was the company bugler during the defence of Rorke's Drift, where he was slightly injured when a bullet grazed his scalp. For his service he received the South Africa Medal with 1877-8-9 clasp, which is now at the regimental museum.

While serving at Gibraltar in 1880 he was fined for drunkenness. He re-engaged in India on 18 December 1880 to complete 21 years service. He reached the rank of corporal on 22 January 1884, and having gained a 2nd Class Certificate of Education he was awarded two pence a day good conduct pay on 1 May 1884, and received a third good conduct badge on 1 January 1886. However, he was reduced to private and forfeited good conduct pay in April 1886. He served in Burma from 9 July 1886–7 December 1887, when he returned home. He was promoted lance-corporal at Brecon on 2 January 1888, and his good conduct pay was restored on 24 July that year.

He married Margaret Bury Ellis at the Brecon Registry Office on 17 April 1889, and they had four children. Ellen Margaret was born in 1889, James Hardy in 1891, William George in 1892 and Ellis John in 1894 (after James's death).

He became a sergeant with the 3rd Volunteer Battalion, South Wales Borderers on 15 April 1890, being appointed to the permanent staff on 22 September 1891. He was promoted colour-sergeant on 4 March 1892, and soon afterwards he was permitted to continue his service beyond 21 years. However, he was diagnosed as suffering from an aortic aneurism, which caused his sudden death at his home, 20 Armoury Terrace, Ebbw Vale, on 18 September 1893, aged 34, and he was buried in Ebbw Vale Cemetery.

His sons served with the South Wales Borderers. James served with the 1st Battalion from 1905 until 1930, when he retired as a QMS, and he re-enlisted for service in the Second World War. Ellis and William served with the 2nd Battalion in Gallipoli, where they were both killed in action in 1915, and their names appear on the Helles Memorial.

John Key

John Key joined the army at Secunderabad in India on 28 August 1871, and as 2389 Private Key he was posted to the 2nd Battalion, 24th Regiment. He was appointed drummer in 1873, but returned to private on 25 September 1877.

He received orders for active service in South Africa and sailed to the Cape in February 1878, where he was appointed lance-corporal on 3 May 1878, and soon after taking part in the Cape Frontier War he was promoted corporal on 3 July 1878. During the Zulu War he was present at the defence of Rorke's Drift. He was appointed lance-sergeant in A Company on 19 February 1879, and transferred to H Company on 31 March 1879. For his service he was awarded the South Africa Medal with 1877-8-9 clasp. He was promoted sergeant on 20 March 1880, and was placed on the unattached list at Secunderabad on 1 March 1884.

Michael Kiley

Michael Kiley joined 25 Brigade at Brecon on 24 April 1877; as 1386 Private Kiley he was posted to the 2nd Battalion, 24th Regiment. He received orders for active service in South Africa and sailed to the Cape in February 1878. He was confined by civil power on 7 October 1878, being sentenced to five days imprisonment with hard labour. He made remittances to Helen Kiley and Mary Sullivan. He was one of several soldiers to be transferred to G Company on 29 January 1879, and on the following 11 March he was confined in cells on a charge of insubordination, was tried by court martial and was sentenced to receive 50 lashes and fined £1. He was confined by civil power on 26 September 1879. He was sent to the general depot on 1 January 1880. For his service he received the South Africa Medal with 1877-8-9 clasp, which is now the property of the regiment.

David Lewis

James Owens was born on 29 May 1852 at Gorsgoch, Llanboidy, Whitland, Carmarthenshire. He was one of two sons in the family of seven children born to David Owens, a farm labourer, and his wife Anne (formerly Thomas). He was educated at Whitland Church School, where he is said to have taken pride in his handwriting and could write in copperplate. In his early teens he travelled to Swansea, where he gained employment at the tinworks at Swansea Docks, before becoming a weaver. He married Emma McIndoe in Swansea on 28 March 1875. Emma was a widow with two children, who was eleven years his senior. They had two children, Amy and David Lewis, born on 12 November 1876.

Soon after his son's birth he went to Brecon to enlist on 9 December 1876. He used a false name, and as 963 Private David Lewis he was posted to the 2nd Battalion, 24th Regiment, having his allowances made payable to his sister,

James Owens (David Lewis), standing third from left in the middle row, with several Rorke's Drift men at Brecon on 1 April 1934. Middle row, far left: Thomas Moffat; second left: John Fielding (Williams) VC. Front row, far left: Alfred Saxty; second left: Frank Bourne; third right: Caleb Wood; second right: John Jobbins.

Emma. He was described as being five feet nine inches tall, with a fresh complexion, grey eyes, and brown hair. He sailed to the Cape in February 1878, fighting in the Cape Frontier War and the Zulu War. For his service he received the South Africa Medal with 1877-8-9 clasp.

He began to show signs of a heart problem and was invalided to England, where he was discharged on 4 August 1879, his character being described as indifferent. An injury assessment board held at the Royal Hospital, Chelsea on 12 August 1879 confirmed that he was suffering from valvular disease of the heart, caused by being under canvas for six months and constantly exposed to climatic vicissitudes. It was considered that he ought to earn after a time, and he was awarded a pension of six pence a day for six months, which was cancelled by the Adjutant General's list dated 11 August 1879.

He returned to his family in Swansea as James Owens and resumed his work as a weaver. Early in 1928 he went into work on his day off to collect his wages, and while he was there he saw a girl using a machine without a safety guard. As he was pointing out the danger a serious accident occurred and he lost an eye. On 7 May 1928 he applied to the Royal Hospital for financial help in obtaining a glass eye, which cost 28 shillings. He was present at many funerals of Rorke's Drift men and attended a number of reunions at Brecon.

He died on 1 July 1938 at his son's home, 12 Kemble Street, Brynmill, Swansea, aged 87, and he was buried with military honours at Bethel Cemetery,

Sketty, Swansea. A wreath was sent by a number of surviving Rorke's Drift men, Frank Bourne, Patrick Hayes, Thomas Lockhart, George Edward Orchard, William Cooper, and George Maybin's son, William.

Henry Lines

Henry Lines was born on 12 April 1844 at Chipping Warden in Northamptonshire, the second of ten children born to Edward Lines, a sawyer, and his wife Ann (formerly Lovell). Henry began his working life as an agricultural labourer, before enlisting in Birmingham on 11 October 1864; as 1528 Private Lines he was posted to the 2nd Battalion, 24th Regiment. He was described as five feet five inches tall, with a fresh complexion, hazel eyes, and dark-brown hair. He had a somewhat chequered army career. He was posted to Mauritius on 23 August 1865 and then moved to and from various stations in India and Burma between 1865 and 1869. He lost and regained good conduct pay several times, and had reached the rank of sergeant on 13 August 1869, when, on 14 January 1870, he was tried and sentenced to six months imprisonment, and reduced to private.

Private Lines re-engaged in Secunderabad on 10 July 187, for such term as would complete 21 years service. He was posted to the Warley Depot in Birmingham where he arrived on 4 January 1873, and then to Aldershot on 19 December 1873. He also attended the Hythe School of Musketry, where he received a good shooting prize. He was posted to Dover, and on 1 June 1876, he was appointed lance-corporal, reverting back to private three months later. He was hospitalised numerous times during his army career for almost every ailment a British soldier on overseas duty was prone to, including syphilis, fever, dysentery, jaundice, bronchitis, contusions, abscesses, bubo, an inflamed gland of the groin, and orchitis – inflammation of the testicles.

He received orders for active service in South Africa, and sailed to the Cape in February 1878, being appointed lance-corporal on board ship on 16 February 1878, but he reverted back to private on 16 April 1878. He took part in the Cape Frontier War, and during the Zulu War he was present at the defence of Rorke's Drift. For his service he received the South Africa Medal with 1877-8-9 clasp.

He gained a 3rd Class Certificate of Education in September 1881 and was promoted corporal on 31 January 1882. However, he was tried by Court Martial on 7 March 1883 for breaking out of barracks, being sentenced to three days imprisonment and reduced to private. He was posted to Gosport and was discharged on 18 December 1883 'due to a reduction in his second term, and a reduction in rank from the rank of corporal'; his conduct was described as good. He received a pension of eleven pence a day and gave his intended place of residence as Chipping Warden.

Henry found work as an agricultural labourer, and lodgings in Lower Boddington, not far from Chipping Warden. However, in 1885 he was living with Ann Berry at 102 Maysoule Road in Battersea, London, and they married at the local parish church on 27 October 1885. They moved back to Lower Boddington where they took up residence in Bradshaw Cottages. By 1901 they had moved to Bake House, Lower Boddington, where Henry still worked as a general farm labourer, and he continued to state his age as three years less than it actually was. Henry Lines died of bowel cancer on 22 April 1904 at his home, 18 Lower Boddington, aged 60, and he was buried in plot 243 in St John's Churchyard in Upper Boddington.

David Lloyd

David Lloyd was born at Dowlais, Merthyr Tydfil, Glamorgan, in about 1858. He had worked as a collier and had previously served with the Royal South Wales Borderers Militia when he enlisted for the regular army at Brecon on 5 June 1877; as 409 Private Lloyd he was posted to the 2nd Battalion, 24th Regiment. He was five feet four-and-a-half inches tall, with a fresh complexion, grey eyes and brown hair. His religion was Church of England. He received orders for active service in South Africa, and sailed to the Cape in February 1878. For his service he received the South Africa Medal with 1877-8-9 clasp.

He served on Gibraltar and in India, where he was granted a penny a day good conduct pay on 10 July 1882. He returned to Britain on 1 December 1883, transferred to the Army Reserves, Cardiff district, and then to the Brecon district on 25 May 1884. He married Mary Price at Merthyr Tydfil on 21 January 1885. He discharged on 5 June 1889, his habits being described as intemperate and his conduct as bad.

Thomas Lockhart

Thomas Lockhart was born 15 March 1857 in St Michael's Parish, Ancoats, Manchester. He worked as a fitter before enlisting at Derby on 6 February 1877, and as 1176 Private Lockhart he was posted to the 2nd Battalion, 24th Regiment at Brecon. He was described as being five feet nine-and-a-half inches tall, with a fresh complexion, dark-grey eyes and brown hair. His religion was Church of England. He sailed to the Cape in February 1878. For his service he received the South Africa Medal with 1877-8-9 clasp.

He was granted one penny a day good conduct pay from 7 February 1879. He served on Gibraltar in 1880, then returned to Brecon. He transferred to the 1st Battalion, which seems to have prompted a difficult time for him. He forfeited his good conduct pay on 5 September 1881, and in the same month he broke out of barracks at Colchester, where he was attacked by 'soldiers who remain unknown of the Colchester garrison, who waylaid and maliciously ill-treated him without provocation or notice'. This presumably means he was punched about the face and head, because he was admitted to hospital at Colchester on 30 September 1881 with a contusion (black eye), and suffering from the effects of an epileptic fit. An invaliding board held at Colchester on 6 February 1882 declared that he was suffering from a permanent condition of epilepsy induced by an injury to the head. This had caused a fracture of the orbit (eye-socket), and the displacement of certain other bones. He was left with a scar on his left temple. The injury may have affected his eyesight because it was considered that his disability would seriously interfere with his powers of supporting himself.

He was declared unfit for further service and discharged on 6 April 1882. His conduct was described as fair and his habits regular. A second Injury Assessment Board held at the Royal Hospital, Chelsea on 13 June 1882 confirmed the previous findings. A Court of Inquiry concerning the incident found that the injury had taken place when he was absent and not on duty, and he was awarded a pension of six pence a day for eight months.

His intended place of residence was 41 Butler Street, Ancoats, Manchester, but he later emigrated to South Africa, where he lived in the gold-mining town of Krugersdorp in the Transvaal. In July 1938 he was one of the Rorke's Drift survivors who sent a wreath to the funeral of fellow defender, James Owens (David Lewis). He was one of the last survivors of the defence of Rorke's Drift when he died at Krugersdorp on 25 June 1943, aged 85.

Joshua Lodge

Joshua Lodge was born on 1 September 1856 at 11 Fletcher's Square, City Road, Hulme, Manchester, the only son and oldest child of four born to Henry Lodge, an iron moulder, and his wife Elizabeth (formerly Tetlow). All the Lodge children were christened at Manchester Cathedral. Shortly after Joshua's birth they moved to Stanby Street, Hulme, and then to Eagle Street, off Oldham Road in Manchester.

Joshua left his job as an engine fitter to enlist into the army at Ashton-under-Lyne on 3 March 1877, and as 1304 Private Lodge he was posted to the 2nd Battalion, 24th Regiment at Chatham. Two weeks later he received orders for active service in South Africa, and sailed to the Cape in February 1878. He took part in the Cape Frontier War, and the Zulu War. He received the South Africa Medal with 1877-8-9 clasp.

He received one penny good conduct pay from 1 March 1879, and from 17 March he made a remittance of £1 a month to his mother. He served on Gibraltar in 1880 and in India, where he reached the rank of corporal on 1 January 1882, but he was reduced to private soon afterwards. He returned to England on 1 May 1883, and after being confined in cells he was discharged to the Army Reserves at Gosport on 28 June 1883. He received his final discharge from the military service at Manchester on 28 June 1889, at which point he gave his intended place of residence as the Albion Inn, 2 Bank Street, Red Bank, Manchester.

In 1906 he was stated to be living at 17 Broughton Street, Ancoats, Manchester, and he was working in an iron foundry. However, it seems that he had declined into alcoholism, and was admitted to the Ancoats Hospital where he died on 26 July 1906, aged 49. The cause of death was given as 'rupture of an artery in the cortex, accelerated by excessive drinking.' He was buried at Phillip's Park Cemetery, Manchester (Church of England section I, grave 2302). There is no memorial stone.

Thomas Lynch

Thomas Michael Lynch was born in Limerick in Ireland in September 1858. He left his job as a letter sorter with the post office to enlist in London on 20 November 1876, and as 942 Private Lynch he was posted to the 2nd Battalion, 24th Regiment. He was just over five feet four inches tall, with a fresh complexion, blue eyes and brown hair. His religion was Roman Catholic.

He received orders for active service in South Africa, and sailed to the Cape in February 1878. He took part in the Cape Frontier War, and on 21 November 1878 he was granted a penny a day good conduct pay. During the Zulu War he was present at the defence of Rorke's Drift, and for his service he received the South Africa Medal with 1877-8-9 clasp.

He served on Gibraltar in 1880 and in India, where he was appointed drummer on 1 June 1882, and his good conduct pay was increased to two pence on 21 November 1882. He returned to Britain on 20 January 1883 and transferred to the Army Reserves as a drummer on 30 March 1883. He joined the Cameron Highlanders on 11 October 1884, before transferring to the permanent staff with the 4th Battalion, Argyle and Sutherland Highlanders on 14 January 1885, with whom he gained a 3rd Class Certificate of Education. He was confined by civil power for seventeen days in March 1888, and forfeited a penny a day of his good conduct pay. He was discharged from the Stirling depot on 25 April 1888, in consequence of his having been convicted of theft, his character being described as indifferent. His next of kin was his mother of Covent Garden in London.

John J.A. Lyons

John Jeremiah Augustus Lyons was born on 23 August 1844 at Sowhill in Trevethin, Monmouthshire. He was the oldest surviving child of John Lyons (or Lions), and his wife Mary (formerly Gahean, sometimes spelt as Gain or Gane). Following the death of his father in 1857, John and his mother moved to lodgings at Morgan's Houses, Gibson's Square, Trevethin, where John went to work as a labourer, before joining the Hanbury Corps of the Monmouthshire Rifle Volunteers. He joined the 57th Regiment in 1864, and in the following year he was on active service in New Zealand to put down a Maori uprising, for which he received the New Zealand Medal with 1863-65 clasp. He was then posted to India, where he transferred to the 63rd Regiment. He transferred to the 24th Regiment in about 1874, and as 1112 Private Lyons he was posted to the 1st Battalion, being appointed lance-corporal on 13 February 1877. He transferred to the 2nd Battalion on 22 February 1877, and was promoted to corporal on 26 November 1877.

Front: Kate Lyons.
Centre from Left : Daughter Margretta,
wife Elizabeth and daughter Ellen
Rear from Left: Cpl John Lyons and son
James.

John J. Lyons with his family. He was dangerously wounded during the defence of Rorke's Drift, when a Zulu slug hit him in the neck. He had the slug mounted on a watch chain which he wore for special occasions.

He received orders for active service in South Africa, and sailed to the Cape in February 1878, and took part in the Cape Frontier War. He made remittances to his mother and wrote to her on a regular basis. During the Zulu War he was dangerously wounded during the defence of Rorke's Drift. For his service he received the South Africa Medal with 1877-8-9 clasp. In a letter published in the *Cambrian* on 13 June 1879 he stated

> after we had been fighting between two and three hours, I received a shot through the right side of the neck, the ball lodged in the back striking the spine, and was not extracted until five weeks afterwards. My right arm was partially disabled. I said 'Give it to them, Allen, I am done, I am dying ...' All I could do as I lay on the ground was encourage the men, and I did so as long as I could open my mouth.

According to Lieutenant Chard

> [I] saw Corporal Lyons hit by a bullet which lodged in his spine and fall between an opening we had left in the wall of biscuit boxes. I thought he was killed, but looking up he said 'Oh Sir, you are not going to leave me here like a dog?' We pulled him in and laid him behind the boxes where he was immediately looked to by Reynolds.

During the operation to remove the slug several pieces of vertebrae had to be removed and the procedure had to stop without the removal of the bullet, and artificial resuscitation had to be given to ensure his survival. A footnote to the doctor's report stated: 'The gallant fellow bore the excruciating pain of the operation without making the slightest murmur, though he was not under the influence of chloroform or any other anaesthetic.'

Corporal Lyons arrived back in England at Spithead on 8 June, and was taken to Netley Military Hospital. He was given a civic reception when he finally returned to Pontypool. He was discharged from the army as medically unfit for further service on 22 September 1879, and an Injury Assessment Board held at the Royal Hospital in Chelsea on 30 September 1879 found him to be 'suffering from the effects of a gunshot wound to the neck in the action at Rorke's Drift. The condition will long continue critical and he can do light work only.' He was awarded a pension of six pence a day for six months. He had the slug mounted on a chain, which he wore for special occasions.

A newspaper report on 12 December 1879 stated that he had joined the Corps of Commissionaires in London. However, by the end of 1880 he had returned to Wales. He obtained employment as a labourer at an iron works, and lived at 9 Mary Ann Street, Cardiff. Living nearby was a spinster named

Elizabeth Ann Evans, and they married at the registry office in Cardiff on 3 January 1881, and lived at Albion Hill, Pontypool. They moved house regularly before settling at 70 Wharf Road, Newport. John had a variety of jobs, including as a coal miner and a postman in the Eastern Valley postal service. They had six children, William John was born in 1881, Philip Henry in 1882, Thomas Augustus in 1885 (died 1892), James Jeremiah in 1888, Ellen Jane in 1892, Margaretta in 1894. Philip was killed in action while serving with the Royal Marines in the Dardanelles, and James was wounded while serving in Gallipoli with the South Wales Borderers.

John Lyons died of pneumonia and heart failure at his home on 1 May 1923, aged 79, and was buried with military honours in an unmarked grave in St Woolos Cemetery, Newport, where fellow Rorke's Drift men John Murphy and Alfred Saxty are laid to rest. Unfortunately, his medals have been mislaid, but in 1936 Elizabeth donated the bullet and watch chain to the Regimental Museum at Brecon.

James Marshall

James Marshall was born on 9 November 1857 in the Hitchin Union Workhouse, and was christened at St Mary's Church in Hitchin, on 15 January 1858. He was the middle son of three born to Dinah Marshall, who was unmarried. However, she married John Bates in 1861, and James took his stepfather's surname, although no formal adoption took place. Two more children were born before John Bates was killed in a farming accident. In 1871 the family were living at 17 Hitchin Hill.

He left his job as a chimney sweep to enlist in the army on 4 December 1876 at Bow Street Magistrates Court in London, and as 964 Private James Marshall he was posted to the 2nd Battalion, 24th Regiment at Brecon. His description was given as five feet six inches tall, with a fresh complexion, hazel eyes and brown hair, and his religion was Church of England. He was hospitalised at Dover in May 1877 suffering with gonorrhoea, and in the following September he was charged with fraudulent enlistment, it having been found that he was two years younger than he had stated, and he was imprisoned for nearly three months, and his former service towards good conduct pay and pension was forfeited.

He received orders for active service in South Africa and sailed to the Cape in February 1878. On 19 October he was sentenced to 21 days imprisonment for 'loss of necessaries'. During the Zulu War he was badly wounded at the defence of Rorke's Drift. For his service he received the South Africa Medal with 1877-8-9 clasp.

James Marshall was one of three Nottinghamshire Rorke's Drift men who have their final resting place in Shaw Street Cemetery in Ruddington.

According to Caleb Wood

When the Zulu's became thick round the hospital, one soldier named Marshall, whom we all regarded as a bit peculiar, and different from the rest of us, stood his ground for a second or two while we were taking our position ten yards away. We shouted 'Come here you silly …!' When he saw where we were he turned about and came, but at the risk of his life, for he was followed by the enemy. Hastily turning around with his fixed bayonet, he brought down three Zulus with the point from the guard.

He served on Gibraltar in 1880 and in India, and spent several stints in hospital suffering with febricula, a mild form of malaria. He arrived back in England on 29 May 1883 and was discharged to the Army Reserves on 29 June 1883, his character being described as 'fair, latterly good.' Having been given a place of residence in East Chatham, James eventually settled in Nottinghamshire.

He settled in Redmile Road, Elton, near Nottingham, where he worked as a labourer. He married Martha Upton (formerly Millington), who had two daughters, Mabel and Mary Ann, on 21 June 1887, at Hyson Green Parish Church near Nottinghamshire. They had six children. Rosella was born in 1888, Jesse Millington in 1890, James Leonard in 1891, Grace May in 1893, William Herbert in 1900 and Noel Millington on Christmas Day 1905. During the First World War Jesse served with the Royal Engineers, and James became a sergeant with the South Nottinghamshire Hussars. During the Second World War Noel served as a fireman with the Royal Air Force.

By 1890 they had moved to Parson's Buildings in Mansfield, shown on the census as 'Forest Cottages', and James worked as a cowman. The family then moved over the county border to Bottesford in Leicestershire, where James worked as a farm labourer. They moved back over the county border to Village Street, Thoroton, Nottinghamshire, where James and Martha rented a shop, along with an allotment where he grew fruit and vegetables to sell in the shop, and they kept pigs. Shortly after the turn of the century they moved to 11 Maud Street, Nottingham, and in 1907 they moved to 71a Gawthorne Street in Nottingham, before moving to 17 Clipstone Lane, Ruddington, James finding employment as a gardener. Martha died in 1916, and in 1918 James left the village and returned to Nottingham, where he obtained employment as an office caretaker. He died of pneumonia at his home, 12 Bertha Terrace, Brierley Street, and was buried alongside his wife in Shaw Street Cemetery, Ruddington (section 11, grave 2).

Henry Martin

Henry Herbert Martin was born on 3 April 1857 at West Lydford in Somerset. He was the fourth child of ten born to Thomas Martin and his wife Anne Maria (formerly Appleby). Having received some education at the Binegar Church of England School he was able to read and write, and worked as an agricultural labourer and in a quarry before leaving home to lodge in Monnow Street, Monmouth. He joined the Royal Monmouthshire Militia on 23 November 1875, his description being given as just under five feet six inches tall, and his religion was Protestant. He gave his age as 21, although he was actually only eighteen and a half. He enlisted for the regular army at Newport, Monmouthshire on 10 February 1876; as 756 Private Martin he was posted to the 2nd Battalion, 24th Regiment, at Brecon on 10 March 1876. He sailed to the Cape in February 1878. He took part in the Cape Frontier War and the Zulu War. He received the South Africa Medal with 1877-8-9 clasp.

He served on Gibraltar in 1880 and in India, where he began receiving one penny good conduct pay from 4 September 1880. He served in Bombay and Poona before being shipped back to England as time expired on 28 October 1881. While awaiting his discharge at Brecon he was fined five days' pay and forfeited his good conduct badge and pay. He was discharged to the 1st Class Army Reserves on 11 February 1882. He returned to his parents at New Inn, West Lydford. He was recalled for duty at Brecon on 2 August 1882

Henry Martin was one of ten children who, apart from his six years in the army, never ventured away from his rural life in the Somerset countryside.

for a short period before receiving his final discharge from the army on 10 February 1883.

He gave his intended place of residence as Lenor's Grove in Shepton Mallet, Somerset, but he moved to Pilton in Somerset where he obtained lodgings at Carnards Grove. He married Mary Jane Warment at the parish church in Pilton on 24 April 1885, and they lived with Polly's parents at Beard Hill, Pilton. By 1901 Polly had lost her hearing and they had moved to Belvedere Cottage, Gurney Slade, Somerset, where Henry worked in a slate quarry, eventually becoming a foreman. He attended the South Wales Borderers Regimental Association reunion dinner held at the Victoria Barracks in Portsmouth on 30 May 1929, along with John Williams VC, John Jobbins and Henry Gallagher. He was active in establishing the Ashwick and Binegar branch of the Royal British Legion Club, which opened on 10 December 1930. When the Duke and Duchess of York visited Wells on 27 May 1933 to inspect the annual parade of the British Legion, Henry was introduced to them.

Henry Martin died of cardiac failure, chronic bronchitis and asthma on 25 January 1937 at his home in Gurney Slade, aged 79, and he was buried in an unmarked grave in Binegar Churchyard.

Charles Mason

Frederick Herbert Brown was born on 5 December 1854 at 20 Barbican, St Giles, Cripplegate, London. He was the youngest of four children born to Charles Brown, a City of London police officer based at Bishopsgate, and his wife Mary Ann (formerly Mason). By 1861 they had moved to 3 Greenwood Rents in Bishopsgate. His mother died in 1864, and his father, who had become a detective constable, married Ann Johnson, and another child was born to the family. The 1871 census shows that the family lived at 53 Bartholomew Close, Bishopsgate, and at that time Frederick worked as a lamp maker.

He left his job as a solder maker to enlist at Bow Street Magistrates Court on 26 February 1877, and as 1284 Private Charles Mason he was posted to the 2nd Battalion, 24th Regiment at Brecon. He was described as just over five feet six inches tall, with a fresh complexion, hazel eyes and brown hair. He had lost several upper teeth (probably in a workshop), and his religion was Church of England. He gave his next of kin as his sister, E. Schooley of 57 Skinner Street. He was hospitalised with a sprain injury, treated for tonsillitis, and he was fined for drunkenness, all early in his army career in 1877, but he gained his 4th Class Certificate of Education at Chatham.

He received orders for active service in South Africa, and sailed to the Cape in February 1878. On 8 February 1879 he wrote a letter home from Rorke's Drift in which he stated that he had been on guard duty before the Zulus attacked them. For his service he received the South Africa Medal with 1877-8-9 clasp. He was actually issued with two South Africa medals by mistake, the edges being engraved with both upright and sloping lettering.

He served on Gibraltar in 1880, where he began to receive one penny a day good conduct pay, and in India, where he was hospitalised on several occasions and his good conduct pay was increased to two pence a day. He embarked for England on 1 May 1883 and was discharged to the 1st Class Army Reserves on 28 June 1883, his character being described as fair, latterly good, and his intended place of residence was given as Finsbury in London.

However, on 30 October 1884, he returned to the Colours as a private in the South Wales Borderers, his good conduct pay being resumed at two pence a day. He was posted to Ireland and then to India, where his unit arrived on 28 September 1885, returning to Ireland on 12 October 1886. He returned to the depot at Brecon on 13 April 1887, being placed in 'D' company. He was hospitalised several more times and lost all his good conduct pay. He discharged on 26 February 1889, his character being described as 'latterly good for ten months since April 1888', giving his intended place of residence as the Lion Coffee Tavern, 105 The Struet, Brecon.

Reverting to his real name of Frederick Herbert Brown, he visiting his sister, Caroline, and gave her a Rorke's Drift Bible and the illuminated address he had received from the Mayor of Durban, and then he faded into obscurity. An emigration and passport application in the name of Frederick Brown, aged 37 years, male, unmarried, gives a departure date of 15 April 1890 from Liverpool, destined for Halifax, Canada, and the 1891 census for Canada shows a Frederick H. Brown living and working in Montreal, Quebec, before crossing the border into the US. It is thought that he returned to England and settled in Old Southgate in London where he died after an accidental fall in 1936, aged 81. His grandson, Captain Reginald Schooley, was killed in action while serving with the Royal Welch Fusiliers during the D-Day landings in Normandy in June 1944.

Michael Minehan

Michael Minehan was born in 1845 at Castlehaven, near Castletownsend, County Cork, Ireland. He had joined the West Coast Artillery Militia on 9 May 1864, and left his job as a groom to enlist into the regular army at Bandon in County Cork on 14 October 1864. As 1527 Private Minehan he was posted to the 2nd Battalion, 24th Regiment, described as just under five feet ten inches tall, with a fair complexion, blue eyes and dark brown hair. He served in India from 12 October 1866–3 January 1873, having been granted two pence a day good conduct pay by the time he re-engaged at Secunderabad on 7 October 1871 to serve 21 years. He forfeited a penny of his good conduct pay, but he was receiving three pence a day by 18 February 1875. He was admitted to hospital in April 1875 after being injured in a fight.

He received orders for active service in South Africa, and sailed to the Cape in February 1878, taking part in the Cape Frontier War. He forfeited a penny of his good conduct pay in July 1878, and another penny while he was stationed at Rorke's Drift on 9 January 1879. Minehan was posted in the kraal to the east of the defences which was not so well lit up by the light of the burning hospital. A Zulu crawled under the straw and grabbed him by the leg, and Minehan retaliated by prodding the straw with his bayonet, and one of the thrusts killed the warrior. For his service he received the South Africa Medal with 1877-8-9 clasp.

Captain Penn-Symons was with the force which relieved the garrison on 23 January, and Minehan, unable to speak properly from exhaustion, had taken him to the kraal to show him the body of the Zulu and relate his story. In his memoirs Penn-Symons wrote that 'Minehan was a great pal of mine; he was right-hand man, front rank of B Company, who knew his drill well and had often kept me straight.'

He served on Gibraltar in 1880 and in India, where his good conduct pay was restored to three pence a day on 9 January 1881. A testimonial regarding Private Minehan was written by Major Bromhead in India on 24 March 1884. He received treatment for cholera on 2 April 1884, and on being examined by a medical board he was invalided to England on 30 April 1884. He was examined by a medical board at Netley Hospital, and discharged as unfit for further service on 2 September 1884. His character was described as good, clean and temperate, and he gave his next of kin as his sister, M. Regan of Castletown.

Michael Minehan died on 26 May 1891, and lies buried in the churchyard at Castletownsend. A wrought iron marker stating that he was 'one of the gallant defenders of Rorke's Drift', was placed at the grave site, but a document in the regimental archive dated 1997 states that the church was derelict and the marker had rusted and broken in two.

Thomas Moffatt

Thomas Moffatt was born on 5 December 1855 in High Street, Runcorn, Cheshire, the son of Thomas Maffatt and his wife Catherine (formerly Rowley).

Thomas Moffatt was Runcorn born and bred, and he died in the town at the age of 80. He and his wife Martha had ten children and 29 grandchildren.

Thomas Moffat's daughter, Nora, holding the testimonial address which was presented to her father in 1880 by the Mayor of Durban, for the part he had taken in the defence of Natal.

A son named Thomas had been born previously, but he died early in 1855 and the new baby was named after him and baptised at home immediately after his birth. Thomas senior died of consumption 1858, and after moving to Mill Street in Runcorn, Catherine died of tuberculosis in 1869, leaving Thomas as a teenage orphan.

He joined the army at Liverpool on 30 November 1876, and as 968 Private Moffatt, he was posted to the 2nd Battalion, 24th Regiment. For his service in the Cape Frontier War and Zulu War he received the South Africa Medal with 1877-8-9 clasp. In the re-shuffle that followed the defence of Rorke's Drift he was transferred to 'G' company on 29 January 1879. He served on Gibraltar in 1880 and in India, from where he returned to England on 27 January 1883. He was discharged to the Army Reserves on 19 July 1883, returning to his native Runcorn.

He found lodgings at 9 Mill Street and employment as a dock worker with the Bridgewater Canal Company on the Runcorn Waterways. When the teenage daughter of his landlord, Martha Plant, moved to Widnes, Thomas also moved to the town, where he found lodgings at 55 James Street, and they kept in touch. They married on 6 December 1892 at St Mary's Parish Church in Widnes. They made their home at 2 Back Brunswick Street, Runcorn, and Thomas worked as a rope gatherer on the canal, later moving to Mersey Street in Mount Pleasant, Runcorn.

They had ten children. Catherine was born in 1895, Thomas Joseph in 1897, Eliza in 1900, John in 1903, Mary in 1904, Francis in 1906, James in 1909, Edward in 1911, Nora in 1916, and William in 1919, after they had moved to 9 Brunswick Street, Runcorn. They went on to have 29 grandchildren.

King George V opened the new bridge between Runcorn and Widnes in 1925, and Thomas Moffatt and fellow Rorke's Drift man Thomas Taylor were presented to the King, along with 'Todger' Jones VC. Thomas suffered from nightmares about the events at Rorke's Drift, and in his later years cataracts impaired his vision. He was often seen about town talking to Todger Jones. He died of myocardial degeneration and arterial sclerosis on 18 November 1936, aged 80, and he was buried with military honours in Runcorn Cemetery (section 13, grave 138). His devoted dog, Toby, died a week later. A renovation and rededication service was held at his graveside in 1999, and that of Thomas Taylor, which included a troupe of Zulu dancers in regalia.

Augustus Morris

Augustus Morris was born a Roman Catholic in Dublin in 1857. He left his job as a labourer to enlist in Liverpool on 3 March 1877, and as 1342 Private A. Morris he was posted to the 2nd Battalion, 24th Regiment at Brecon. He was described as being five feet seven inches tall, with a fair complexion, dark-grey eyes and red hair.

He and his older brother Frederick received orders for active service in South Africa, and sailed to the Cape in February 1878. They were both present at the defence of Rorke's Drift. For his service he received the South Africa Medal with 1877-8-9 clasp. He was appointed lance-corporal on 5 February 1879 and was awarded one penny a day good conduct pay from 6 March 1879. He reverted to private on 24 October 1879.

He served on Gibraltar in 1880 and in India, where he gained a 4th Class Certificate of Education in September 1881, his good conduct pay was increased to two pence a day from 6 March 1883, and he was permitted to extend his service to ten years on 4 September 1883. He served in Burma to 7 December 1887, being appointed lance-corporal on 12 June 1886. He received the Indian General Service Medal, 1854, with Burma 1885-87 clasp. He transferred to the 1st Class Army Reserve as a lance-corporal on 18 December 1887, and discharged from the army on 5 March 1889, his character being described as 'very good' and his habits 'temperate'.

His next of kin was given as Mrs Hughes, sister, of Oliver Street, Bootle, Liverpool. A death certificate in the Regimental Archive records the internment of Augustus Morris in November 1914, aged 52, of 6 Johnstone Street,

Bootle, Liverpool, at Kirkdale Cemetery (C of E, section 9, public grave 119). There is a discrepancy about the age and religion, but the age given may be wrong and he could have changed his religion. There is no Oliver Street in Liverpool, but his sister may have lived in Olivia Street, Bootle, where close by up to 1889 lived Augustus Morris, coppersmith, of 11 Stewart Grove.

Frederick Morris

Frederick Morris was born in Dublin in 1855, the older brother of fellow Rorke's Drift man, Augustus Morris. He enlisted in Liverpool on 4 December 1876, and as 529 Private F. Morris he was posted to the 2nd Battalion, 24th Regiment at Brecon. For his service he received the South Africa Medal with 1877-8-9 clasp, which is now regimental property, and the Address from the Mayor of Durban in January 1880. He served on Gibraltar in 1880, and in India. Private Frederick Morris died of disease at Secunderabad, India, on 26 September 1883, aged 26, having never returned home.

Thomas Morrison

Thomas Morrison was born in Armagh, County Armagh, Ireland, and enlisted on 8 March 1877. As 1371 Private Morrison he was posted to the 2nd Battalion, 24th Regiment at Brecon. He received orders for active service in South Africa, and sailed to the Cape in February 1878. He took part in the Cape Frontier War, and during the Zulu War he was present at the defence of Rorke's Drift. He made a monthly remittance to a Mrs Shillcock in March 1879. For his service he received the South Africa Medal with 1877-8-9 clasp. He served on Gibraltar in 1880 and in India, returning to England on 26 April 1883.

John Murphy

John Murphy was born at Tredegar in Monmouthshire, where he enlisted on 8 March 1877. He received orders for active service in South Africa, and sailed to the Cape in February 1878. He was confined and sentenced to receive 25 lashes on 11 February 1878, probably while on board ship. For his service he received the South Africa Medal with 1877-8-9 clasp. He served on Gibraltar in 1880, and returned to England from India on 28 October 1883. He lived at 81 Witham Street, Newport. He died on 28 July 1927 and is buried at St Woollos Cemetery in Newport. A plaque was placed at the grave of John Murphy, and new headstones were erected at the graves of John J. Lyons and Alfred Saxty at the cemetery in 1996.

William Neville

William Neville was born on 12 May 1858 in Broom Street, Ince-in-Makerfield, Wigan. He was the last child of six born to William Neville, a spade plater, and his wife Jane (formerly White). He was baptised at All Saint's Parish Church in Wigan on 2 July 1858, where fellow Rorke's Drift man, John Smith, had also been baptised. His father died in 1861 and his mother remarried. At the aged of twelve William became a coal miner's labourer working on the coal face.

He enlisted at Liverpool on 23 February 1877, at the same time as fellow Rorke's Drift man, John Thomas, and as 1279 Private Neville he was posted to the 2nd Battalion, 24th Regiment. He was just over five feet five inches tall, with a fresh complexion, hazel eyes and brown hair. His religion was Church of England.

After service in South Africa he served on Gibraltar in 1880, and in India, where he was granted one penny a day good conduct pay from 6 November 1880. A week after his service continued with the South Wales Borderers on 1 July 1881, he began to show the first signs of being a troublesome soldier when he forfeited his good conduct pay, and he arrived home from India on 28 May 1883. He joined the 1st Class Army Reserve and was passed around several districts, presumably still making life difficult for his superiors. He joined the 20th Regimental District (Bury) on 21 June 1883, being transferred to the 40th District (Warrington) on 24 August 1883. He returned to the 20th District on 7 February 1884, before returning to the depot at Brecon on 1 April 1884.

On 1 June 1884 he married Sarah Elizabeth Graham at Christ Church, Ince-in-Makerfield, Wigan, and they lived at 28 Broom Street, Ince. They had had five sons. William was born in 1885, James in 1887, Thomas in 1890, John in 1891 and Ernest in 1894.

On the morning of 28 November 1885, a woman named Phoebe Benyon was walking to work along the Leeds-Liverpool Canal at Ince when she was attacked by a man who manhandled her and stole threepence. Local newspapers reported the assault as a 'Dastardly Outrage'. William Neville, described as a miner, appeared in court at Wigan on 4 December charged with committing highway robbery and attempted criminal assault in connection with this incident. The woman identified him, but Neville denied the charges and produced witnesses who said he was at home at the time of the crime. He twice went to court at the Liverpool Assizes to face the charges, where, on the first occasion the jury failed to reach a verdict, and on the second he was acquitted.

However, the victim eventually produced a witness of her own, who stated he had seen Neville running from the scene of the crime. He was ordered to appear before the Liverpool Assizes for a third time on 19 May 1886. Local newspapers reported that he had been 'Convicted At Last', and he was sentenced to twelve months in prison with hard labour. He was released from Walton Prison in Liverpool on 18 May 1887, and his army service continued from the following day.

William Neville was discharged on 25 February 1889, his character being described as 'bad' and his habits 'intemperate'. His next of kin was given as Mrs Anderson (mother), of Longbroom Street, Ince. He died of heart failure at his home, 52a Broom Street, Ince-in-Makerfield, Wigan, on 28 August 1895, aged 37, and was buried in public grave (C of E – section C/grave 478), of the Urban District Cemetery at Ince-in-Makerfield, Wigan. There is no memorial stone at his grave.

Robert Norris

Robert Norris was born in Liverpool in February 1858. The only child named Robert Norris baptised in Liverpool from July 1857 to July 1860 was at St David's Church, Brownlow Hill, Liverpool 3, on 11 September 1859. He was the son of Edward and Margaret Norris, of Henry Street, Liverpool 1, but they had moved by the time of the 1861 census. His father was a brass founder. Robert worked as a labourer until the age of nineteen, when he enlisted at Liverpool on 21 February 1877, and as 1857 Private Norris he was posted to the 2nd Battalion, 24th Regiment a month later. He was described as just over five feet seven inches tall, with a fresh complexion, grey eyes and dark-brown hair. His religion was Church of England. He was admitted to hospital in 1877 to be treated for syphilis.

He received orders for active service in South Africa, and sailed to the Cape in February 1878. He took part in the Cape Frontier War, and during the Zulu War he was present at the defence of Rorke's Drift. For his service he received the South Africa Medal with 1877-8-9 clasp.

He served in Gibraltar in 1880, and in India, where he was admitted to hospital in 1881 to be treated for syphilis, the treatment being repeated three times in 1882. His good conduct pay was increased to two pence a day from 22 February 1883 and he returned home from India on 30 May 1883. He transferred to 1st Class Army Reserves at Warrington on 28 June 1883, moving to Brecon on 25 May 1884.

As 1933 Private Norris he joined the 1st Battalion, Royal Sussex Regiment on 5 May 1885, regaining his two pence a day good conduct pay. He later resigned, but re-engaged on 28 June 1885 to complete twelve years service. He gained a 3rd Class Certificate of Education on 14 October 1886 and was promoted corporal on 17 December 1886. However, on 27 July 1887, he was allowed to resign and revert to private at his own request, considering himself unfit for NCO duties. He was allowed to retain his good conduct pay and he re-engaged to complete 21 years service on 29 February 1888. On 25 July 1888, even though he had indicated a lack of confidence in his own abilities, he transferred to the Corps of Military Police.

On 13 June 1889 he was examined by a Medical Board at the Curragh Camp in Ireland, and was found to be suffering from venereal disease of the heart. He was discharged as unfit for further service on 16 July 1889, his character being described as temperate and steady, but he obviously returned to civilian life in very bad health. His next of kin was given as J. Norris, uncle, 15 Hinds Street, Edge Hill, Liverpool.

William Osborne

William Osborne was born in 1858. He enlisted for the army at Pontypool, Monmouthshire on 28 November 1877, and as 1480 Private Osborne he was posted to the 2nd Battalion, 24th Regiment. He received orders for active service in South Africa, and sailed to the Cape in February 1878. He made a monthly remittance to Mrs Osborne in January 1879, and for his service he received the South Africa Medal with 1877-8-9 clasp.

He served on Gibraltar in 1880, and in India, from where he returned to England in October 1883. He lived at Cambrian Row, Blaenavon, Monmouthshire, where he died in February 1931, aged 72, and was buried with military honours in St Peter's Churchyard, Blaenavon.

Samuel Parry

Samuel Parry born in about 1861, one of eight children born to George and Matilda Parry in the Bedwellty District of Sirhowy, near Tredegar, Monmouthshire. He had served in the Monmouthshire Militia at Pontypool when he enlisted for the regular army at Monmouth on 23 May 1877; as 1399 Private Parry he was posted to the 1st Battalion, 24th Regiment at Brecon. He was described as aged eighteen, just under five feet six inches tall, with a 34-inch chest, a fresh complexion, light-brown hair and grey eyes, and his religion was Church of England. His home address was 13 George Street, Blaenavon. He transferred to the 2nd Battalion, and on receiving orders for active service in

South Africa he sailed to the Cape in February 1878. He took part in the Cape Frontier War, being confined in cells from 28 September to 4 October 1878. During the Zulu War he was present at the defence of Rorke's Drift, and for his service he received the South Africa Medal with 1877-8-9 clasp.

He transferred to C Company and was admitted to hospital at Pinetown with fever on 3 January 1880, being examined later that month and recommended for return to England. He served on Gibraltar from 12 February–17 March 1880, and on returning home he was admitted to Netley Hospital where he was found to have chronic rheumatism which had originally manifested at Rorke's Drift, and was attributed to the climate and service as his regiment underwent exposure. It was stated that the disability need not be permanent and eventually he ought to be able to earn a livelihood and his pension appeal was rejected. He was discharged as unfit for further service on 25 May 1880, being described as aged 23 years, and his conduct as fair and temperate. His intended place of residence was Birmingham. It is believed he was living with his widowed mother and blind brother in Long Acre, Aston, Birmingham, at the time of his death, which occurred during the June quarter of 1898, aged 37.

Samuel Pitt

Samuel Pitt was born on 20 October 1855 at Portskewett, Monmouthshire, the oldest of six children born to Jesse Pitt, a land drainer, and his wife Jane (formerly King). The red-haired young man left his home at New Buildings, Trisha, St Brides Minor, Glamorgan on 9 February 1877 to enlist in Cardiff. As 1186 Private Pitt he was posted to the 2nd Battalion, 24th Regiment. He sailed to the Cape in February 1878. He said of Rorke's Drift that

> we pounded away for all we were worth, raining bullets amongst them, but on they came, not fearing death. They were sharp enough, however, to take advantage of every bit of cover they could. By nine o'clock, when darkness had set in, they got to close quarters, and were gripping our bayonets through the spaces left between the bags for firing. It was 'touch and go' at that time, and how they were kept out was miraculous. The Zulus held up their dead comrades for us to fire at, the idea, I think, being to get us to expend our ammunition.

For his service he received the South Africa Medal with 1877–8-9 clasp. He made a remittance of £1 to his widowed father in March 1879. He served on Gibraltar in 1880, where the one penny a day good conduct pay he had at some time forfeited was restored. He returned to England from India on 26 May 1883, and was transferred to the Army Reserves on 21 June 1883.

He married Mary Venn on 23 July 1883 at Bridgend Register Office, and they lived at Coytrahen, Llangynwyd, Bridgend, and Samuel became a miner at Wyndham Colliery, Bridgend. They had six children. Mary Ann was born in 1884 (died aged two), Charles Henry in 1886, Elizabeth Ann in 1889, Kezia in 1891, Jesse in 1894 and Wyndham in 1896. The family moved to Cildendy, Llangynwyd in 1889, and Samuel became a gamekeeper on the Coytrahen Estate. He received his final discharge from the 1st Class Army Reserve at Aberkenfig on 9 December 1889. By 1896 they had moved to 9 Frowen Terrace, Tynewydd, Llangeinor in Ogmore Vale, and Samuel returned to the pit. His wife died of typhoid fever in 1897. By 1901 Samuel had moved the family to 3, Perycal Buildings, St Bride's Minor, where he frequented the White Lion, and in 1909 he was president of the team when they won the Bridgend and District Bagatelle Championships. He was also a life member at the Royal British Legion. The *Western Mail* published a narrative on 11 May 1914 in which Samuel spoke of his experiences at Rorke's Drift.

By 1918 he was living at 47 Wyndham Street, Ogmore Vale, Bridgend, and on 16 March that year he married Rosina David at the Bridgend Register Office. They lived at 13 Carmen Street, Caerau, Maesteg, where Samuel died of acute myocardia and cardiac failure on 21 November 1926, aged 71; he was buried at the Church of St David, Bettws, Newport (row 3, plot 29a).

Samuel Pitt holding the Bridgend and District Bagatelle Championship cup, which he won while he was president of the White Lion pub team at St Bride's Manor in 1909.

Thomas Robinson

Thomas Robinson was born in 1853 at St Patrick's, Dublin. He enlisted at Bow Street Police Court in London on 23 February 1877, and as 1286 Private Robinson he was posted to the 2nd Battalion, 24th Regiment, at Brecon. He was described as being five feet nine inches tall, with a fresh complexion, grey eyes, and brown hair. His religion was Church of England.

He received orders for active service in South Africa, and sailed to the Cape in February 1878. He took part in the Cape Frontier War. He was charged with 'disgraceful conduct in losing a pair of boots' and was imprisoned for three months from 27 April 1878. During the Zulu War he was present at the defence of Rorke's Drift. For his service he received the South Africa Medal with 1877-8-9 clasp.

He served on Gibraltar in 1880 and in India, from where he returned on 25 May 1883, having gained a penny a day good conduct pay and a 3rd Class Certificate of Education. He transferred to the 1st Class Army Reserve on 21 June 1883 and discharged from Brecon on 25 February 1889. His conduct was described as 'very bad, latterly good.' He stated that his next of kin was his brother.

Edward Savage

Edmund Savage was born on 19 April 1858 at Water's Court, Newport, Monmouthshire, and he was baptised at St Mary's Church, Stow Hill, Newport. He was the third child of four born to Timothy Savage, a mason's labourer, and his wife Ellen (formerly Flinn). By 1860 they had moved to 12 Granville Street, St Woollos, Newport, and his father was killed while working as a wharf labourer in 1864. By 1871 the family had moved to 18 Canal Parade in St Woollos.

He had previously served in the Royal Monmouthshire Militia when he enlisted for the regular army at Cardiff on 8 February 1877. As 1185 Private Savage he was posted to the 1st Battalion, 24th Regiment, later transferring to the 2nd Battalion. He was five feet four-and-a-half inches tall, with a fresh complexion, blue eyes and light brown hair. His religion was recorded as Roman Catholic, and he had a tattoo on his right arm. His home address was given as 54 George Street in Newport. He was hospitalised at Dover and Chatham several times during 1877.

He sailed to the Cape in February 1878, taking part in the Cape Frontier War, after which he was hospitalised in September and then confined to cells in November. He received the South Africa Medal with 1877-8-9 clasp.

He was in the hospital at Rorke's Drift on 22 January suffering with a knee injury, and was a patient in the hospital during the defence of the garrison. An account of his experience appeared in newspapers in Brecon and Manchester in July 1879.

> Savage describes the warning given to the unfortunate inmates of the hospital. Seeing the danger drawing nearer, though suffering from an injured knee, he jumped out of the window into the fort. He assisted in the defence, lying on his side and taking aim at the Zulus through an opening in the biscuit boxes. In the night time, when under fire, Savage heard a fellow soldier of the name of Fagan, cry out for water, and managed to crawl along to help his disabled comrade-in-arms, who died before daylight the next morning. Savage says he never spent such a miserable night in all his life. There was a momentary danger of being shot dead, and the likelihood of perishing from cold and hunger. He had no recollection of ever having gone through such hardships as whilst an invalid at Rorke's Drift.

Edward was transferred to G company on 29 January 1879, and he remained at Rorke's Drift for twelve weeks before transferring to E company on 3 April 1879. He was hospitalised in Pietermaritzburg for recurring fever, and on being recommended for a change of climate, he returned to England on 26 June 1879, and was admitted to Netley Military Hospital. He was posted to the 1st Battalion, 24th Regiment at Gosport on 24 February 1880, and to Colchester in the following November, being hospitalised on several occasions suffering with syphilis. He was posted to Salford near Manchester on 29 August 1882, and spent more time in hospital at Chester, from 29 November–8 December 1882, being treated for inflammation of the glands.

He was discharged to the 1st Class Army Reserve at Brecon on 9 February 1883, and gave his intended place of residence as 11 Halkett Street, Cardiff. His character was described as fair. He married Johanna McCarthy on 26 March 1883 at St Marie's School Chapel, Canton, Cardiff, and they lived in 7 Edward Street, Canton. His wife died of tuberculosis in 1886. He married Mary Thomas, a widow with two daughters, Sarah Ann and Emma Jane, at the Cardiff Register Office on 28 June 1887, and they lived at 137 Wellington Street, Canton, where Edward was employed as a road labourer. They had four children. Edward John was born in 1888, William in 1889, Timothy George in 1891 and Beatrice Maud in 1892.

Edward was discharged from the 1st Class Army Reserves to the D list Reserves on 11 February 1889. However, his health went into decline, and he was admitted to the Bridgend County Asylum at Angelton, Bridgend on 13 May 1892, and he was given his final discharge on 20 June 1892. He died in the

Bridgend Asylum on 30 January 1893, aged 32, the cause of death being given as general paralysis. He was buried with his first wife in St Cathay's Cemetery in Cardiff, in common grave number R464.

Alfred Saxty

Albert Saxty was born on 11 March 1859 in Minety near Chippenham in Wiltshire. He was the fourth child of five born to Thomas John Saxty, a police-man on the Great Western Railway, and his wife Grace Thomas (formerly Collett). The family moved to Buckland Dinham in Somerset in 1864, where Thomas continued to work for the GWR, and Albert left school to start work at the age of ten. His elder brother, John, joined the army, and Albert enlisted on 12 September 1876. As 849 Private 'Alfred' Saxty, he was posted to the 2nd Battalion, 24th Regiment at Brecon, described as five feet seven-and-a-half inches tall, with a fresh complexion, blue eyes and light-brown hair. His reli-gion was Roman Catholic. Army life seems to have suited him and promotion was quick, and he reached the rank of lance-sergeant on 1 February 1878, the day he embarked for active service in South Africa. He took part in the Cape Frontier War, reverting to corporal on 11 July 1878, and gaining a 2nd Class Certificate of Education. During the Zulu War he was present at the defence of Rorke's Drift. He was promoted to sergeant on 23 January 1879, and for his service he received the South Africa Medal with 1877-8-9 clasp.

He served on Gibraltar in 1880, and had to undergo medical treatment onboard HMS *Orantes* while on the way to India, which was followed up as soon as he arrived in Secunderabad. He was found to be drunk on piquet duty on 6 May 1881, and after being confined in cells he was tried by District Court Martial and sentenced to 56 days imprisonment with hard labour. He was reduced to private, fined £1, his pay was stopped and he lost all his good conduct pay. He was released on 13 July 1881 and despite of his misdemeanour his superiors saw something in him, as his good conduct pay was restored on the day of his release, and he had reached the rank of sergeant by 2 December 1885. He re-engaged on 4 October 1887, and as 2595 Sergeant Saxty he was posted to the 1st Battalion, Bedfordshire Regiment, for such term as would complete 21 years of service. He transferred to the 2nd Battalion on 1 August 1888. He transferred to the 2nd Battalion, Royal Inniskilling Fusiliers on 14 August 1891 as 3760 Sergeant Saxty.

He married in Rangoon in his given name of Albert Saxty on 30 December 1885, his new wife being seventeen-year-old Maria Copeland. Maria died less than a year later of septicaemia following the birth of Albert junior on 1887. Albert was killed in action in the Dardanelles during the First World War.

Alfred Saxty, front row, far left, with an array of heroes pictured at Brecon for the 'Laying of the Colours' in 1934. Back row, second left: John Williams (Fielding) VC; front row, second left: Frank Bourne, DCM; front row, second right: Caleb Wood; and front row, far right: John Jobbins.

Sergeant Saxty's service record states that he married Mary Cole in Wellington on 1 August 1888. They had four children. Wilfred St Clare was born in 1890, Mabel Bridget Grace in 1892, Robert Lionel Anthony in 1893 and Leo Desmond Cole in 1894.

He was tried and convicted for an unrecorded misdemeanour in September 1894, being sentenced to be reduced to the rank of corporal and to forfeit his good conduct pay. The sentence was remitted by the GOC Rangoon on 2 October 1894, but within a month he was tried and sentenced to be reduced to the rank of corporal and to forfeit his good conduct pay. He was discharged at his own request in Burma on 28 February 1894.

Alfred began work on the railways in Burma, but a few years later he left home and did not return, leaving all his possessions, including his medals. He was officially pronounced dead seven years later and his wife remarried and had a daughter, Alma Leslie born in 1908.

Alfred reappeared on 12 June 1930, when he was admitted to the Royal Hospital in Chelsea, which was not far from where his wife lived, who had returned to England to live with her daughter in Kensington. During his time at the hospital Alfred applied for replacements for his lost medals. He reverted to outpatients at his own request on 4 October 1933, and left the Royal Hospital to live with his sister at 1 Blewitt Street in Newport, Wales. He attended the ceremony for the 'Laying up of the Colours' in Brecon Cathedral in 1934, and he attended the Northern Command Tattoo in Gateshead in the same year. Alfred died of a heart attack while visiting a friend at 131 Stow Hill, Newport on 11 July 1936, aged 77. He was buried with full military honours in Saint Woollos Cemetery, Newport (RCD block 32, grave 127). New headstones were placed at his grave, and that of John J. Lyons, along with a plaque on the grave of John Murphy at the cemetery in 1996.

George Shearman

George Shearman was born on 5 November 1847 at Hayes, Middlesex, and lived at St Margaret's, Twickenham, Middlesex, when he enlisted at the Westminster Police Court, London on 4 November 1864. As 1618 Private Shearman he was posted to the 1st Battalion, 24th Regiment. He was five feet five-and-a-half inches tall, with a fresh complexion, grey eyes and brown hair. He transferred to the 2nd Battalion on 31 January 1865. He served in India from 16 June 1865, where he turned eighteen on 5 November 1865. He was awarded a penny a day good conduct pay on 7 March 1871, and obtained a 3rd Class Certificate of Education.

George re-engaged at Secunderabad to complete 21 years service on 6 July 1872. He returned home on 2 January 1873, being promoted corporal on 2 June 1874. He was tried for being drunk on 11 July 1874, and imprisoned until 27 February 1875, being reduced to private, lost his good conduct pay, and was deprived of a day's pay. He retrieved himself, as his good conduct pay was restored in 1876, and he was promoted lance-corporal on 17 February 1877. However, he was reduced to private and forfeited his good conduct pay in September 1877.

He sailed to the Cape in February 1878. He was appointed lance-corporal on 5 February 1879, but reverted to private in the following November. For his service he was awarded the South Africa Medal with 1877-8-9 clasp.

He served on Gibraltar in 1880, and his good conduct pay was restored on 2 August 1880, just prior to sailing for service in India. He was promoted and demoted, and gained and forfeited good conduct pay several times, and was imprisoned for being drunk on duty while serving in India. However, he reached the rank of sergeant on 15 August 1885, and by this time he had obtained a 2nd Class Certificate of Education, gained his first good conduct badge, and was allowed to continue his service beyond 21 years. He returned home from Burma on 17 November 1886. He was confined for absence on 19 November 1886, and at his trial on 30 November he was reduced to corporal and forfeited his good conduct badge. He was discharged at Gosport on 14 December 1886.

John Shergold

John Shergold was born on 11 November 1839 at 2 Exeter Buildings in Chelsea, London, the second child of six born to James Shergold, a shoemaker, and his wife Rosina (formerly Wartnaby). They moved to 4 New Court, New Street, Brompton, 5 Palace Place, Fulham, and 7 Oakham Street, Chelsea, before John left home and travelled to Coventry, where he enlisted on 28 February 1858. As 914 Private Shergold he was posted to the 2nd Battalion, 24th Regiment, at Aldershot. He was five feet four inches tall, with a fresh complexion, hazel eyes, and brown hair, and had a 31-inch chest.

He was imprisoned for what must have been a serious misdemeanour on 2 May 1859, before spending 46 days in hospital in Aldershot later that year being treated for syphilis, this being the first of many treatments for one complaint or another during his army career. He was stationed in Cork from 7 January 1860, and arrived at Mauritius on 23 May 1860, where he was hospitalised suffering with cholera on 27 January 1862. He was hospitalised several times on Mauritius suffering from the effects of gonorrhoea. He forfeited his good conduct pay, which was reinstated on 14 December 1864. He arrived in Rangoon

44 Gladstone Street in Battersea, London, where John Shergold lived with his wife and son.

on 10 November 1864, where at various times he was hospitalised with fever, an infected cut, bronchitis and a swelling on his heel.

His good conduct pay was increased to two pence on 4 March 1867, and he re-engaged at Rangoon on 26 March 1868, for such term as would complete 21 years service. He arrived in India on 16 February 1869, where he was hospitalised for gonorrhoea for fifteen days, and after forfeiting his good conduct pay it was reinstated at two pence on 12 February 1872. He arrived back at the Warley depot on 4 January 1873. His good conduct pay was increased to three pence a day at Aldershot on 19 December 1873, which increased to four pence per day while he was at Dover on 4 March 1876. He was posted to Chatham in 1877, where he was back in hospital being treated for a sprain.

He had married Emily Birch on 6 September 1873 at the Church of St Philip in Battersea, and they had a son named William John, born in 1880. On receiving orders for active service in South Africa, his wife sailed to the Cape with him in February 1878. For his service he received the South Africa Medal with 1877-8-9 clasp.

He was hospitalised with debility and rheumatism on 9 November 1879, brought about by service and conditions. The medical board recommended he should be sent to Netley Military Hospital, later confirming that he was suffering from chronic rheumatism. John left hospital on 6 April 1880, and on the same day he discharged from the army as 'weakly and worn out' and 'unfit for further service.' He was described as being five feet five-and-three-quarter inches tall, and he was awarded a pension of one shilling and two pence per day. He and his family lived at 44 Gladstone Street, Battersea, and John found employment as a railway porter. He fell at work and suffered a head injury, and he was taken to St George's Hospital where he died of his injuries on 18 February 1884, aged 44. The cause of death was given as 'abscess in the brain from injury to the head. Fell accidentally from a buffer when at work at Victoria Station of the London, Brighton, and South Coast Railway Company. 3 Weeks.'

George Smith

George Henry Smith was born on 26 January 1840 at Bird Cage Fields, Stamford Hill, north London, the sixth child of seven born to George Smith, a dairyman's labourer, and his wife Susannah (formerly Willshire). The family moved to Moore's Field Cottages, Stamford Hill, and by 1851 they had moved to 6 South Row, Stamford Hill.

He enlisted in the Royal London Militia on 14 April 1860, before joining the regular army on 29 May 1860 at Worship Street Police Court, Finsbury. As 1387 Private G. Smith he was posted to the 2nd Battalion, 24th Regiment. He was

George Smith, with his wife Fanny. George seems to have had a weak constitution as he spent much of his army service in military hospital suffering with a variety of ailments. In spite of this he lived to the age of 85.

five feet four inches tall, with a sallow complexion, grey eyes and brown hair. He had small pox marks, and a bald spot on the back of the head from a burn. He arrived at Cork on 31 May 1860, where he was awarded a penny a day good conduct pay on 30 May 1863. He arrived at Mauritius on 6 November 1863, where he spent some time in hospital suffering from severe constipation caused by intestinal obstruction, and later inflammation of the testicle caused by an injury. He was sent to Port Blair in India, where he was admitted to hospital in December 1865, being treated for dysentery, and he was re-admitted to hospital early in 1866, again being treated for inflammation of the testicle caused by an injury. He was twice admitted to hospital in Rangoon suffering from boils and then with a fever. He re-engaged on 10 January 1868 to complete 21 years, and his good conduct pay increased to two pence a day from 30 May 1868. He arrived in Port Blair on 22 June, and in the following September he was hospitalised with a swelling of the groin caused by a sprain. He was admitted to hospital again on 3 October for a fever.

He forfeited one penny of his good conduct pay on 4 December 1868. He was posted to Madras on 27 January 1869, and by 5 March he had moved to Secunderabad, where he was hospitalised with tonsillitis, followed by a couple of bouts of enteric fever, attributed to a defective malaria injection. George was to have several more bouts of fever. He was promoted to corporal on 4 August

The house at 22 George Street in Brecon, where Sergeant George Smith lived with his family at the time of the Zulu War in 1879.

1871, he obtained a 3rd Class Certificate of Education on 15 April 1872 and began receiving good conduct pay at the rate of three pence a day from 30 May 1872. He was posted to England and arrived at the Warley depot on 4 January 1873, before being posted to the new depot at Brecon on 1 April 1873. He completed the course at the Hythe School of Musketry on 31 December 1873. He was hospitalised at Brecon in 1874 suffering from inflammation of the eye caused by a common cold. He was promoted to lance-sergeant on 1 April 1876.

George married Fanny Martin on 13 June 1877 at the Wesleyan Chapel in Brecon, and they lived in Free Street. They had five children. Louisa was born in 1878, Elizabeth in 1881, Llewellyn George in 1882, Arthur Joseph in 1886 and Daisy in 1889. Llewellyn was killed in action during the First World War in 1917.

George was promoted to sergeant on 1 February 1878, the day he embarked for active service in South Africa. He took part in the Cape Frontier War, after which he was once again admitted to hospital with fever, and no sooner had the fever been dealt with than on the same day he began to suffer from another bout of orchitis, being discharged as fit for duty on 29 November 1878.

During the Zulu War he was present at the defence of Rorke's Drift, from where he wrote a letter to his wife on 24 January.

I am thankful that I have been saved from the cruel slaughter and bloodshed that we had all gone through the last four days. The Zulus got hold of four boys of the 1st/24th band and cut them up in bits, and destroyed everything they could get their hands on. After destroying all they could, they made for Rorke's Drift, and at about 2.30pm the same day we were attacked by about 3,000 of them, and had to build up a fort... how we ever escaped I can hardly tell you. I myself had given up all hopes of escaping. We have counted the number of Zulus that were shot by my company, and they were over 800, so that they dearly paid for what they killed of our men. I cannot tell you a quarter of the horrors that have taken place. My dear wife, I trust you will feel thankful to God for having preserved my life. My company was very highly praised for the noble stand they made in keeping the place, and the cool manner in which they defended it.

On 4 February 1879 he was transferred to 'A' Company in the re-shuffle which followed the massacre at Isandlwana. For his service he was awarded the South Africa Medal with 1877-8-9 clasp.

He served on Gibraltar in 1880, and just four days after arriving in India in August 1880 he was hospitalised suffering yet another bout of fever caused by climate, and two days after his discharge he was re-admitted suffering with orchitis. He was re-admitted for the same complaint three days later. The authorities finally realised that he had a weak constitution and he was invalided home on 11 March 1881. He began to suffer with a condition which was diagnosed as hoops disease, and he was admitted to Netley Hospital in June 1881. In spite of this he was permitted to serve beyond 21 years by authority dated 22 August 1881. He transferred to the Permanent Staff, 3rd (Volunteer) Battalion, South Wales Borderers at Devonport on 28 December 1881. He remained in Brecon until 24 September 1882, when he was posted to the Provisional Battalion, Colchester and from 30 May 1883 he received five pence good conduct pay.

George was discharged from the 3rd South Wales Borderers' staff on 31 July 1883. His character on discharge was described as good, clean and temperate, and his conduct was very good. He was awarded a pension of one shilling and ten pence a day, and gave his intended place of residence as c/o Sarah Martin, 79 Lombard Street, London. He had earned five good conduct badges, and received the Long Service Good Conduct Medal and the Meritorious Service Medal.

By the turn of the century he was living at 15 Roman Road in Islington, where he was employed as an estate agent's assistant. George Smith died of a cerebral haemorrhage at his home, 31 Grafton Road, Islington on 20 January 1925, aged 85, and he was buried in public grave number Z26 16834 in Islington Cemetery. The grave has no memorial and the area is described as a nature reserve, which is overgrown.

John Smith

John Smith was born on 28 December 1851 at Wood's Houses, Chapel Lane, All Saints, Wigan, and he was baptised at All Saints parish church in Wigan, where fellow Rorke's Drift man William Neville had also been baptised. He was the son of John Smith, a spinner in the cotton industry, and his second wife Mary (formerly Hallam). His father moved to Kay's Cottages in Wigan to work for the Lancashire and Yorkshire Railway. However, he was working as a brakes man when he was killed in a railway accident at Trinity Street Station in Bolton in 1856.

Mary and her two children left the family home in Wigan and returned to Bolton, where most of the Smith family had settled, and they rented a house at 1 Shepherd Street, Little Bolton, before moving to lodgings in Waterloo Street, Little Bolton. However, Mary died of tuberculosis in 1867, and when his sister had left home John had to fend for himself.

Having joined the 7th Royal Lancashire Militia, John decided to enlist into the regular army which he did at Ashton-under-Lyne, on Christmas Eve 1876. As 1005 Private Smith he was posted to the 2nd Battalion, 24th Regiment. He was five feet seven-and-a-half inches tall, with a chest measurement of 36 inches. He had a fresh complexion, blue eyes and brown hair, with a scar on his right forefinger, a scar on his forehead and on his chin.

He received orders for active service in South Africa and sailed to the Cape in February 1878. At the defence of Rorke's Drift he received an assegai thrust in the abdomen, the only man fighting at the barricades to receive a spear wound. He was granted one penny a day good conduct pay from 14 April 1879, and on 8 July 1879 he received treatment in hospital at Pietermaritzburg for a minor sprain, the result of an accident. He was examined on 8 August and was recommended for a change of climate. He was sent home, and arrived at Netley Hospital in Southampton on 20 September 1879, being discharged as fit for duty on 10 October. He was posted to Brecon where he was admitted to hospital in December 1879 for a sprained ankle. He was discharged on 15 February 1880, being recommended for further treatment.

John was discharged to the 1st Class Army Reserves, Bury District, on 21 July 1880, having served 3 years and 178 days, and he gave his intended place of residence as Bury, Lancashire. A note on his service papers stated that he had

> an outstanding claim for compensation for kit lost at Isandlwana, Zululand; ditto for shirt and trousers issued for fatigue work at Fort Melville, Rorke's Drift; ditto for tunic left by order in squad bay at Pietermaritzburg when ordered to the front in 1878.

He possibly found it difficult to settle into civilian life, as less than eight months later he re-enlisted for the 46th Brigade General Depot Duties on 1 March 1881, and as 2333 Private Smith he was sent to join the 2nd Battalion, 97th (Royal West Kent) Regiment. Four days later he boarded a ship with his new regiment and was once again on his way to South Africa, where a Boer uprising was causing major problems for the British forces.

He was on the march in Natal on 10 March 1881 when he was lifting something heavy and a hernia in his groin ruptured. He was admitted to hospital for treatment on 26 May, where he remained until 31 August, being re-admitted on 10 September 1881 for the same problem, remaining there until 6 October, at which point he was shipped back to Dublin and hospitalised on 21 March 1882. He was examined by a medical board on 8 June 1882 and declared unfit for further service due to an inguinal hernia.

John was discharged from the army in Dublin on 25 June 1882, with a pension of six pence a day, and his papers state that during his service with both regiments he had three entries in the Regimental defaulter's book, but had never been tried by court marshal. He gave his intended place of residence as Wigan in Lancashire.

Thomas Stevens

Thomas Stevens was born in 1854 in St John's, Exeter. He left his job as a bricklayer to enlist into the army at Brecon on 9 March 1876, and as 777 Private Stevens he was posted to the 2nd Battalion, 24th Regiment. He was described as five feet five-and-a-half inches tall, with a dark complexion, brown eyes and black hair. His religion was Church of England. He obtained a 3rd Class Certificate of Education on 18 July 1877, and was promoted corporal on 12 August 1877. However, he was tried for being absent on 19 January 1878 and reduced to private.

He received orders for active service in South Africa and sailed to the Cape in February 1878. He took part in the Cape Frontier War and the Zulu War. For his service he received the South Africa Medal with 1877-8-9 clasp.

He served on Gibraltar, where he was granted a penny a day good conduct pay on 28 April 1880, but this was forfeited while he was in India on 12 September 1881. He returned to Brecon on 25 November 1881, being transferred to the 1st Class Army Reserves on 17 March 1882. He was recalled to the South Wales Borderers on 2 August 1882, and re-transferred to the Army Reserves at Salford on 28 August 1882. He married Ellen Calvert at Merthyr Tydfil in Glamorgan on 1 September 1883, and received his final discharge on 6 March 1888, giving his next of kin as his father, Robert Stevens, Robin Hood Inn, Dowlais in Glamorganshire.

William Tasker

William Tasker was born in 1846 at St Martin's, Birmingham. He left his job as a buffer to enlist at Sheffield on 25 September 1866. He was posted to the 2nd Battalion, 24th Regiment as 1812 Private Tasker. He was just over five feet ten inches tall, with a fair complexion, grey eyes and fair hair. He served in India from 4 November 1867, gaining and forfeiting good conduct pay until it was restored on 27 June 1872. He returned home on 3 January 1873 and re-engaged to complete 21 years service on 20 August. However, he deserted on 10 March 1874, and on rejoining two weeks later he was imprisoned from 30 March–10 May 1874, forfeited good conduct pay and former services towards good conduct and pension. However, he was appointed lance-corporal on 13 August 1875, and his good conduct pay was restored on 12 March 1877. He was caught drunk on picquet duty on 26 May 1877, for which he was reduced to private and forfeited good conduct pay, and he was imprisoned for 28 days with hard labour from 2 June 1877, being released after 20 days.

He received orders for active service in South Africa and sailed with his battalion to the Cape in February 1878. He took part in the Cape Frontier War, and at Rorke's Drift he was wounded when a splinter from a Zulu slug which glanced off his forehead and broke the skin. For his service he received the South Africa Medal with 1877-8-9 clasp.

His good conduct pay was restored on 1 January 1880. He served on Gibraltar in 1880, and in India, where his good conduct pay was increased to two pence a day from 15 January 1882, He returned home on 27 January 1883, and his previously forfeited service towards good conduct pay and pension was restored on 4 July that year. He married Elizabeth Ridney at the Brecon Register Office on 29 September 1883. His good conduct pay was increased to three pence a day on 15 January 1884. He was prematurely discharged for the benefit of the public service on 31 January 1885, his character being described as clean, good and temperate. e suffered a heart attack, collapsed and died in the street at Bordesley Green in Birmingham, on 7 July 1898.

Frederick Taylor

Frederick Taylor was born at Mangotsfield, near Bristol in about 1858, and he had previously served in the Royal Monmouth Militia when he enlisted for the regular army at Newport, Monmouthshire on 9 December 1876. As 973 Private F. Taylor he was posted to the 2nd Battalion, 24th Regiment.

He received orders for active service in South Africa and sailed with his battalion to the Cape in February 1878. He received the South Africa Medal with

1877-8-9 clasp for service in the Cape Frontier and Zulu Wars. Sadly, he died of disease at Pinetown, Natal on 30 November 1879, and his medal was issued to his next of kin on 29 September 1881.

Thomas Taylor

Thomas Edward Taylor was born on 9 September 1856 in the Hatton Village Cottages, at Hatton near Warrington, the son of Thomas Taylor, an agricultural labourer, and his wife, Ellen (formerly Andrews).

He enlisted at Liverpool on 11 November 1876, and as 889 Private Taylor, he was posted to the 2nd Battalion, 24th Regiment. He was described as being five feet seven-and-a-half inches tall, with a chest measurement of thirty four-and-a-half inches. He had brown hair and his religion was Church of England. He sailed to the Cape in February 1878 and was awarded the South Africa Medal with 1877-8-9 clasp. He served on Gibraltar in 1880, and in India, being credited with Home Service from 27 January 1883.

He married Lucy Maddock at Daresbury Church (the Lewis Carroll Church) on 29 December 1884, and they lived at St George's Cottages, Weston, Runcorn, where Tom gained employment as a stone quarry labourer at the Weston Quarry. They had seven children. Sarah C. was born in 1886, Thomas Bradshaw in 1887, Florence Louisa in 1889, John Percy in 1892 (drowned aged

King George V opened the new bridge between Runcorn and Widnes in 1925, and Thomas Taylor was one of the military men chosen to be presented to him.

fifteen), Margaret Elizabeth in 1894, Elsie Maude in 1898 and Lucy Lillian in 1901 (died aged three). In 1891 they lived at Quarry Bank Lea in Weston, and in 1901 at Bankes Row, Weston.

King George V opened the new bridge between Runcorn and Widnes in 1925, when he and fellow Rorke's Drift man, Thomas Moffatt, were presented to the King, along with 'Todger' Jones VC. Lucy died in 1903 and Tom died of bronchitis and heart failure on 17 April 1926, aged 69, at 5 St John's Cottages, Weston. He was buried in Runcorn Cemetery (section 5/363). In 1999 a renovation and rededication service was held at his graveside and that of Thomas Moffatt, which included a troupe of Zulu dancers in regalia. His medal and the illuminated address presented to him by the Mayor of Durban remain with the family.

John Thomas

Peter Sawyer was born on 21 May 1850, at Princes Terrace, Bootle-cum-Linacre in Liverpool. He was the oldest child of four born to Samuel Sawyer and his wife Elizabeth (formerly Collier), who already had three children. By 1861 the family had moved to Brickfields, Great Crosby in Liverpool. At the age of eleven Peter joined his father and brother working as labourers in the Brickfields. However, by 1869 both his parents were dead, and having to fend for himself, he took lodgings at Haigh's Cottage, Waterloo Park, Liverpool.

He joined the 2nd Royal Lancashire Militia (Duke of Lancaster's Own Rifles), before enlisting for the regular army at Liverpool on 23 February 1877. Another recruit enlisting at the same place and on the same day was William Neville. He used a false name, and as 1280 Private John Thomas he was described as five feet five-and-three-quarter inches tall, with a sallow complexion, dark blue eyes and brown hair. His religion was Roman Catholic.

He sailed to the Cape in February 1878. He took part in the Cape Frontier War, being hospitalised with pneumonia on 29 June 1878. He was transferred to Natal where he was re-admitted to hospital, the cause of his illness being 'exposure in service.' During the Zulu War he was present at the defence of Rorke's Drift. He was awarded one penny a day good conduct pay on 26 February 1879, and on 15 May of that year he was promoted to lance-corporal. For his service he received the South Africa Medal with 1877-8-9 clasp.

He served on Gibraltar, where on 5 June 1880 he forfeited his good conduct pay, and in India, where his good conduct pay was restored on 5 June 1881, but he forfeited it again in the following month. He appeared before the Cantonment Magistrate in Secunderabad on 26 May 1882 to sign a document stating that he had enlisted under a false name. However, the pay and muster rolls continued to state his name as John Thomas up to the date of his discharge.

His good conduct pay was restored again on 4 July 1882. Arriving in England on 30 May 1883, he received his final discharge at Gosport, and was posted to the 1st Class Army Reserves on 28 June 1883. His character was described as good and his habits as temperate. His intended place of residence was the post office at Devizes, c/o Mrs Bryant, Melksham, Wiltshire.

He married Annie Louisa Kelsey at the Portsea Register Office on 5 July 1883, giving an address as Smith's Lane, Portsea. However, they travelled to Peter's home city and lived at 3 Sweden Street, Great Crosby, Liverpool, where he obtained employment as a bricklayer's labourer. By 1901 they had moved to 78 Sweden Street, Great Crosby, and shortly afterwards to 21 Sweden Street. Peter died of cardiac thrombosis on 16 May 1903, aged 52, and he was buried in an unmarked communal grave at Kirkdale Cemetery in Liverpool (section 16, grave 166). One of his descendants sent a wreath in his name to the funeral of Rorke's Drift man, George Edward Orchard.

John Thompson

John Thompson attested for 25 Brigade at Brecon on 3 May 1877, and as 1394 Private Thompson he was posted to the 2nd Battalion, 24th Regiment on 16 January 1878. He sailed to the Cape in February 1878 and fought in the Cape Frontier War and the Zulu War. He was appointed lance-corporal on 5 March 1879, being reduced to private on 6 December that year. For his service he received the South Africa Medal with 1877-8-9 clasp. He served on Gibraltar in 1880, and returned to England from India in October 1883.

Michael Tobin

Michael Tobin was born in 1856 at Windgap, County Kilkenny, Ireland. He enlisted at Monmouth on 6 November 1876, becoming 879 Private M. Tobin. He was posted to the 2nd Battalion, 24th Regiment at Brecon. He was five feet nine-and-a-half inches tall, with a fresh complexion, grey eyes and brown hair. His religion was Roman Catholic.

He received orders for active service in South Africa, and sailed to the Cape in February 1878. He fought in the Cape Frontier War, being granted good conduct pay on 7 November 1878. During the Zulu War he was present at the defence of Rorke's Drift. For his service he received the South Africa Medal with 1877-8-9 clasp. He was found drunk on guard duty on 4 July 1879, the day the Zulus were defeated at Ulundi. He was sentenced to receive 50 lashes, which was later remitted, but he forfeited his good conduct pay was imprisoned from 8 July 1879, being released in Gibraltar on 30 June 1880, his good conduct pay being restored on 8 July 1880. He arrived in India on 11 August 1880, where his good conduct pay was increased to two pence from 12 November 1882. He returned home on 27 January 1883 and transferred to the 1st Class Army Reserves on the following day.

He married Margaret Mohan at his home town of Windgap in February 1886, and discharged at Brecon on 10 November 1888. His character was described as conduct good, habits temperate. He gave his next of kin as his father, M. Tobin of County Tipperary, and his intended place of residence as Ninemile House, County Tipperary. He discharged from Section D, Army Reserves on 10 November 1892.

Patrick Tobin

Patrick Tobin was born in 1857. He enlisted for 25 Brigade at Newport, Monmouthshire on 17 September 1875. He was posted to the 2nd Battalion, 24th Regiment on 21 March 1877 as 641 Private P. Tobin. He received orders for active service in South Africa, and sailed to the Cape in February 1878. He took part in the Cape Frontier War and the Zulu War. For his service he received the South Africa Medal with 1877-8-9 clasp. He appears to have been appointed lance-corporal in 1880, while in Gibraltar, but incorrectly named Michael Tobin, and he may have been appointed corporal in India in April 1881, again incorrectly named, the muster rolls appear to confuse him with 2698 Lance-Corporal John Tobin. He returned home from India on 28 October 1881.

William Todd

William John Todd was born in Liverpool in about 1857. He enlisted on 2 March 1877 and was posted to the 2nd Battalion, 24th Regiment as 281 Private Todd. He sailed to the Cape in February 1878 and received the South Africa Medal with 1877-8-9 clasp. He served on Gibraltar in 1880, and returned home from India on 26 April 1883.

Robert Tongue

Robert Tongue was born on 3 June 1857 in Ruddington, Nottinghamshire. He was the child of John Tongue and his second wife Elizabeth (formerly Powdrill).

Robert Tongue with his wife, Mary, and their two-year-old daughter Evelyn, pictured in 1896.

Robert Tongue in later life.

His father had a son from his first marriage. John Tongue died within five years, and Elizabeth remarried and had three more children before she died in 1877.

Having previously served with the Nottingham Militia, he left his job as a framework knitter and enlisted for the regular army on 26 February 1877. He became 1315 Private Tongue and was posted to the 2nd Battalion, 24th Regiment at Brecon, giving his half-brother Thomas as his next of kin. He was five feet seven inches tall, with a fresh complexion, grey eyes and brown hair. His religion was Wesleyan.

He sailed to the Cape in February 1878. He took part in the Cape Frontier War and the Zulu War. For his service he received the South Africa Medal with 1877-8-9 clasp.

He received good conduct pay from 1 March 1879 and obtained a 4th Class Certificate of Education. He was in hospital several times for minor ailments during his service. He served on Gibraltar in 1880 and in India, where his good conduct pay was increased to two pence a day on 1 March 1883, and from where he returned home on 29 May.

He married Mary Wright at Ruddington Parish Church on 27 June 1884, and they took a house in Church Street, Ruddington. They had nine children. Florence was born in 1884, Beatrice in 1885, Edith in 1887, Ethel in 1889, and Agnes in 1891, but these first five daughters all died of childhood-related diseases before the age of ten. Evelyn was born in 1894, and the first son, John George, was born in 1896. Mary was born in 1898 and Jesse Arthur in 1904.

Robert began working as a road repair man until he went into declining health. During the First World War he and his wife welcomed many Commonwealth soldiers into their home in Wilford Road in Ruddington, and wrote letters of encouragement to them while they were on active service. Robert died on 29 January 1918, aged 60, and he was buried in an unmarked grave at Shaw Street Cemetery in Ruddington. His son, John George, was killed in action soon after his death. A headstone was erected at his grave during a dedication ceremony in 2004.

John Wall

John Wall was born in 1859, at St James's, Deptford in Kent. He served with the West Kent Light Infantry Militia before enlisting for the regular army at Chatham on 1 December 1877. He was posted to the 2nd Battalion, 24th Regiment as 1497 Private Wall. He was just over five feet five inches tall, with a fresh complexion, blue eyes and brown hair.

He received orders for active service in South Africa, and sailed to the Cape in February 1878. Colour-Sergeant Bourne later wrote 'One day I heard a man named Wall ask my batman "if the kid was in."' This was a reference to the fact that Bourne was a senior ranking NCO at the age of only 23. He took part in the Cape Frontier War, and on 19 October 1878, he was sentenced to 21 days in prison with hard labour. During the Zulu War he was present at the defence of Rorke's Drift. For his service he received the South Africa Medal with 1877-8-9 clasp, which was returned to the Mint on 7 November 1882.

He served in Gibraltar in 1880, and in India, where he was in hospital at Secunderabad from 4 May–12 August 1881. He was treated for dyspepsia, the diagnosis later being changed to mania. He returned home and was admitted to Netley hospital on 25 November 1881, being treated for mania, attributed to intemperance. His condition had not improved and it was considered that he was unable to contribute to his own support. He was discharged from the army at Netley on 27 December 1881, after a disturbing military career in which his name appeared in the defaulters book on ten occasions, he was twice convicted by court martial, and his character was described as 'bad and dirty.' An Injury Assessment Board held at the Royal Hospital in Chelsea on the day of his discharge had no sympathy for him when it confirmed the original findings but rejected a pension award. His intended place of residence was the Lunatic Asylum at Barming Heath in Maidstone, Kent.

Alfred Whetton

Alfred Whetton was born on 24 May 1841 at St Luke's Parish, Islington, London. He joined the army at Westminster on 24 March 1859, and as 977 Private Whetton, he was posted to the 2nd Battalion, 24th Regiment. He was five feet five-and-a-half inches tall, with a fresh complexion, hazel eyes and brown hair. Only a month after enlistment he went absent without leave on 27–28 April 1859. He was tried on 2 May 1859 and was in confinement until 23 May 1859, the day on which he turned eighteen and the sentence was remitted. He served on Mauritius and was granted good conduct pay on 24 May 1862, which had risen to three pence by 24 May 1871. He re-engaged at Secunderabad in India on 15 April 1869 to complete 21 years service.

He received orders for active service in South Africa, and sailed to the Cape in February 1878. He took part in the Cape Frontier War, where his good conduct pay was increased to four pence a day from 24 May 1878, and during the Zulu War he was present at the defence of Rorke's Drift. For his service he received the South Africa Medal with 1877-8-9 clasp.

He served on Gibraltar, where his good conduct pay was increased to five pence a day from 24 May 1880, and three days later he claimed his discharge on completion of his second term of limited service. His character was described as very good, he was in possession of five good conduct badges, and he received the Long Service Good Conduct Medal with a gratuity of £5. His intended place of residence was 5 Tower Hamlets Road, Newham in London. He died at Shoreditch in London on 6 April 1891, aged 50.

William Wilcox

William Wilcox was born on 17 August 1860 at Higher Welsford, Hartland, Devon. He was the sixth child of seven born to Richard Wilcox, an agricultural labourer, and his wife Ann (formerly Harris), who died in childbirth in 1866. William had left home by 1871 to take up employment as a general servant at Hescoth Farm.

He enlisted for the army at Cardiff on 9 February 1877 and was was posted to the 2nd Battalion, 24th Regiment at Dover as 1187 Private Wilcox. He was five feet seven-and-a-half inches tall, with a sallow complexion, hazel eyes, and dark hair, and his religion was given as Roman Catholic (though he later married in the Church of England). It is known that William was a servant for one of the regiment's officers.

He received orders for active service in South Africa, and sailed to the Cape in February 1878, being hospitalised with pneumonia from 15–28 February. He received the South Africa Medal with 1877-8-9 clasp.

He received good conduct pay from 10 February 1879, but he was tried for desertion and theft of government property and sentenced to imprisonment from 25 November–30 December 1879, all former service towards pensions and his good conduct pay being forfeited. He was in prison in Pinetown charged with 'disgraceful conduct' when the Battalion embarked for Gibraltar, and he was shipped back to England to serve the remainder of his sentence in Forton Military Prison at Alverstoke in Hampshire, from where he was released on 27 September 1881. He was posted to the 1st Battalion in Colchester, and then to Salford on 29 August 1882, and it was from there that he was discharged to the 1st Class Army Reserves on 10 February 1883, giving his intended place of residence as New Oldfield Road, Salford. He received his final discharge on 9 February 1889.

On his return to Devon he found that his father had re-married. He obtained employment as an agricultural labourer, and by 1891 he was working at Docton Farm, having developed a passion for any kind of engine. He married Lily Vanstone on 27 February 1892 at the Bideford Register Office, and they rented a home in Limebridge, Hartland, where their only child, Maud Mary, was born in 1892. By 1901 they were living at Limebridge Cottages. Lily died in 1917 and William gave up his home and moved into a caravan at Brightly Quarry.

He died at Newbridge in Dolton, north Devon, on 29 May 1925, aged 64. The cause of death was given as 'valvular disease of the heart and mitral incompetence', and he was buried in Dolton Churchyard.

John Williams

John Fielding was born in Merthyr Road, Abergavenny in Monmouthshire on 24 May 1857. He was the second of ten children born to Michael Fielding, a gardener, and his wife Margaret (formerly Godsil), his parents being of Irish descent. The family settled at 3 Penywain Cottages in Llantarnum when John was five. He went to work at the Patent Nut and Bolt Factory in Cwmbran in 1865. He entered the Royal Monmouth Militia in 1877, but when he decided to join the regular army his family disapproved and tried to stop him. Using the name John Williams he enlisted into the 24th Regiment at Monmouth on 22 May 1877. 1393 Private J. Williams was posted to the 2nd Battalion at Dover. He was just under five feet six inches tall, with a fresh complexion, blue eyes and light-brown hair. His religion was Church of England. He received orders for active service in South Africa, and sailed to the Cape in February 1878. He

John Fielding used the surname 'Williams' when he joined the army. He was mentioned in dispatches and was awarded the Victoria Cross for his part in rescuing patients from the hospital at Rorke's Drift. He was the last surviving Rorke's Drift VC when he died in 1932.

John Fielding (left) and
Henry Hook, two of the
four soldiers of the 24th
Regiment who were awarded
the Victoria Cross for valour
during the hospital siege at
Rorke's Drift.

was charged at King William's Town on 20 April 1878 with quitting barracks
improperly, and admonished.

At Rorke's Drift Private Williams was posted in a corner room of the building, which had no communication with the interior, and where he and Private
Joseph Williams were in charge of three patients. When the Zulus made a fierce
assault on the hospital they managed to keep the enemy away from an exterior door by shooting through loopholes, and through panels in the flimsy
door. When they ran out of bullets the Zulus closed and smashed their way
in. Joseph Williams and two patients were dragged away and slaughtered, but
John had succeeded in breaking through an interior wall with two patients. He
entered a room that Private Hook was occupying with more patients. Hook
kept the warriors back while Williams broke through two more partitions, and
they were able to help most of them through the window to the inner barricade. For his conduct at the defence of Rorke's Drift, Private John Williams
was mentioned in dispatches, and was awarded the Victoria Cross, which was
announced in the *London Gazette* on 2 May 1879. He also received the South
Africa Medal with 1877-8-9 clasp.

He was granted good conduct pay from 23 May 1879, but he was charged
with being absent from duty at Pietermaritzburg on 25 October 1879 and
admonished. He served on Gibraltar, where he was charged with being drunk

John Fielding is presented before King George V and Queen Mary, as one of the 324 holders of the Victoria Cross who marched to Buckingham Palace to attend the first VC reunion party in 1920.

on 13 February 1880, returning to barracks at 4:30pm and was admonished. He received his VC from Major-General Anderson at the Almeda Parade Ground, Gibraltar on 1 March 1880. He arrived in India on 12 August 1880, where he was charged at Secunderabad with being in bed at 7:00am on 18 August 1881, against orders. He was charged at Secunderabad for committing a nuisance in the water room on 1 May 1882, being confined to barracks for five days. His good conduct pay was increased to two pence a day from 23 May 1883, and he obtained a 4th Class Certificate of Education. He returned from India on 30 November 1883.

He transferred to the 1st Class Army Reserve at Brecon on 13 December 1888, his character being described as very good. His intended place of residence was 3 Stercus Row, Cwmbran, Monmouthshire and his next of kin was his father, of 4 Abbey Row, Llantarnum. At some time he was a sergeant in 3rd Volunteer Battalion, South Wales Borderers. He attested for general service infantry at Newport on 23 May 1889, and discharged on termination of his engagement on 22 May 1893, becoming attached to the civilian staff at Brecon Barracks, and living at 146 Llantarnum Road, Cwmbran, Newport. He went back to work at the Nut and Bolt Factory, and he met Elizabeth Murphy, who had a daughter named Annie. They married at St Alban's Catholic Church in Pontypool on 15 April 1884, and together they had five children. The 1891 census shows them living at 43 Morgan John Street, Llantarnum, and the 1901 census shows them living at 10 Pritchard Terrace, Llantarnum Road. He was appointed recruiting officer at the barracks during the First World War, where he received the tragic news that the eldest of his three sons, Tom, had been killed in action at Mons in 1914, serving with the South Wales Borderers.

He was present at a VC garden party held by King George V and Queen Mary at Buckingham Palace on 26 June 1920, and he attended a VC dinner in the House of Lords on 9 November 1929, which was hosted by the Prince of Wales. After his wife died on 29 May 1914 he led a quiet life in Llantarnam Road in Cwmbran. Described as 'a rather tall, charming man', he retired from Brecon Barracks on 20 May 1920, and left the Nut and Bolt Factory in 1922. He eventually went to live with his married daughter, Margaret, at 28 Cocker Avenue, Cwmbran.

On 24 November 1932, the last surviving Zulu War VC was visiting his daughter, Elizabeth at Tycoch in Cwmbran. While he was there he suffered heart failure and died in the early hours of 25 November 1932. He was 75. His funeral cortege was half a mile long, including a place of honour for survivors of the Zulu War, and there were floral tributes from the families of Fred Hitch and Harry Hook. He was buried with military honours provided by the South Wales Borderers, who erected a memorial at his grave in St Michael of All Angels Churchyard in Llantarnum.

Joseph Williams

Joseph Williams enlisted at Monmouth on 23 May 1877, and as 1398 Private J. Williams, he was posted to the 2nd Battalion, 24th Regiment. He received orders for active service in South Africa and sailed to the Cape with his battalion in February 1878. He took part in the Cape Frontier War, and during the Zulu War he was present at the defence of Rorke's Drift, where he was killed in action defending the hospital. He and Private John Williams were posted in a far corner room of the building in charge of three patients, which had no communication with the interior. When the Zulus made a fierce assault on the hospital, they kept them away from an exterior door by shooting through loopholes and panels in the door. When they ran out of bullets the Zulus closed and smashed their way in, and he and two patients were taken and killed. According to Reverend Smith

> Private Joseph Williams fired from a small window at the far end of the hospital. Next morning fourteen warriors were found dead beneath it, besides others along his line of fire. When their ammunition was expended, he and

his companions kept the door with their bayonets, but an entrance was subsequently forced and, he, poor fellow was seized by the hands, dragged out and killed before the eyes of the others.

He was buried in the cemetery at Rorke's Drift and his name is inscribed on the monument. His effects were recorded for claim by his father. For his service he received the South Africa Medal with 1877-8-9 clasp.

Thomas Williams

Thomas Williams attested for 25 Brigade on 6 March 1877 and was posted to the 2nd Battalion, 24th Regiment on 3 December 1877 as 1328 Private T. Williams. Thomas took to the army well and promotions came quick. He was appointed lance-corporal on 8 January 1878 and corporal on 1 February 1878, the day he embarked for active service in South Africa, and he was appointed lance-sergeant while serving in the Cape Frontier War. In the Zulu War he was mortally wounded during the defence of Rorke's Drift. 'There were two mortally wounded men to attend to and Doctor Reynolds did all he could to save them, but did not succeed.' He was buried in the cemetery at Rorke's Drift and his name appears on the monument. For his service he received the South Africa Medal with 1877-8-9 clasp.

Joseph Windridge

Joseph Lenford Windridge was born on 14 May 1842 at 10 Keppel Street, Southwark, Surrey (now Greater London). He was the eldest child of four to Daniel Windridge, a hatter, and his wife Martha (formerly Clark). The family had moved to Newington in Surrey by 1845, and in the following year they moved to Daniel's hometown of Atherstone in Warwickshire.

Joseph left his employment as a compositor to enlist into the army on 26 January 1859, and as 735 Private Windridge he was posted to the 2nd Battalion, 24th Regiment. He gave his age as eighteen, which was something that many young men did at the time to bluff their way into the military. He was just over five feet six inches tall, with a fresh complexion, hazel eyes and brown hair. He served on Mauritius from May 1860 to October 1865, being promoted corporal on 6 May 1861, and on 3 March 1862 he attained the rank of sergeant. He was appointed quartermaster-sergeant on 21 December 1863. In October 1865 the battalion embarked for India, where they remained until 2 January 1873. He re-engaged at Rangoon to complete 21 years service.

Having returned to England, he married Annie Hannah Letitia Sullivan on 16 August 1874. He is described as being a widower, suggesting that he had married while on overseas duty. He reverted to colour-sergeant on 21 June 1873, and on 4 January 1876 he reverted to sergeant. On 14 July of that year he was appointed colour-sergeant, followed by promotion to quartermaster-sergeant on 17 January 1877. He reverted back to sergeant at his own request on 27 April 1877, having been appointed orderly room clerk on 1 April 1877, when he was recommended for the Long Service Good Conduct Medal. He married for a third time at the Holy Trinity Church in Dover on 14 June 1877. His new wife was nineteen-year-old Helena Catherine Rawlinson. Helena Lenford was born in 1878.

He received orders for active service in South Africa and sailed with his battalion to the Cape in February 1878. He took part in the Cape Frontier War, and at Rorke's Drift he was placed in charge of some caskets of rum in the store, with orders to shoot any man who tried to get near them. However, being fond of a drink himself, he used his better judgement and delegated this responsibility to Sergeant Millne. Lieutenant Chard stated that 'Sergeant Windridge showed great intelligence and energy in arranging the stores for the defence of the Commissariat stores, forming loopholes, etc.' He was said to have taken great satisfaction in issuing each survivor with a tot of rum when relief came in the morning. For his service he received the South Africa Medal with 1877-8-9 clasp.

On 6 July 1879 Joseph went 'absent without leave', being charged and tried on the following day. He was reduced in rank, which was remitted, but he had to forfeit his good conduct pay. On 16 November 1879 he was confined for drunkenness, and was tried and reduced to private three days later. He served on Gibraltar in 1880, before being posted to Secunderabad in India, where he reached the rank of sergeant on 3 March 1882. Sergeant Windridge was discharged at Gosport on 7 August 1883, having served for over 24 years, and during his service he had been admitted to hospital on eight occasions. He was entitled to four good conduct badges and his conduct was described as 'very good'.

He gained employment as a clerk to a lamp maker, and the family made their home at 32 Paddington Street, St George's Parish, Aston, Birmingham. Selina was born in 1881, but she died when she was eight years old. Joseph Lenford was born in 1883, but died in 1884. Twin boys, Lenford Rawlinson and Henry Rawlinson, were born in 1885, Martha Clarissa in 1886, Josepha Rawlinson in 1888, Joseph Rawlinson in the spring of 1890, and in December of that year came Ann. In 1891 Joseph moved his family to live at 156 Clifton Road, Aston, where Dolly was born in 1892, followed by Amy in 1894 and William in 1895. Sadly, six of their children died of tuberculosis in March 1896.

The 1901 census shows Joseph staying with his nephew at Velos Yard in Atherstone. He died on 30 August 1902, aged 60, at the home of his sister, 59 Tower Street, Aston, Birmingham. He had suffered a stroke, and the cause of death was given as apoplexy. He was buried in Witton Cemetery in Aston (plot 97, grave 54737), which has remained unmarked.

Caleb Wood

Caleb Wood was born on 24 April 1858 at 4 Oliver's Row, Ruddington near Nottingham. He was the second of five children born to William Wood, a framework knitter, and his wife Ellen (formerly Daft). Caleb received his education at the small village school in Ruddington, and by the time he was twelve he was working with his father and elder brother as a framework knitter. Like Robert Tongue he left this type of work to join the army. He attested on 6 March 1877, and as 1316 Private Wood he was posted to the 2nd Battalion, 24th Regiment.

He sailed to the Cape in February 1878, fought in the Cape Frontier War and during the Zulu War, and transferred to G Company on 29 January 1879. For his service he received the South Africa Medal with 1877-8-9 clasp. He served on

Caleb Wood was a member of the silver band at his local church, where he served the Church Army Mission.

Gibraltar in 1880, and in India, where he was appointed drummer on 1 February 1881, and from where he returned home on 1 May 1883 and took his discharge.

He took lodgings in Cambridge Street, New Radford near Nottingham. He met Emily Jones (formerly Whitworth), who had a two-year-old daughter, Catherine Annie, and they married at the New Radford Parish Church on 25 December 1883. He returned to the regular army at Newport for a short period of time, but by 1888 he had returned to civilian life and made the family home at Tibshelf, a village three miles from Hardstoft, where he gained employment as a coal miner at the number one deep pit in Tibshelf. On 26 January of that year Caleb and Emily's first child, William John, was born. Soon after the birth, Caleb took his family to live at Lower Brook Street in Long Eaton, where he found work as a coal miner at the local pit. He then took his family to live at 7 Sawley Road, and Caleb changed his occupation to that of a twist hand in the lace industry. Arthur Charles Jepson was born in 1895, and Wilfred Roy was born in 1899. By 1900 they had moved to Cossall, near Ilkeston in Derbyshire, and Caleb remained employed in the lace making trade. They moved to Digby Street, Ilkeston, and from there to Lower Chapel Street. Caleb joined the silver band at the local church, and he also joined the Voluntary Fire Service. Caleb and Emily were active members of the Church

Caleb Wood wearing his cinema commissionaire's uniform and his South Africa medal, poses proudly with his two eldest sons, Arthur and William.

Army Mission, and in his capacity as such, Caleb was invited to give a talk on Rorke's Drift to help raise money for the Church Land Fund on 19 April 1913. An account of his service in South Africa appeared in the *Ilkeston Pioneer* on 26 December 1913, and he was occasionally asked to go into schools to give talks about his life and the events at Rorke's Drift. He became a commissionaire at the King's Cinema in Ilkeston in 1915. His two eldest sons served with the Sherwood Foresters during the First World War, and Arthur was awarded the Military Medal for bravery during the Somme Offensive in July 1916.

By 1922 they had moved back to Ruddington and Caleb returned to the trade of framework knitter. In 1934 they moved into a cottage at 2 Asher Lane in Ruddington. He attended the Northern Command Tattoo held at Ravensworth Castle in Gateshead, and the 2nd Battalion, South Wales Borderers, recreated the action at Rorke's Drift. Caleb, now almost blind and visibly frail, appeared in the arena at the end of the sketch with fellow defenders Frank Bourne DCM, Alfred Saxty, John Jobbins and William Cooper. Also in 1934 he attended the ceremony for the laying-up of the regimental colours at Brecon Cathedral.

Caleb Wood died at his home on 20 February 1935, aged 77, and he was buried in the Shaw Street Cemetery in Ruddington. A new headstone was placed at his grave during a rededication service held at his gravesite in 2004. His great-granddaughter, Kris Wheatley, is the author of the series of booklets entitled *Legacy*, containing biographical tributes to defenders.

A Company, 2nd Battalion, 24th Regiment

John Lyons

John Lyons was born at Kallaloe, near O'Brien's Bridge, County Clare, Ireland in March 1837. He worked as a labourer before joining the British Army to escape the horrors of the terrible potato famine. He enlisted into the 87th Foot – later the Royal Irish Fusiliers (Princess Victoria's) – at Ennis in County Clare on 30 March 1859. He was described as being just under five feet eight inches tall, with a fresh complexion, grey eyes and red hair. On 1 July 1861 he transferred to the 2nd Battalion, 24th Regiment, as 1441 Private Lyons. He then served on Mauritius until 5 October 1865, and in India from 6 October 1865–5 January 1973. He was granted one penny a day good conduct pay from 31 March 1862, which had risen to four pence a day by 31 March 1875.

He received orders for active service in South Africa and sailed to the Cape in February 1878. He took part in the Cape Frontier War, and during the Zulu

War he was one of the oldest soldiers present at the defence of Rorke's Drift. He was admitted to hospital at Rorke's Drift for ten days from 25 February 1879, being treated for Bright's Disease, which was caused by severe exposure to wet and cold weather, and he was recommended to return to England. For his service he received the South Africa Medal with 1877-8-9 clasp, and a copy of the Address by the Lord Mayor of Durban was forwarded on to him in Brecon.

He was admitted to Netley Military Hospital in Southampton on 10 June 1879 and was examined by a Medical Board on 16 July. He was found to be 'suffering from general debility at the Cape, 1879. A very clear and honest case of a worn-out soldier, scarcely able to earn anything for his family.' He was discharged as unfit for further service on 4 August 1879. His character was described as 'very good' and his habits 'temperate'. His intended place of residence was Manchester.

There is a John Lyons, who died on 1 January 1900, aged 60, buried in Philips Park Cemetery, Bradford Ward in Manchester (Roman Catholic - section F grave 103). He had worked as a bricklayer's labourer, and died at 41 High Burton Street, St George's Parish, Hulme, Manchester, cause of death being acute pneumonia and cardiac failure. His son, James H. Lyons, was present at his death. The age given on his death certificate does not correspond with the ages stated on his service papers, but this is a common problem area with Victorian soldiers, and this is almost certainly the John Lyons who was a defender of Rorke's Drift.

John Manley

John Manley was born in 1849 and attested for the British Army at Cork in Ireland on 17 April 1864. He was aged fifteen years three months and was five feet one inch tall. He served in India, being appointed drummer in December 1866, reverted to private in 1868, and as 1731 Private Manley was posted to the 2nd Battalion, 24th Regiment in about December 1868. He was appointed drummer on 1 January 1869, and reverted to private on 7 August 1876.

He received orders for active service in South Africa and sailed with his battalion to the Cape in February 1878. He took part in the Cape Frontier War, and during the Zulu War he was present at the defence of Rorke's Drift. When the battalion sailed to Gibraltar on 1 February 1880, he was sent to Netley Hospital, from where he was discharged. For his service he received the South Africa Medal with 1877-8-9 clasp, which was issued on 17 June 1881.

The *Gloucester Journal* carried a report on 7 February 1885 that John Manley, a soldier aged 34, was charged with criminally assaulting Eliza Jenkins on 9

January 1885, at Stoke Bishop, near Bristol, while 'the worse for drink'. The report stated that he

> had served 20 years in the army. He had served in India and was one of the defenders of Rorke's Drift. He had been reduced from the rank of corporal for drunkenness, but that was the only thing against him. He had an attack of sunstroke and was invalided home. He was a married man with two children. Apparently in tears, he stated that he had no recollection of the offence and 'tendered his deepest regret for having molested her.'

Colour-Sergeant Strait of Gloucester gave him a good character. He pleaded guilty to an attempted assault, for which a jury found him guilty, and he was sentenced to be imprisoned for eighteen months with hard labour.

John Meehan

John Meehan was born in Limerick, Ireland and attested for the army in about March 1871. He appears on the Muster Roll for 1 January 1873, and as 2483 Private Meehan he was posted from the depot at Warley, being appointed drummer on 7 August 1876. In June 1877 he was sentenced to 42 days imprisonment with hard labour, of which eleven days were remitted. He was awarded a good shooting prize in 1878. He received orders for active service in South Africa and sailed with his battalion to the Cape in February 1878. For his service he received the South Africa Medal with 1877-8-9 clasp. He served on Gibraltar in 1880 and returned from India for discharge on 29 January 1883. He died in Limerick.

John Scanlon

John Scanlon was born in County Sligo in Ireland and attested for 25 Brigade on 16 January 1877. As 1051 Private Scanlon he was posted to the 2nd Battalion, 24th Regiment on 11 May 1877. He sailed to the Cape in February 1878 and was a patient in the hospital when he was killed in action by a Zulu slug at the defence at Rorke's Drift. He is buried in the cemetery at Rorke's Drift and his name is inscribed on the monument. His effects were claimed by his mother. For his service he received the South Africa Medal with 1877-8-9 clasp.

Arthur Sears

Arthur John Sears was born on 29 January 1854 at Harmondsworth near Sunbury-on-Thames in Middlesex, where his family had been established for hundreds of years. He was the sixth son in a family of eight born to John Sears, an agricultural labourer, and his wife Ann (formerly Ives), who had started their married life in a house called 'Greensleeves' in Sunbury. Soon after Arthur's birth the family moved to Nursery Road in Sunbury, and by 1861 they lived at a house called 'The Ceson' in Sunbury.

Arthur and two of his brothers, Henry and Joseph, chose the army life, and Arthur enlisted at Little Warley in Essex on 14 February 1873. He was described as being five feet nine inches tall, with grey eyes and light-brown hair. His muscular development was good, and his religion was Church of England. As 2404 Private Sears, he was posted to the 2nd Battalion, 24th Regiment. His brother Joseph also joined the 24th Regiment. He was detached to the School of Military Music at Kneller Hall in 1874–75, and in 1878 he was appointed bandsman.

He sailed to the Cape with his battalion in February 1878 and was present at the defence of Rorke's Drift. For his service he received the South Africa Medal with 1877-8-9 clasp.

On his retirement from the army, Arthur Sears became a keeper at Kensington Park Gardens in west London.

Back Row: Mildred Clara,		Alice Emma		Arthur John
Ft Row: Charles Thomas,	Emma (nee Park),	Florence,	Ex Sgt Arthur Sears,	Walter
		Cyril (on mother's knee)		

A wonderful family photograph of Arthur and Emma Sears and their seven children, taken in about 1904. His son, Arthur, is wearing the uniform of the Royal Fusiliers. Arthur senior died two years after this picture was taken.

He married Emma Park, the orphaned daughter of a Royal Artillery officer, at St John's Episcopalian Church in Secunderabad on 14 August 1882. They had seven children. Mildred Clara was born in 1883, Arthur John in 1885, Alice Emma in 1889, Charles Thomas in 1895, Florence in 1897, Walter Edward in 1900 and Cyril Leslie in 1903.

He obtained a 3rd Class Certificate of Education and was promoted corporal on 6 March 1883, and sergeant on 1 May 1884. He re-engaged in Madras on 30 January 1885, for such term as would complete 21 years service. He was posted to Rangoon in Burma on 9 May 1886, and from there to Tongou on the 2 November 1886. He was appointed sergeant-drummer on 1 June 1888. He returned to India in 1889, being stationed at Bareilly and Allahabad, and in October 1893 he and his family boarded HMS *Serapis* for the journey to England. He discharged on 14 February 1894, having been awarded the Burma Medal with 1887-89 clasp and the Long Service Good Conduct Medal. He was granted a weekly pension of eleven shillings.

Arthur began working for the Royal Parks Department as PK24 (park keeper) at Kensington in June 1895. He left the department for health reasons in 1905. He died on 15 December 1906 at 85 Stephendale Road, Fulham in London, aged 51, having been suffering from tubercular phthisis. He was buried in Fulham Cemetery (section C18, grave 6A).

D Company, 2nd Battalion, 24th Regiment

Robert Adams

Robert Adams had served in the East Middlesex Militia when he attested for the army on 21 December 1876, and was posted to the 2nd Battalion, 24th Regiment as 987 Private Adams. He received orders for active service in South Africa and sailed to the Cape with his battalion in February 1878. He took part in the Cape Frontier War, and was sent to the General Depot on 1 November 1878, returning to the service companies on 21 December 1878. During the Zulu War he was killed in action as a defender of Rorke's Drift, having been a patient in the hospital.

During his escape from the hospital Gunner Evans stated

> I was then standing in the doorway of the hospital, and witnessed five Zulus come in front of the doorway, jumping in their mad frenzy and flushed with their late victory. Just at this moment my newest mates were Adams and Jenkins of the 24th Regiment. What became of these men I can't say, I never saw them again after …

Robert and Drummer Hayden were two of the bedridden patients being defended by Privates John and Joseph Williams in a dangerously exposed room at the far end of the hospital. According to Private Hook 'John Williams had held the other room with Private William Horrigan for more than an hour, until they had not a cartridge left. The Zulus then burst in and dragged out Joseph Williams and two of the patients, and assegaid them.' These two men were Private Adams and Drummer Hayden of D Company. Hayden's body was found badly mutilated and it is likely that Robert Adams suffered the same terrible fate. He was buried in the cemetery at Rorke's Drift and his name is inscribed on the monument. His effects were recorded for claim by his next of kin. For his service he received the South Africa Medal with 1877-8-9 clasp.

James Chick

James Chick attested for 25 Brigade on 8 March 1877, and as 1335 Private Chick he was posted to the 2nd Battalion, 24th Regiment at Brecon on 11

May 1877. He acted as assistant schoolmaster during 1877. He received orders for active service in South Africa and sailed to the Cape in February 1878. He took part in the Cape Frontier War, and during the Zulu War he was killed in action as a defender of Rorke's Drift. He had been a patient in the hospital and was killed at the barricades by a Zulu slug. He was buried in the cemetery at Rorke's Drift and his name is inscribed on the monument. For his service he was entitled to receive the South Africa Medal with 1877-8-9 clasp. There is no trace of a claim for his effects.

Patrick Galgey

Patrick J. Galgey was born in Ireland in 1851, the son of Patrick Galgey, a chandler. The 1875 subscribers list to Cusacks. The History of Cork shows a Patrick Galgey of 2 Clifton Terrace, Cork, who may be Drummer Galgey's father.

Patrick junior attested in Cork as a boy soldier on 12 March 1865. He received a bounty of £1, and he was described as aged fourteen years, and being four feet seven-and-three-quarter inches tall. As 1713 Private Galgey he was posted to the 2nd Battalion, 24th Regiment. He was appointed drummer on 1 February 1866, which meant he received an extra penny a day. He remained in Cork for five years before being posted to India to join his company on 5 April 1869 at the age of eighteen. He was reduced to private in Secunderabad on 1 July 1870, but was re-appointed drummer in Secunderabad on 23 February 1872, and from 30 April 1872 he was in receipt of good conduct pay. He returned to the Warley depot on 1 October 1872. The muster rolls for 1 July 1873 show that he attended the Gravesend School of Musketry before postings at Warley, Aldershot, Dover and Chatham.

He received orders for active service in South Africa and sailed to the Cape with his battalion from Portsmouth in February 1878. He took part in the Cape Frontier War, and during the Zulu War he was present at the defence of Rorke's Drift. For his service he received the South Africa Medal with 1877-8-9 clasp. He served on Gibraltar in 1880, where he was demoted to private, and he was discharged on 2 March 1880, having completed his army service of fifteen years.

By 1881 Patrick was living at Top Row in New Town, Aberysrtuth, Monmouthshire, and he had gained employment as a labourer. Moving to London, he took lodgings at 24 Brand Street, Marylebone, and found work as a tailor's porter. He met Catherine Evans, who was seventeen years older than him, and they lived together at 88 Newnham Street in Marylebone. They married at Marylebone register office on 29 June 1891. By 1901 they had moved to 33 Great Quebec Street, Marylebone. They next moved to 8 Circus Street, north-west London, but Catherine began to suffer the effects of senile dementia, and died on 15 January 1913. Six months later, on 5 August 1913, Patrick married Maria Eyles, who was aged 44. Patrick died in Paddington Hospital on 11 August 1935, aged 84, the cause of death being given as a cerebral hemorrhage and arterial sclerosis. He was buried in an unmarked grave at Paddington Old Cemetery, Willesden Lane, London (section 3W, grave 9926).

Garret Hayden

Garret Henry Hayden was born in Ireland in 1852, the son of Charles Hayden, a cabinet maker. He enlisted in Dublin on 9 December 1865, and his description notes stated that he was five feet five inches tall. He gave his age as eighteen but later information suggests that he enlisted as a boy soldier at the age of thirteen and the latter figure has been mistaken for an eight by transcribers. As 1769 Private Hayden he was posted to the 2nd Battalion, 24th Regiment in India on 11 July 1867. He was appointed drummer on 1 October 1868, but he reverted to private on 10 September 1873. He married Margaret Ann Jones at Brecknock Register Office on 5 May 1877, when he gave his occupation as bugler, 2/24th Regiment. They set up home at 9 John Street in Brecon. Their only child, Mary Ellen, was born at the Barracks on 17 February 1878, and as Garret had received orders for active service in South Africa, and had sailed to the Cape on 2 February 1878, it must be assumed that he missed the birth of his daughter. Before leaving Britain, Garret had given his wife a small brooch as a keepsake, which is still owned by the family, and has been identified as the sept badge of the Irish 'Clan Dennis'.

He took part in the Cape Frontier War, and during the Zulu War he was killed in action during the defence of Rorke's Drift. He was a bedridden patient in a room of the hospital being defended by Privates John and Joseph Williams, and was dragged out and killed. According to Sergeant Smith

> We had thirteen killed and about eight wounded. Amongst the former was poor Drummer Hayden, who lived at the top of John Street. He was stabbed in hospital in sixteen places, and his belly cut open right up in two places, and part of his cheek was cut off.

He was buried in the cemetery at Rorke's Drift and his name is inscribed on the monument. His effects were claimed by his father. For his service he was entitled to the South Africa Medal with 1877-8-9 clasp.

Several of his descendants saw distinguished military service. His great-grandson, Kenneth Jones, served with the Welsh Guards. During the Falklands

War in 1982 he was aboard HMS *Sir Gallahad* waiting to disembark as part of British land forces when Argentinian fighter planes attacked the ship and he was badly burned.

E Company, 2nd Battalion, 24th Regiment

James Ruck

James Ruck attested for 25 Brigade on 18 January 1877, and as Private Ruck he was posted to the 2nd Battalion, 24th Regiment at Brecon. He was promoted corporal on 12 January 1878, and received orders for active service in South Africa. He sailed to the Cape in February 1878, and took part in the Cape Frontier War, being reduced to private on 17 July 1878. During the Zulu War he was present at the defence of Rorke's Drift, being promoted to lance-corporal on the day after the defence, and transferred to G Company on 31 January 1879. He was promoted to corporal on 30 April 1879, but reduced to private. For his service he received the South Africa Medal with 1877-8-9 clasp. He was promoted to corporal on 15 May 1881 while in India, but reduced to private, and was placed on the unattached list while serving at Madras on 28 November 1886.

James Taylor

James Taylor was born in the village of Meltham near Huddersfield in West Yorkshire in March 1855. He moved across the Pennines to Manchester, where he worked as a clerk, until he enlisted into the army at Hulme Barracks in Manchester on 13 March 1874, apparently aged nineteen. He was just over five feet eight inches tall, with a fresh complexion, blue eyes and brown hair, and had a small scar on his forehead. His religion was Church of England. As 92 Private Taylor he was posted to the 2nd Battalion, 24th Regiment.

His records suggest that his education helped him, but he seems to have found it difficult to adjust to army life. He was appointed corporal on 3 March 1875, but he was confined for drunkenness on 27 May that year and reduced to private. He was appointed corporal on 4 August 1876 and was granted one penny a day good conduct pay from 27 March 1877. He was promoted lance-sergeant on 26 October 1877, but reverted to corporal the following month. He received orders for active service in South Africa and sailed with his battalion to the Cape in February 1878. He took part in the Cape Frontier War, being promoted lance-sergeant on 11 July 1878, and during the Zulu War he was present at the defence of Rorke's Drift. He was promoted sergeant on 23 January 1879. For his service he was awarded the South Africa Medal with 1877-8-9 clasp.

He served on Gibraltar in 1880, where he was confined in cells on 17 March 1880, and three days later he was tried by Regimental Court Martial and reduced to private. He served in Bombay in India, where his good conduct pay was increased to two pence a day from 20 March 1883. He was promoted lance-sergeant on 3 September 1884, but was deprived of this rank on 19 February 1885. He was tried by Regimental Court Martial on 22 September 1885 and sentenced to 21 days imprisonment with hard labour, being reduced to private and forfeiting one good conduct badge. However, the sentence was later remitted. He re-engaged at Madras on 23 November 1885 to complete 21 years service. He went with the battalion to Burma on 9 May 1886, being granted three pence a day good conduct pay from 19 September 1888, and for his service he received the Indian General Service Medal with Burma 1887-89 clasp. He returned to India on 10 November 1888, where he remained until 17 November 1893. He had reached the rank of orderly room sergeant from 5 June 1891 and was granted four pence a day good conduct pay from 1 March 1892. He also gained a 2nd Class Certificate of Education. He discharged on 8 March 1894, his conduct being described as good and his habits regular.

He lived with his wife Sarah and their two children at 33 Parkfield Road, Rusholme, Manchester, for about 20 years. His daughter, also named Sarah, went to live at St Asaph in Denbighshire, and in 1915 he took his family to live in the village of Trefnant near Denbigh, making their home at 'Siop Bach', and James returned to his previous occupation as a clerk, with the firm of Richard Evans. He died on 15 November 1915 from a malignant disease of the throat and exhaustion, aged 64, and he was buried with military honours in Trefnant Churchyard. His South Africa campaign medal is with the regimental museum in Brecon.

John Williams

John Williams was born at Cadoxton near Neath in Glamorganshire. He had previously served with the Glamorgan Artillery when he left his job as a collier to enlist into the regular army on 28 November 1876 at Pontypool, and as 934 Private Williams he was posted to the 2nd Battalion, 24th Regiment. He sailed to the Cape in February 1878. He died of disease at Rorke's Drift on 5 February 1879 and is buried in the cemetery there. His name is inscribed on the monument, and for his service he received the South Africa Medal with 1877-8-9 clasp, issued on 29 March 1881.

F Company, 2nd Battalion, 24th Regiment

Robert Cole

Robert Edward Cole was born on 28 November 1858 at Brompton Barracks, Chatham in Kent, where his father George Cole was serving with the 24th Regiment. His mother was Eliza (formerly Roche). Although the register of births was first introduced in 1837, it did not become compulsory until 1871. When Eliza and George registered their youngest son in 1858, they chose to do so with the regiment and not the civil authorities. His birth certificate is therefore held by the GRO in their 'foreign births' section, even though Robert was born in England. His father was medically discharged from the army in 1864, having served his country for most of his adult life. George and his family moved into a temporary home at 12 Nova Scotia Street in Birmingham, gaining employment as a day labourer, and by 1871 they had moved to their permanent home at 7 Lench Street, Aston, Birmingham. Robert had two siblings and all three children obtained employment with the British Small Arms Company (BSA) in Aston.

Robert attested for the army on 29 October 1877, and as 1459 Private R. Cole he was posted to the 2nd Battalion of his father's old unit, the 24th Regiment, at Brecon. He was five feet six inches tall, with grey eyes and brown hair. His religion was Church of England, his trade a gun maker, and he gave his next of kin as his brother, George Cole, of 7 Poplar Place, Sherbourne Road, Birmingham.

He was twice hospitalised in Chatham and received treatment for scabies and 'glands' just prior to receiving orders for active service in South Africa. He sailed to the Cape in February 1878, taking part in the Cape Frontier War. Robert did not accompany the rest of the men of 'F' company when they invaded Zululand, as he was in hospital suffering from typhoid fever. During the defence of Rorke's Drift he had to be assisted from the hospital, where Michael McMahon saw him having difficulty in reaching the safety of the inner perimeter and ran to his aid, and Private Hitch also assisted in his escape by giving covering fire. For his service he received the South Africa Medal with 1877-8-9 clasp.

He was again hospitalised in Natal for 40 days, being treated for syphilis. He served on Gibraltar in 1880 and in India, where he was admitted to hospital on numerous occasions suffering with a variety of ailments. However, he had put his time to good use by gaining a 4th Class Certificate of Education, and he received one penny a day good conduct pay from 19 June 1882. He arrived back in England on 1 December 1883, and was discharged to the 1st Class Army Reserve at Brecon. He held one good conduct badge and his character was described as 'good' and his habits were 'temperate'. He was finally discharged in 1893.

He returned to work at BSA, and on 23 August 1884 he married eighteen-year-old Elizabeth Gibelin at St Bartholomew's Church, and they lived at 2 Court, Lower Tower Street, Birmingham. They had five children; Eliza was born in 1886, Gertrude in 1888, Robert in 1890 (died aged two), Elizabeth in 1893 and Edith in 1896. They moved to 7 Floodgate Street in Birmingham, but they moved back to their home area and lived at 11 Court, 3 Lower Tower Street, and Robert became a licensed hawker of fruit and vegetables. He died at his home on 19 August 1898, aged 40, the cause of death being given as 'malignant disease of the lungs, and asthenia', the latter being the same condition as had been suffered by his father. He was buried in an unmarked public grave in Witton Cemetery in Birmingham (section 164, grave 54737).

William Cooper

William Cooper was born on 16 July 1855 at Whybro's Yard in Tottenham, London. He was the second of three sons born to William Cooper, a horse keeper, and his second wife Elizabeth (formerly Angel). His father had several children by his first wife. By 1861 they lived at number 3, Factory Yard,

William Cooper (far right of picture), poses with four fellow Rorke's Drift men during the Northern Command Military Tattoo held at Ravenswood Castle in Gateshead in 1934. The others are Alfred Saxty, Caleb Wood, Frank Bourne and John Jobbins.

Edmonton, but both parents had died by 1865. William went into boarding at 6 Harewood Cottages, Edmonton, and earned a living as a domestic servant. He enlisted into the army and was posted to the 2nd Battalion, 24th Regiment at Warley on 1 January 1873 as 2453 Private Cooper.

He sailed to the Cape in February 1878. He and Private Robert Cole were sent to Rorke's Drift with a ration party on 21 January 1879, and he was present at the defence of the post on the following day. He was sent to the general depot at Helpmekaar on 28 March 1879, as time expired, where he appeared before a discharge board at Pietermarizburg on 4 April 1879, and on 19 May he embarked for England, where he was sent to Netley Hospital and discharged to the 1st Class Army Reserves. For his service he received the South Africa Medal with 1877-8-9 clasp.

He obtained employment as a brewer's drayman and found lodgings in Leslie Grove, Croydon. He married Eliza Rhoades on 30 June 1881 at St James Parish Church in Croydon, and they made their home at 10 Grove Terrace, Cross Road, Croydon. They had two children; Jessie was born in 1882 and William Joseph was born in 1885. He was killed in action serving with the Royal Artillery in France during the First World War. By 1891 William and Eliza had moved to 48 Borough Hill in Croydon, and William worked as a brewer's draymen. They moved to the village of Cocking in West Sussex for a while, and William attended the Northern Command Tattoo in Gateshead in July 1934. They eventually made their home at 6 Cranmer Road in Worthing, which was closer to their daughter. However, the Second World War was raging and William had stated that he was worried about the conflict. He was also having trouble with failing eyesight. On 19 February 1942 Eliza found him lying dead with his head in the oven. He was 86. His funeral took place at the Woodvale Crematorium in Worthing, and his ashes were scattered in the Garden of Remembrance (section 6134).

G Company, 2nd Battalion, 24th Regiment

John Connolly

John Connolly stated that he was born at Castletown, Berehaven, County Cork in Ireland in 1859, the son of a fisherman named John Connolly, although his service papers record that he was born at Trevethin, Pontypool, Monmouthshire. He had served with the Monmouthshire Militia when he enlisted on 24 November 1876 at Newport, where he had been working as a labourer, and as 906 Private Connolly he was posted to the 2nd Battalion, 24th Regiment. He was five feet six-and-a-half inches tall, with a fresh complexion, blue eyes and light-brown hair. He had a cross tattooed on his left forearm and his religion was Roman Catholic. He gained a 4th Class Certificate of Education.

He sailed to the Cape in February 1878, taking part in the Cape Frontier War. He was sentenced to 168 hours imprisonment with hard labour on 27 August 1878. During the Zulu War he was present at the defence of Rorke's Drift. 'Having been injured in the left leg at the knee when loading a wagon at the Tugela River [5 January 1879] I was in the hospital at Rorke's Drift under treatment and in bed ...' Henry Hook reported that

> All this time Williams was getting the sick through the hole into the next room, all except one, a soldier of the 24th named Conley (Connolly) who could not move because of a broken leg. Watching my chance, I dashed from the doorway and, grabbing Conley, I pulled him after me through the hole. His leg got broken again, but there was no help for it. As soon as we left the room the Zulus burst in with furious cries of disappointment and rage. Now there was a repetition of the work ... Again I had to drag Conley through, a terrible task because he was a very heavy man.

Surgeon Reynolds reported that Hook and Connolly 'made their way into the open at the back of the Hospital by breaking a hole in the wall with a pickaxe and then through a small window looking into what may be styled the neutral ground.' He was admitted to hospital in Natal on 25 February 1879, suffering from synovitis due to a partial dislocation of the left knee, and being recommended for a change of climate he was invalided home on 11 March 1879. He sailed back to England on HMS *Tamar*, and on 3 May he gave an account of his experience at Rorke's Drift to Captain Liddell, at the request of Lady Frere.

> I crawled out of the window by placing mealie bags, and made for the bush by sitting down and pushing myself along feet first. After going fifty yards I got into the bush and laid down to keep out of sight. The Zulus kept passing me all night, but either did not see me or thought me dead. About 5am I crawled back into the entrenchment.

For his service he received the South Africa Medal with 1877-8-9 clasp.

He was admitted to Netley Hospital on 10 June 1879, and on being examined on 21 July he was declared unfit for further service and discharged on 4 August 1879. His character was described as fair and his intended place of residence was Hereford. An injury assessment board held at the Royal Hospital in Chelsea considered the injury to be permanent, and insofar as employment he could do nothing at the moment, and awarded him a pension of six pence a day for six months. He appeared before an assessment board for a second time on 2 September and his award was increased to twelve pence a day for twelve months, which was made permanent in 1880. He is believed to have returned to Castletown and died there some time after 30 November 1905, when his pension was reduced to ten pence a day.

Private Connolly's account of the action and how he escaped from the hospital has been described as dubious, based on the fact that it seems to contradict the account of Henry Hook. Although I find it disappointing that Connolly fails to mention Hook, the man who almost certainly saved his life, the events he speaks of could well have happened after Hook dragged him through the second hole.

Robert Maxfield

Robert Maxfield was born in 1855 at Llangarron in Herefordshire. He enlisted at Newport on 30 July 1875. He was posted to the 2nd Battalion, 24th Regiment at Brecon in the following month as 623 Private Maxfield. He received orders for active service in South Africa, and he was promoted to sergeant on 1 February 1878, the day he embarked to sail with his unit to the Cape. He took part in the Cape Frontier War, being awarded a good shooting prize in 1878. During the Zulu War he was a patient in the hospital at Rorke's Drift suffering with fever, where he was killed by the Zulus. According to Henry Hook

> Privates William Jones and Robert Jones ... kept at it with bullet and bayonet until six of the seven patients had been removed. They would have got the seventh, Sergeant Maxfield, out safely but he was delirious with fever and, although they managed to dress him, he refused to move. Robert Jones made a last rush to try and get him away like the rest, but when he went back into the room he saw that Maxfield was being stabbed by the Zulus as he lay on his bed.

He was buried in the cemetery at Rorke's Drift and his name is inscribed on the monument. For his service he received the South Africa Medal with 1877-8-9 clasp. His effects were claimed by his mother, brothers and sisters.

William Partridge

William Partridge was born on 27 June 1858 in Broad Street, Ross-on-Wye, Herefordshire, the oldest child of four born to William Partridge, a sawyer and carpenter, and his wife Sarah (formerly Williams). They moved back to their native Monmouthshire.

Having served with the Monmouthshire Militia, William enlisted for the regular army at Monmouth on 5 June 1877, and as 1410 Private Partridge, he was posted to the 2nd Battalion, 24th Regiment, being described as just over five feet six inches tall, with a fresh complexion, grey eyes and brown hair. His religion was Church of England. He sailed to the Cape in February 1878. He took part in the Cape Frontier War, being appointed lance-corporal on 1 August 1878, but he reverted back to private on 1 December 1878. It was during this campaign that he was batman to Colour-Sergeant Bourne, who stated

> One day I heard a man named Wall ask my batman 'if the kid was in', a day or two later I asked Partridge who 'the kid' was, and received the answer 'why, you are of course!'

During the Zulu War he was present at the defence of Rorke's Drift. For his service he received the South Africa Medal with 1877-8-9 clasp.

He served on Gibraltar, from where he embarked on 23 February 1880 to return home. An injury assessment board held at the Royal Hospital in Chelsea in November 1881 confirmed that he was suffering from chronic rheumatism, which would materially affect his ability to earn an income. His condition was attributed to having been brought about by climate and exposure during the Zulu War, and he was awarded a pension of seven pence a day for twelve months. He was discharged as unfit for further service at Devonport on 10 November 1881. He gave his intended place of residence as Llangstone in Newport in Monmouthshire, the home of his father, William, who by this time was the local parish clerk.

He married Mary Letitia 'Polly' Reeves on 13 November 1880 at the Brecon Register Office. Polly was the sister-in-law of William Allan VC. They had six children; Sarah Eleanor, known as 'Nellie', was born in 1882, William Henry in 1885, Elizabeth in 1889, Lily in 1891, but she only lived for a few days, Beswick in 1894 and Jessie in 1899. They lived at 46 Lancaster Street in Blaina where William found employment as a stoker. At the time of the First World War he and William Henry were working at the same pit, before William junior enlisted for service with the Royal Warwickshire Regiment. William died on 16 April 1930, aged 71, the cause of death being myocardial degeneration. He was buried in Blaenau Cemetery in Gwent (section 7, grave 349).

H Company, 2nd Battalion, 24th Regiment

Thomas Evans

Thomas Evans was born at Cilybebyll near Pontardawe near Swansea in about 1855, the son of a stoker. By 1871 he was living with his family at Llwynypia near Tonypandy in Glamorganshire. He was aged fifteen and was working as a collier.

He enlisted at Monmouth in 1876, and as 954 Private Evans he was posted to the 2nd Battalion, 24th Regiment. He sailed to the Cape with the battalion in February 1878. During the Zulu War he became attached to the Mounted Infantry. He escaped from the massacre at Isandlwana and was present at the defence of Rorke's Drift. He was tried for quitting his picquet without permission and confined for fourteen days from 31 January 1879. For his service he received the South Africa Medal with 1877-8-9 clasp.

He served on Gibraltar in 1880, where he began to drink heavily and get into trouble with the authorities. He began to make a monthly remittance of seven shillings and six pence to his wife Mrs Evans from 30 April 1880. He was fined seven shillings and six pence for drunkenness on 12 May 1880, and was fined ten shillings for drunkenness on 27 May 1880, being confined in cells, but he still managed to increase the remittance by three pence from 31 May 1880, although this was reduced to seven shillings at a later date. He was confined in cells on 3, 14 and 17 June 1880, and he was fined for drunkenness on 10 July 1880.

It has been suggested that Private Evans was not present during the defence. However, Private Waters stated that

> The first news I had of what happened at Isandlwana was when one of the Mounted Infantry, named Evans, came galloping up to the mission house and said that a part of the camp across the river had been destroyed by the Zulus …

Corporal Lyons noted that he 'saw Private Evans, of the Mounted Infantry, riding up at full gallop, without either coat or cap on.' In a letter dated 28 January 1879, written in Welsh to his wife who lived at Tonypandy in the Rhondda Valley in Glamorgan, he himself said that

> The Zulus crossed into Natal, and attacked another station with such fire against them that they failed to force an entrance, and when they saw what number of men amongst them was being killed they set fire to the hospital and then retreated. I was in the midst of this fight, and about 100 of us killed about 600 of the enemy …

His name appears on three lists of defenders, and there is no evidence to suggest that he decamped after bringing the report to the post.

2nd Battalion, 90th Light Infantry

James Graham

Daniel Sheehan was born near Cork in Ireland in July 1851. He left his job as a clerk to enlist into the army on 5 December 1870, and was posted to the 2nd Battalion, 6th Regiment. He was just under five feet eight inches tall. He gained a 2nd Class Certificate of Education, and by the end of January 1876 he had been promoted to sergeant, gaining a sergeant instructor's certificate of musketry. However, he went absent without leave in the following June, for which he was tried and sentenced to be reduced to private. On 15 December 1876 he transferred to the Army Reserves at Liverpool District, having committed to six years at the time of his attestation.

He re-enlisted at Bin in Ireland as 1123 Private James Graham, being posted to the 2nd Battalion, 90th Light Infantry. He said that he was born at St Mary's near Dublin, and stated that he had no previous military service. However, he was found out and convicted of fraudulent enlistment on 2 May 1877, lost his pension and good conduct pay, and was confined in military prison until 26 June 1877.

He received orders for active service in South Africa and arrived at the Cape on 11 January 1878. He took part in the Cape Frontier War, and while still on active service he was tried by court martial for desertion from the Liverpool District and had to forfeit the six years service, pension and good conduct pay he had accumulated in the name of Private Sheehan. Nevertheless, he continued his military service as James Graham, and by the time he took part in the defence of Rorke's Drift he had been promoted to corporal.

He later served in India, where he was promoted sergeant in May 1880, and all his forfeited service and pensions were restored to him on 16 March 1883. He married Mary Ann Daly at Barreilly in India in February 1885. He reached the rank of colour-sergeant with the 1st Lanark Rifle Volunteers on 19 March 1887, and was discharged on 15 December 1891 after 21 years service. He died at Farnborough in Hampshire on 24 February 1899.

Army Medical Department and Hospital Corps

James Reynolds

James Henry Reynolds was born at Kingstown (now Dun Laughaire) in Ireland on 3 February 1844, the son of Laurence Reynolds, JP of Dalyston House, Granard, County Longford. He was educated at Castle Knock and at Trinity College in Dublin, from where he graduated Bachelor of Medicine and Bachelor of Surgery in 1867. He entered the Medical Staff Corps as Assistant-Surgeon on 31 March 1868, and joined the 36th Regiment on 24 March 1869. He received a commendation for his efficient service during an outbreak of cholera in the regiment in India. He was appointed to the Medical Staff in 1870, becoming Surgeon Reynolds in 1873.

When the 1st Battalion, 24th Regiment sailed to South Africa in 1874, he went with them as part of the medical team. He took part in the campaign in Griqualand West in 1875, and during the 9th Cape Frontier War he was stationed at the Impetu depot with the 24th Regiment when the garrison was besieged for several weeks until relief came in January 1878. He was appointed for service with the British troops preparing for hostilities against the Zulus,

Surgeon James Reynolds had been in South Africa for five years when the Zulu War began. He worked tirelessly to attend to the wounded throughout the Zulu attack at Rorke's Drift, for which he was awarded the Victoria Cross.

and on 22 January 1879 he was on medical duties at Rorke's Drift. He was helped by a servant named William Pearce, who was aged about 27 and was born in Devonport, Plymouth, Devon.

On 22 January 1879, he and Reverend Otto Witt were preparing their horses to go and visit a local missionary when the first sounds of hostilities were heard. He later said

> At about 12:30pm, we were surprised at Rorke's Drift by hearing big guns in the neighbourhood, and almost immediately I commenced climbing up the big hill of the Oscarberg, in company with the Missionary Witt, and Mr Smith [afterwards] Army Chaplain. We expected to get a view of what was happening, but on looking across the Buffalo River from the top we discovered that Isandlwana mountain [five miles away] shut from our view the scene of action.
>
> At 1:30pm, a large body of natives marched over the slope of Isandlwana in our direction. These men we took for our own native contingent. Soon afterwards appeared three horsemen on the Natal side of the river galloping in the direction of our post, and feeling they might possibly be messengers for additional medical aid, I hurried down to the hospital and arrived there as they rode up. They looked frightfully scared, and I was startled to find one of them riding Surgeon-Major Shepherd's pony. Their report was the camp at Isandlwana had been taken by the enemy and all our men massacred …

Surgeon Reynolds worked tirelessly throughout the Zulu attack at Rorke's Drift. Whenever a man was injured 'the doctor was by him at once'. When the Zulus forced their way over the barricade in front of the hospital veranda, the doctor and his men grabbed as much as they could carry, and worked hard to establish a new casualty station at the storehouse veranda. When the doctor had no patients to attend to he took ammunition to the men who were defending the hospital, exposing himself to enemy fire.

Private Hitch wrote that 'As we got the sick and wounded out they were taken to a veranda in front of the storehouse, and Doctor Reynolds, under a heavy fire and clouds of assegais, did everything he could for them.' There were two mortally wounded men to attend to and it was stated that 'Doctor Reynolds did all he could to save them, but did not succeed.'

His award of Victoria Cross was announced in the *London Gazette* of 17 June 1879, and he was promoted to surgeon-major, dated 23 January 1879. He remained at Rorke's Drift after the battle, and Henry Harford wrote

> I shall not easily forget one particular night when Doctor Reynolds and I met in the dark having literally been washed out of our sleeping place, and

mooched about, endeavouring to find a more sheltered spot. Suddenly we hit on the idea of lying down under the eaves of B Company's [storehouse] roof, so coiled ourselves up in our soaking-wet blankets, thanking our stars that at all events there would be no river running under us, when presently swish came about half a ton of water clean on top of us – B Company were emptying their tarpauline!

He was at the decisive Battle of Ulundi to witness the defeat of the Zulus, and he arrived back in England on board the *Eagle* on 2 October 1879. For his service he was awarded the South Africa Medal with 1877-8-9 clasp. In July 1879 he was awarded the British Medical Association's gold medal, and he was elected Honorary Fellow of the Royal College of Physicians, Ireland, and Honorary Doctor of Law, Dublin. On 17 October 1879 he and John Chard were guests of honour at a dinner held at the Wanderers Club, Pall Mall, London, 'In recognition of their splendid defence of Rorke's Drift.'

In 1880 he was appointed senior medical officer for the expedition to aid Captain Charles Boycott during the Irish Land War. He married Elizabeth McCormick in 1880, and in 1891 he was living at Cheriton Cliffs, St Paul's Parish, Sandgate, at Hythe in Kent, with his four children, George, Percy, Henry

Surgeon Reynolds risked his life on several occasions as he carried ammunition to the men in the hospital, and attended to the wounded under enemy fire.

The grave of James Henry Reynolds in Kensal Green Roman Catholic Cemetery, London. It was renovated and re-set in 1991.

and Lily, who had all been born in Ireland. He also had a daughter named Elizabeth.

He was promoted lieutenant-colonel on 1 April 1887 and brigade-surgeon lieutenant-colonel on 25 December 1892. He retired from military service on 8 January 1896, and while on the retired list he was employed as Senior Medical Officer at the Royal Army Clothing Factory at Pimlico in London. He retired from this post in May 1905. A keen sportsman, he was a member of the Army and Navy Club from 1890 until his death. On 9 November 1929, he and John Fielding were guests of honour as the two senior VC holders at a dinner hosted by the Prince of Wales in the Royal Gallery at the House of Lords.

The 1901 census records him as living alone at 156 Cambridge Street in Belgravia, London, and he was living at the Rubens Hotel in Westminster when he became ill and was admitted to the Empire Nursing Home in Victoria, London. He died of pleurisy and influenza on 4 March 1932, aged 88, and was buried in St Mary's Roman Catholic Cemetery, Kensal Rise, London (grave NE 504). The granite cross memorial which marks his grave became blackened and had subsided badly, so it was cleaned and re-set in 1991. His medals are with the Royal Army Medical Corps Museum in Aldershot.

A number of items which Surgeon Reynolds had used at Rorke's Drift were auctioned at Spinks in 2001. They included two Gladstone bags engraved with his initials, a travelling wooden medicine chest containing unused ointment tubes and glass bottles, and two leather pocket cases containing the surgical instruments he used in the field. The lot included his revolver, an eighteenth-century pocket watch he had been given by his grandfather, a silver medal which had been presented to him by the Royal Welch Fusiliers and dress miniatures of his Victoria Cross and South Africa campaign medal.

Michael McMahon

Michael McMahon was born at Rathkeale in Limerick in Ireland in about 1856, and as 3359 2nd Corporal McMahon he was probably with the same Army Hospital Corps unit as Privates Luddington and Miller (see below) which was posted at Devonport until October 1878, when it received orders for active service in South Africa. It arrived on 7 November 1878 and he served under Surgeon Reynolds during the defence of Rorke's Drift. As the hospital patients were being evacuated across the compound to the inner defences, several Zulus scaled the ramparts and attacked them. McMahon was one of the men who ran out to help them, assisting Private Robert Cole in particular. Doctor Reynolds stated that 'I am glad to say that the men of AHC behaved splendidly.' For his gallantry Corporal McMahon was mentioned in dispatches, and on 15 January 1880 he was recommended to receive the Distinguished Conduct Medal. However, this was cancelled two weeks later 'for going absent without leave and stealing certain items.' For his service he received the South Africa Medal with 1879 clasp.

Thomas Luddington

Thomas Levi Luddington was born on 14 December 1855 at Lavendon, close to the northern border of Buckinghamshire. He was the fourth son in a family of ten children born to James Baker Luddington and his wife Ann (formerly Brittain). His mother died in childbirth in 1858. The family moved to London, and the 1861 census shows them living at 34 Dean Street in Islington where James was employed as a 'dust controller's labourer'.

Thomas left his job as a locksmith to enlist for the British cavalry at Westminster on 30 April 1874, and as 1509 Trooper Luddington he was posted to the 8th Hussars. He was described as five feet six-and-a-half inches tall, with a fresh complexion, hazel eyes, and brown hair. His religion was Church of England, and it was stated that he had 'rather flat feet'. He transferred to 48 Brigade on 30 June 1874; as 91 Private Luddington he was posted to the

2nd Battalion, 2nd Regiment. He transferred to the Army Hospital Corps at Aldershot on 1 September 1876 with the regimental number 3037. He was posted at Devonport until October 1878, when he received orders for active service in South Africa, arriving on 7 November 1878. During the Zulu War he served under Surgeon Reynolds at the defence of Rorke's Drift. For his service he received the South Africa Medal with 1879 clasp.

He was promoted to 2nd corporal in June 1879 and obtained a 4th Class Certificate of Education, being classed as a professional AHC, and he arrived back at Aldershot on 18 March 1880. He was posted to Malta from 15 September 1880 until August 1881, when he purchased his discharge and arrived in England on 2 October 1881. However, he re-enlisted at the Westminster Police Court on 6 October 1881. The Army Hospital Corps had been re-designated as the Medical Staff Corps, and he was posted to Aldershot as 4580 Private Luddington, later reverting to his old regimental number of 3037.

He arrived at Devonport on 17 April 1883, where he married Jessie Harper, a widow with a daughter, on 28 April 1884. He received orders for active service in Egypt on 27 August 1884, from where he took part in the Nile Expedition to try to relieve General Gordon at Khartoum. For his service he received the Egypt Medal with Nile 1884-85 and Gemaizah 1888 clasps, and the Khedives

Thomas Luddington's son played international rugby union for England, gaining gained thirteen caps. He was killed in action serving with the Royal Navy in 1941.

Bronze Star. He passed the exams for his 2nd Class Certificate of Education on 10 April 1886, and on 1 May 1886 he was promoted to corporal, returning to Aldershot from Egypt in March 1889. The 1891 census shows Thomas as being stationed at Aldershot with his wife, step-daughter Ethel Linda Harper (Luddington), and Thomas, who is stated to be a nephew, but it is known that he was born to Jessie while Thomas was in Egypt. William George Ernest was born in 1894, and soon afterwards Thomas and Jessie were married for a second time in Stoke Damarel in Devonport. He discharged on 3 May 1896, having received the Long Service and Good Conduct Medal.

Thomas became the landlord of the Naval Reserve public house at 6 Pembroke Street in Stoke Damerel, where George Francis was born in 1897. By 1900 he was the landlord of the Friendship Inn at 19 Cannon street in Devonport, before moving to 15 Fort Street, where Jessie died in 1911. Thomas died of a heart attack, brought about by chronic bronchitis, in a lodging house at 5 Prospect Row in Devonport on 22 March 1934, aged 78, and he was buried with his wife in Weston Mill Cemetery (section: general B, grave: 4498). A new headstone was erected at the grave during a rededication service in 2009.

William George Ernest Luddington became captain of the Royal Navy rugby union team, and he was capped thirteen times for England, during which they suffered only one defeat, winning the Grand Slam on two occasions. He was killed in action in 1941 while serving in the Malta convoys on HMS *Illustrious*. His name is inscribed on the Plymouth Naval Memorial, and items of rugby memorabilia associated with him are on display at the Museum of Rugby in Twickenham.

Rowland Miller

Rowland Herbert Miller was born on 25 May 1855 at Te Aro, Cuba Street, Wellington, New Zealand. He was the fourth son of six born to Edward Miller and his wife Frances Ann (formerly Brown), who had emigrated from England in 1853 to set up as sheep farmers, before Edward gained a senior position at the Wellington branch of the Bank of New South Wales, and he also became the mathematical examiner to Wellington College. All six Miller boys attended Mr Fennimore's School in Willis Street, and went on to grammar school, where Rowland gained a First in history and a Second in Latin.

Rowland travelled to England, where he enlisted into the British Army at Horfield in Bristol on 2 July 1874, and as 248 Private Miller he was posted to the 37th Brigade, being described as five feet nine inches tall, with a fresh complexion, blue eyes and dark brown hair, with a slight burn mark on the back of his hand. He left the infantry, and on 1 October 1876 he signed on for twelve years with the Army Hospital Corps as 3169 Private Miller. He was promoted corporal on 3 January 1878. He married Elizabeth Ellen Few on 2 April 1878 at Northgate, Canterbury in Kent, and they had one son, Rowland Herbert Henry, born in 1885.

He was posted at Devonport until October 1878, when his unit received orders for active service in South Africa, where it arrived on 7 November 1878. He served under Surgeon Reynolds during the defence of Rorke's Drift. Lieutenant Chard reported that 'There was a short but desperate struggle during which Mr Dalton shot a Zulu who was in the act of stabbing a corporal (Roland Miller) of the Army Hospital Corps, the muzzle of whose rifle he had seized …' He was promoted sergeant on 2 July 1879. However, in the same year he received the devastating news that one of his brothers had committed suicide, and another had killed his parents and then taken his own life. For his service he received the South Africa Medal with 1878-9 clasp.

He returned to England on 15 May 1880. British forces were struggling with a serious uprising by the Transvaal Boers, and on 24 January 1881, the day they had suffered heavy losses at Spion Kop, Rowland was posted to South Africa with British reinforcements. He returned to England twelve months later. On 10 August 1882 he was posted to Egypt for his last tour of overseas duty, and returned to Aldershot on 9 June 1883. Unfortunately, by this time he was beginning to have difficulties with his sight. In spite of this he was promoted to 2nd staff sergeant on 8 April 1886. However, he appeared before a medical board in London on 14 May 1886, which concluded that he was suffering with hypermetropia and astigmatism of the eyes and was no longer fit for overseas duties. On 8 June 1886 he re-engaged with the Medical Staff Corps, but on 19 January 1887 he was in hospital under observation for mental weakness.

He married Mary Brehaut on 18 December 1889 at South Stoneham in Southampton, and they had three children; William Edward was born in 1891, Madeline Frances Mary in 1893 and Gertrude Ellen in 1895, but the latter only survived for eighteen months. The family home was Alderney House, Grand Bouet, Guernsey, and after discharging from the army in 1895 it is thought that Rowland found employment in a nursery and market garden owned by Mary's uncle. The 1901 census has Rowland and his family living at 135 Upton Park, West Ham, London, where he was working as a watcher for the Customs and Excise, but they later moved back to Alderney. His time of death can be estimated as between 1925 and 1932.

Commissariat and Army Service Corps

James Dalton

James Langley Dalton was born in 1831 in the parish of St Andrews in Holborn, London. He gave up his job as a clerk in a stationers' shop to enlist into the army at Victoria in London on 20 November 1849, being just under six feet tall, with a fresh complexion, hazel eyes and red hair. As 965 Private Dalton he was posted to the 85th Regiment at Waterford in Ireland. The 1851 census lists him as a soldier of the 85th Regiment stationed at Fulwood Barracks in Preston, and he was later stationed at Hull and Portsmouth. In 1853 the battalion embarked for service at Mauritius, where he was promoted to corporal on 1 July 1853, and drew his first entitlement to good conduct pay on 21 December 1854. He left the island three years later having been promoted sergeant on 7 September 1855. In 1856 he sailed with his regiment to the Cape, taking part in the 8th Cape Frontier War. He re-engaged at Pembroke Docks on 21 December 1859 for a further eleven years of service.

He transferred to the Commissariat Staff Corps at Aldershot on 31 March 1862, being appointed colour-sergeant on 1 June 1863. While stationed in

James Langley Dalton had gained much experience during his 30 years with the colours, which he put to good use when being instrumental in organising the defences at Rorke's Drift. He was highly praised for the initiative he showed during the engagement, in which he was seriously wounded. He was awarded the Victoria Cross for his valour.

Aldershot until 1867, he attended the Hythe School of Musketry in 1864, and on 7 February 1866 he was appointed clerk and master-sergeant. His last tour of overseas duty was at Montreal and Quebec in Canada from 1868 to 1871, and it was during this period that General Wolseley embarked on the Red River Expedition. While serving in Canada, the reorganisation of the Commissariat in 1870 saw him transferred to the Army Service Corps on 1 April 1870 as 2nd class staff sergeant, and on the following 1 July he was promoted to 1st class staff sergeant, making him the equivalent of a warrant officer. He discharged from the army in London on 20 November 1871, having received three good conduct badges, and he was awarded the Long Service Good Conduct Medal. Remarks on his discharge papers state 'his conduct has been very good.'

By 1877 he was in South Africa serving as a senior officer. On 13 December 1877 he was appointed to British forces for the 9th Cape Frontier War, for which he was mentioned in dispatches.

> Mr Dalton, Acting Assistant Commissary, has been most energetic. The sole officer at Ibeka in that department, under great difficulties he increased the supplies, and provided three columns in their advances, and the stations in Galekaland, with the utmost regularity.

He volunteered for the Zulu War, and he and Louis Byrne rode through pouring rain on New Year's Day 1879 to join the British forces assembling at Helpmekaar, and then moved up to Rorke's Drift. The chapel building at the mission station had been commandeered by the Army as a storehouse and the arduous task of filling it with supplies soon began. James Dalton was highly praised for the part he played in the action at Rorke's Drift, and he is mentioned in several accounts by fellow defenders, praising his valour and initiative.

Private Hook:

> Mr Dalton came up and said if we left the Drift every man was certain to be killed. He had formerly been a Sergeant-Major in a line regiment and was one of the bravest men that ever lived.

Mr Dunne:

> Dalton the lionhearted, as brave a soldier as ever lived, had joined us, and hearing the terrible news said, 'Now, we must make a defence!' It was his suggestion which decided us to form a breastwork of bags of grain, boxes of biscuits, and everything that would help to stop a bullet or keep out a man.

Doctor Reynolds:

> My first move was to consult with Lt Bromhead, and Commissary Dalton, Lt
> Chard not having as yet joined us from the pontoon. We quickly decided that,
> with barricades well placed around our position, a stand could best be made
> where we were. At this period, Mr Dalton's energies were invaluable.

Lieutenant Chard:

> There was a short but desperate struggle during which Mr Dalton shot a
> Zulu who was in the act of stabbing a corporal [Roland Miller] of the Army
> Hospital Corps, the muzzle of whose rifle he had seized, and with Lieutenant
> Bromhead and many of the men behaved with great gallantry; Mr Dalton
> dropping a man each time he fired his rifle. While firing from behind the
> biscuit boxes, Mr Dalton, who had been using his rifle with deadly effect,
> and by his quickness and coolness had been the means of saving many men's
> lives, was shot through the body. I was standing near him at the time, and
> he handed me his rifle so coolly that I had no idea until afterwards that he
> had been wounded so severely. He waited quite quietly for me to take the
> cartridges he had left out of his pockets. We put him inside our mealie sack
> redoubt, building it up around him.

A sketch of one of the commissariat wagons which was utilised as part of the south
barricade facing the hill. British sharpshooters were posted behind it to return the fire of
the Zulus who were hidden among the caves and terraces of the Oscarberg armed with
rifles taken from the bodies of the soldiers killed at Isandlwana.

Reverend Smith:

> Mr Dalton, who is a tall man, was continually going along the barricades, fearlessly exposing himself and cheering the men, and using his own rifle most effectively. A Zulu ran up near the barricade. Mr Dalton called out 'Pot that fellow!' and himself aimed over the parapet at another, when his rifle dropped and he turned round, quite pale, and said that he had been shot. The doctor was by his side at once, and found that a bullet had passed quite through above the right shoulder. Unable any longer to use his rifle, he did not cease to direct the fire of the men who were near him.

Henry Harford:

> Mr James Dalton, who in the absence of Lieutenant Chard, devised all the rapid arrangements for the defence, as well as working like a Trojan himself with the men at the barricades and did much gallant work during the night. I noticed that directly Mr Smith or Mr Dalton showed themselves they received an ovation from the men, which was unmistakable.

Private Hitch later said 'Mr Dalton was very active up till he was wounded,' and Corporal Lyons noted 'Mr Dalton deserved any amount of praise.'

He had been so severely wounded that he was sent to recuperate at Pietermaritzburg for six months. The medical records of Surgeon Blair-Brown are interesting to note

> James Dalton was hit in the right shoulder. The bullet entered about half-an-inch above the middle of the clavicle, and made it's escape posteriorly at the lower border of the trapezious muscle. The course taken was curious, regularly running round the shoulder and down the back, escaping all the important structures. The wounds, like all those received at Rorke's Drift, were wide and open and sloughing when seen by me on 26 January. After the slough came away the usual tenax was applied. I had no antiseptic to use. I thought of quinine, which I knew was a wonderful preserver in animal tissue, and used a solution of that, experimenting in this case. It seemed to answer, as the wounds got well after being injected several times with it.

When the 2nd Battalion marched into Pietermaritzburg on 16 October 1879, it was recorded in the *Natal Witness* that

> The spectators in Church Street could not make out why one company of the noble 24th suddenly raised a deafening cheer when coming to the club-

house. The fact was that B Company, the gallant defenders of Rorke's Drift, under Major Bromhead VC, had recognised amongst the spectators Assistant Commissary Dalton, one of the leaders on that night. May we ask why Mr Dalton, who originated the defences at Rorke's Drift, and who was wounded whilst gallantly leading a portion of the men, has not yet received the Victoria Cross?

The award of Victoria Cross to James Dalton was announced in the *London Gazette* on 17 November 1879, and he received the medal from Major-General Hugh Clifford during a parade of the troops at Fort Napier in Pietermaritzburg on 16 January 1880, 'Amid surroundings well calculated to make it impressive to participators and spectators alike.' He also received the South Africa Medal with 1877-78-79 clasps. For his gallantry Dalton had been awarded a permanent commission as sub-assistant commissary on 21 November 1879, back-dated to his temporary appointment in December 1877, and he subsequently became senior commissariat officer at Fort Napier. He was promoted assistant-commissary from 13 December 1879, and placed on half-pay. He sailed to England in February 1880.

Little is known about the last years of his life. The 1881 census states that he was living in lodgings at 17 Cottage Grove in Lambeth, London, giving his age as 46. A man named Robert Dalton is listed as being a visitor at the address. He eventually returned to South Africa, making his living as a gold prospector. He

The final resting place of James Dalton at the Russell Road Cemetery in Port Elizabeth, South Africa, where he died only eight years after the Zulu War.

owned 1,500 shares in the Little Bess Mine at Barberton during the Transvaal gold rush days of 1884–86. He decided to spend the Christmas of 1886 with his old friend, former Sergeant John Sherwood Williams, at the Grosvenor Hotel in Port Elizabeth, Cape Province. After spending the day of 7 January 1887 confined to his bed, he died suddenly in his room during the night. He was 54 and had remained unmarried. He was buried in Plot E of the Russell Road Roman Catholic Cemetery in Port Elizabeth, and an impressive stone memorial was erected at his grave 'by his old comrade Sergeant John Williams and Friends of Natal.'

The centenary of the defence of Rorke's Drift in 1979 was celebrated with a wreath-laying ceremony at his graveside, and his medals came up for auction in 1986. The Royal Corps of Transport purchased them, and they are now with the Royal Logistic Corps Museum at Aldershot.

Walter Dunne

Walter Alphonsus Dunne was born on 10 February 1853 in Cork in Ireland, the third son of James Dunne of Stephen's Green, Dublin, and he was educated at Queen's University in Dublin. He was a devout Roman Catholic.

He joined the Control Department as sub-assistant commissary (2nd lieutenant) on 9 April 1873, and served with the Commissariat Department in Dublin until October 1877. He was posted to South Africa, where he saw active service with the 1st Battalion, 24th Regiment during the 9th Cape Frontier War of 1878, and in the campaign against Sekhukhune in the north-east of Transvaal, who was defying all attempts to prize him from his mountain stronghold. At the end of 1878, Assistant Commissary Dunne received orders to go to Helpmekaar in Natal where a force was being assembled for the invasion of Zululand, and he arrived exhausted after riding 100 miles across country to take up his duties as Senior Commissary with the 3rd Central Column.

Commissary Dunne was mentioned in dispatches for his service during the defence of Rorke's Drift, and although Lord Chelmsford recommended that Dunne should be awarded the Victoria Cross it was not granted. Major Chard stated that Dunne had supervised the erection of the original defences and was later made responsible for building the inner defences, including the mealie bag redoubt meant as a last rallying point. When building the redoubt, Dunne, a tall man, encouraged the exhausted soldiers while standing on the growing pile of bags high above the defences, drawing fire on himself and ignoring any danger.

He took part in the re-invasion as a deputy commissary of supplies with the flying column, and he was in the square which destroyed the Zulu army at the Battle of Ulundi on 4 July 1879. He was in further action during the renewed

Walter Dunne drew fire on himself but ignored the danger as he shouted encouragement to his fellow defenders. He was recommended for the award of Victoria Cross for his initiative at Rorke's Drift but it was not granted.

Sekhukhuni Expedition, taking part in the successful assault on his stronghold in November 1879, for which he was mentioned in dispatches.

He remained stationed in the Transvaal, and when the Boer uprising began in 1880 he was again involved in a siege, this time by Boer commando units at the garrison town of Potchefstroom, a flashpoint of discontent. The 200 defenders, including women and children, had to survive behind a makeshift perimeter in an area about 30 paces square, their only protection against the elements being a few bell tents. Commissary Dunne sat on the parapet each Sunday reading the Roman Catholic service to the people of that faith. They held out under constant fire for three months until sickness and starvation forced them into dignified surrender in March 1881. The ordeal affected his health and on returning to Natal he was nursed back to strength by friends, including Winifred, the daughter of John Bird CMG, Treasurer of Natal, and they became engaged. After five years of active service in South Africa, Walter returned to England in April 1882 to be stationed at Aldershot.

Just four months later he sailed for active service in north-east Africa, taking part in the decisive victory over Egyptian forces at Tel-el-Kebir on 13 September 1882. He returned to England, and in February 1885 he was posted back to North Africa to join the British forces station at the Red Sea port of Saukin in the Sudan, and was present during the British advance against

Dervish warriors at Hasheen on 19 March 1885. On his return to England he and Winifred were married on 23 July 1885.

He was transferred as a lieutenant-colonel to the Army Service Corps on the establishment of that unit in 1888, serving on Mauritius 1887–89, and he was DAAG of the Southern District 1892–95. He was appointed Commander of the Bath for distinguished service in 1896, and was promoted colonel in 1897, becoming HAAG of the North-East District at York, a position he held until 1899. From January 1900 he was assistant quartermaster general at Army Headquarters in Aldershot, representing the War Office on the Army Medical Advisory Board. He was considered for promotion to major-general in 1905, and in the same year he was appointed Director of Supplies and Transport at Gibraltar, from where he retired from military service in February 1908.

He was active in various public undertakings. While stationed at York he was president of the York Catholic Association and was a supporter of the Catholic Soldiers' Club in London. Colonel Dunne died at The English Convent Home in Rome, on 2 July 1908, aged 55, and was buried at the Verano Cemetery in Rome.

Francis Attwood

Francis Attwood was born on 29 September 1844 at 20 Norman Street, off the City Road, in the St Luke's district of London, the son of Francis Attwood, a shoemaker, and his wife Mary Ann (formerly Boost). He enlisted into the Army Service Corps, being given the service number C/2469. In 1878 he received orders for active service in South Africa, and arrived at Cape Town on 25 October of that year.

He had been working as a clerk in Pietermaritzburg when he was sent to the mission station at Rorke's Drift in January 1879, 'as a punishment' for his tendency to be argumentative. He wrote six letters to an aunt and uncle while in South Africa, and the second one, written in Helpmekaar on 2 January 1879, stated

> The Sergeant-Major I am with and I do not agree very well. We are continually quarrelling, and he takes every advantage he can of me, but I will try that he does me no injury if I can help it.

Although he was considered to be a stubborn man by nature, he had been promoted to corporal by the time he arrived at Rorke's Drift. After helping to remove the bags and boxes from the store to be used at the barricade, he took his place at one of the upper windows of the building to shoot at Zulus who were rushing forward trying to throw lighted spears on the roof to set it on

Francis Attwood had been sent to Rorke's Drift as a punishment for his tendency to be argumentative, and was awarded the Distinguished Conduct Medal for his part in the action.

fire. Francis was promoted sergeant dated from the day of the defence, and for his gallant conduct he was awarded the Distinguished Conduct Medal, which was presented to him in the town square at Pietermaritzburg on 13 September 1879. He also received the South Africa Medal with 1878-9 clasp.

By 1880, Francis had returned to England and was stationed at Aldershot. On being posted to Plymouth he took accommodation for himself and his partner, Amy Jane Wood, a widow with a son, at 5 Cremyll Street in East Stonehouse, Plymouth, where Amy Mary was born in 1883. They then decided to get married, but circumstances dictated that they could not do so in East Stonehouse. They married in the parish church of St John the Evangelist, in the district of St George's, Hanover Square, London, on 25 September 1883, giving their address as 28 Horseferry Road in south-west London. They returned to East Stonehouse, but only five months after their marriage, Francis died after an epileptic convulsion at their home in Cremyll Street on 20 February 1884. He was buried with full military honours at Milehouse Cemetery, Plymouth.

The headstone at Sergeant Attwood's grave was badly damaged during a bombing raid in 1941, and a quarter of a century later Milehouse Cemetery was cleared and the remains of Sergeant Attwood were re-interred in communal ground at Efford Cemetery, Plymouth. A memorial plaque was placed in Stoke Damarel Church, and in 2009 a new headstone was unveiled at his grave.

Louis Byrne

Louis Alexander Byrne was born in Ireland in about 1857, the seventh child of Richard and Maria Byrne, who moved to Cardiff when Richard became a prominent ship owner, introducing the first steamship to that port. Louis and his elder brother, Alfred, had travelled to South Africa, and Louis was employed in a government appointment when the Zulu War began. The Commissary-General was given authority to employ local men who knew the country and could be quickly trained in commissary work, and being accepted as an assistant storekeeper, Louis had ridden up to the border with James Dalton in torrential rain on New Year's Day, 1879. He was killed in action during the defence of Rorke's Drift, and although his body was for some reason buried outside the little cemetery, his name is inscribed on the monument.

Lieutenant Chard said that Byrne 'was greatly instrumental in forming the entrenchment of biscuit boxes, which was in all probability the means of our successful defence.' In his report he stated 'Mr Byrne, who had behaved with great coolness and gallantry, was killed instantaneously by a bullet through the head, just after he had given a drink of water to a wounded man of the NNC [Corporal Scammel].' The *Illustrated London News* for 29 March 1879 reports of him 'behaving nobly.'

Louis Byrne was the son of a prominent Irish ship owner. He had ridden up to Rorke's Drift with James Dalton in torrential rain on the first day of 1879. Described by Lieutenant Chard as having behaved with great coolness and gallantry, he was killed in action by a Zulu slug to the head as he was giving a drink of water to Corporal Scammel.

Army Chaplains Department

George Smith

George Smith was born at Docking, Norfolk on 8 January 1845, the son of William and Frances Smith. A tall man with a great red beard, he was at college in Canterbury before going to South Africa as a lay missionary in 1870. He was ordained deacon in 1871, and priest in 1872. He was appointed to St John's Parish, based at the Estcourt Mission in Natal, where he became well known as a hard-working man. He served as a volunteer during the Langalibalele Rebellion and in 1878 he was appointed acting chaplain to the volunteers. It was in this capacity that he took part in the Zulu War.

On 22 January 1879 he was going about his duties at Rorke's Drift when it was reported that there was possible action at Isandlwana, so, in the company of Surgeon Reynolds and the Reverend Witt he decided to go on a reconnaissance to the top of the Oscarberg Hill to try to get a clearer view of what was happening. They saw a number of colonials returning from enemy territory on the Zululand side of the river, so Surgeon Reynolds went back to the mission station in case they required medical assistance. The two clerics watched a large

George Smith, wearing his South Africa Medal, Egypt medal and Khedives Star. He was a tall man, known to his friends as 'Daddy Smith', because of his great bushy red beard, and to the military as 'Ammunition Smith' because of his action at Rorke's Drift.

number of natives moving slowly up from the Natal bank of the river at such a leisurely pace that they believed them to be colonial troops. However, the increasing force was within rifle range when they saw that the two men on horseback leading them were not Europeans, but had black faces. When they realised that the oncoming mass was a Zulu *impi*, they hastily climbed back down the hill to report the danger to the officers.

During the ferocious Zulu onslaughts he spent his time moving along the barricade, apparently with the aid of a native servant, handing out cartridges from his hat, as well as reproving the curses of the hard-fighting soldiers and stopping to give spiritual consolation to the wounded. Private Jobbins stated that 'All that night a Minister was praying in the fort they would go away.'

Colonel Harford was with the column which arrived at Rorke's Drift on the morning of 23 January, and wrote that

> The part which the Reverend Smith played in the defence, and the splendid example he set throughout that terrible night, ought to have earned for him the VC. I noticed that directly Mr Smith showed himself, he received an ovation from the men.

A trooper of the Natal Carbineers named J.P. Symons later said that

> The men of the 24th Regiment who defended the place, spoke very highly of the Reverend George Smith, who, they say, carried ammunition round in his hat for the men. One man told me that a private was swearing because he could not get any ammunition and the Reverend George reproved him, saying he should not swear at such a time as this but to put his trust in God. Patting his rifle the soldier replied, 'I shall put my faith in this now and God afterwards.'

He served throughout the Zulu War, his deeds and reputation earning him the nickname 'Ammunition Smith', and he was in the British square at Ulundi to witness the final defeat of the Zulus. He visited the devastated battlefield at Isandlwana and said many prayers for the soldiers who had been massacred, and held a short service at the bodies of Lieutenants Coghill and Melvill, who had lost their lives while trying to save the Queen's colour of their battalion from falling into enemy hands, and would many years later be awarded the Victoria Cross. In November 1879 he was one of several clergymen who visited the site, with the view to establish a mission church in remembrance of the dead. This became the Zululand Memorial Church.

After a period at home, he served under Sir Garnet Wolseley in his north-east Africa campaigns from 1882–1887. He took part in the Battle of

The Rev. Smith

This charming sketch of Reverend Smith was one of many drawn by Lieutenant Crealock, Lord Chelmsford's military secretary, who was with the troops who relieved the Rorke's Drift garrison on the day after the defence. He is wearing an alpaca frock coat and riding spurs. He carried a revolver, but as a man of the cloth he would have been expected to use it only for self defence.

Tel-el-Kebir in Egypt on 13 September 1882, and in the Battle of El Teb in the Sudan on 29 February 1884, when the British defeated a mass army of Dervish warriors. For his service he received the Queen's Medal for Egypt and the Khedives Bronze Star.

He was chaplain at various military stations at home and abroad from 1887 until his retirement in 1905, including a spell of duty at Fulwood Garrison Church in Preston, from about 1897–1903. It would seem that he was a well-known character, with many friends, who knew him as 'Daddy Smith' because of his great bushy beard. It is believed that he was visited in Preston by Colonel Chard, and the Reverend Smith went to see Chard in Somerset. Both meetings were during the last months of Chard's life, and his former comrade may have wanted his spiritual consolation.

He chose to take a room at the Sumners Hotel, where the manager remembered him as being very popular in the hotel, and staff made sure their 'favourite guest' was always looked after. It has been said that the famous painting of the defence of Rorke's Drift by Alphonse de Neuville once hung in the hotel, which was of particular interest because the names of several of the defenders had been written in by George Smith himself. On his retirement in 1905 he continued to reside at the hotel, although he visited South Africa frequently and was away a considerable time.

In 1918 he became ill with bronchial trouble, and after being confined to his hotel room for six months, died during the night of 26/27 November 1918, aged 63. His death was only a few days after the armistice which ended the First World War, so his funeral was a small military parade, and among the floral tributes was one from the officers of the South Wales Borderers – 'In Memory of Rorke's Drift.' He was buried in the New Hall Lane Cemetery, and a monument was erected in memory of one of the heroes of Rorke's Drift, 'Who was a brave and modest Christian gentleman.'

In July 2009, Bible and ammunition box representations were placed among a floral tribute to George Smith in Miller Park, Preston, along with helmets commemorating the eleven VCs gained in the battle.

Natal Mounted Police

Henry Lugg

Henry Lugg was born on 9 March 1859 at Northlew near Clovelly in Devon. He had travelled to South Africa with fellow Devonians, Edward and Henry Camp, of Barnstable, whose sister, Mary, Harry was courting, and they all joined the Natal Mounted Police on 22 May 1878. The Natal Mounted Police was formed as a para-military force in 1874 by a retired British Army officer named Major John Dartnell, as the first line of defence in the colony, and they had been scouting the Natal-Zululand border since November 1878. Because of a problem with their horses the invasion force had already crossed into enemy territory when they joined the column. They had a skirmish at Sihayo's Kraal, and after the engagement Harry was ordered to ride to Pietermaritzberg with dispatches. He was eager not to miss the further advance into Zululand, so he made a pony express-style ride, using ten horses in relays, and he was back at Rorke's Drift by 17 January. However, his efforts were in vain. As he crossed the river his mount lost its footing and crushed his knee as it fell, causing him to have to go into hospital.

During the defence of the garrison on 22 January he manned a loophole in a kitchen extension of the hospital, from where he could get a good shot at any warriors who reached the outer wall of the building. When the Zulus had moved off he was limping about among the bodies outside the compound when he saw a rifle and went to pick it up. As he did so, a warrior who was lying close by pretending to be dead, suddenly grabbed the weapon and jumped up, jamming the muzzle against Harry's body. Harry heard the trigger click, but the rifle misfired, and before the Zulu could recover he dropped on him and

Henry Lugg, seated second from right, with one of the local volunteer regiments he helped to establish in Natal. He left an account of the defence of Rorke's Drift and a sketch of the post.

stabbed him with his hunting knife. He managed to rescue his spurs from the ruins of the hospital, although they were burnt black, and while hospitalised in Pietermaritzburg the 17th Lancers presented him with a commemorative belt, which he is said to have worn every day.

He and Edwin Camp bought a store and hotel at Umbango in the Port Shepstone area of Durban. They celebrated a double wedding in Durban in 1881, when Harry married Mary Camp, and Edwin married Harry's sister, Marion. Harry became active in the formation of a local volunteer regiment named the Umzimkulu Mounted Rifles in 1884, which was amalgamated with the Alexandra Mounted Rifles, which in turn amalgamated to form the Natal Mounted Rifles in Durban in 1888. The NMR consisted of two units, but in 1894 one was separated and re-designated the Border Mounted Rifles, with Captain Henry Lugg as second in command.

In 1895 he became a district adjutant on Colonel W.J. Royston's staff, who was then commanding the Natal Volunteers. He held an intriguing variety of government posts, including Conservator of Forests, Field Cornet and Collector of Dog Tax. Harry died at the home which he had called 'Lynton', in Port Shepstone, on 27 October 1927, aged 68. He left a widow and five sons, one of whom Harry Camp Lugg became a respected Zulu linguist and writer. In his book *A Natal Family Looks Back* he states: 'The firing was so fast and furious that rifle barrels got red hot,' and in proof of this, the forepiece of the carbine Henry Lugg used during the defence – which was still in possession of the family a century later – was found to have been so badly scorched that a piece had to be cut off the end to prevent it splintering. The family also had his spurs and hunting knife.

Robert Green

Robert Shedden St John Green was born in 1854, the son of Frederick Owen Green and his wife Alice (formerly Shedden), who lived in Waterloo Road, Lambeth, London. He had two brothers, Harold, who was also known as John, and Frederick, who never married and survived into the London Blitz in 1940, and a sister named Alice, who never married and became a registered nurse. She came out of retirement to run the Cheltenham Hospital during the First World War. Frederick Owen Green moved to South Africa, and worked at the South African Glass Works in Cape Town.

Robert and Harold Green were based in Pitermaritzburg when Robert joined the NMP on 31 August 1877, while Harold joined on 14 March 1878. The unit had been scouting the Natal-Zululand border since November 1878. Because of a problem with their horses the invasion force had already crossed into enemy territory when they joined the column, but they took part in the first skirmish with the Zulus at Sihayo's Kraal on 12 January 1879. He and Trooper Hunter were patients in the hospital on 22 January 1879, stricken with rheumatic fever. A roll of defenders compiled by Major Frank Bourne states that Robert was killed, but he escaped from the burning hospital, being wounded as he did so. Reverend Smith later said that

> Trooper RS Green (NMP) also a patient, got out of the little end window within the enclosure. The window being high up, and the Zulus already within the room behind them, each man had a fall in escaping and then had to crawl (for none of them could walk) through the enemy's fire inside the entrenchment. Whilst doing this, Green was struck in the thigh with a spent bullet.

Robert discharged from the NMP on 30 April 1881 and Harold left the unit on 28 April 1884. Robert was a founder partner in Tarry's Tools of Port Elizabeth, and lived in Jagersfontein, Orange Free State. When the Boer War began he was put in charge of the Jagersfontein Commando. He rode across the Orange River and met up with the Seaforth Highlanders marching to Jagersfontein. He was commissioned as a lieutenant in the Seaforths, rode back to Jagersfontein with them and was mentioned in garrison orders for his conduct in the battle which followed. While they were under a truce to gather the dead and wounded the Boers recognised him and in retribution burned down his house and business. The Boers held a drumhead court, convicted him of treason and issued a 'Wanted – dead or alive' notice on him. After that the Free State was too dangerous for him, so he travelled down to Mossel Bay in the Cape as the Seaforth's remount officer. Because of the risk to his life they gave him permits to carry his Jagersfontein Commando Mauser rifle and a revolver to protect himself.

Robert Green died on 21 January 1925, aged 70, and he is buried in Lazaretto Cemetery, Mossel Bay, Cape Province, South Africa.

Sydney Hunter

Sydney H. Hunter was born in September 1856 at Barnet in Hertfordshire, and was residing at Helpmekaar when he joined the Natal Mounted Police. He was in the hospital at Rorke's Drift stricken with fever when the Zulus attacked the post, and he was stabbed six times as he tried to get across the compound to the inner entrenchment. According to Lieutenant Chard

> Trooper Hunter, escaping from the Hospital, stood still for a moment hesitating which way to go, dazed by the glare of the burning hospital, and the firing that was going on all around. He was assegaid before our eyes, the Zulu who killed him immediately afterwards falling.

He was 22, and a document recording his death states that his possessions were 'two saddle rings.' He was buried in the cemetery at Rorke's Drift and his name appears on the monument.

1st Battalion, 3rd Regiment, Natal Native Contingent

James Adendorff

James (Gert Wilhelm) Adendorff was born at Graaff Reinet in Cape Province, South Africa on 10 July 1848. He was a lieutenant in the NNC when the Zulu War began, and escaped from the camp at Isandlwana. Lieutenant Chard reported that

> At 3:15pm that day I was watching at the ponts when two men came towards us from Zululand at the gallop. They shouted out and were taken across the river; and I was then informed by one of them – Lieutenant Adendorff of

Commandant Lonsdale's regiment, who afterwards remained to assist in the defence – of the disaster befallen at the Isandlwana camp, and that the Zulus were advancing upon Rorke's Drift … Seeing the Hospital burning, and the attempts of the enemy to fire the roof of the store (one man was shot, I believe by Lieutenant Adendorff, who had a light almost touching the thatch).

James Adendorff died in South Africa in about 1914.

uMKungu

A native of the Xhosa tribe named uMKungu was serving with the 1st Battalion, 3rd Regiment, Natal Native Contingent, and was a patient in the hospital at Rorke's Drift when the Zulu onslaught began, having had his thigh split by a rifle bullet at Sihayo's Kraal. Henry Hook reported

> I had charge of a small room with only one patient in it, a native whose leg was broken and who kept crying and groaning near me. Fire and dense choking smoke forced me to get out and go into the other room. It was impossible to take the native patient with me, and I had to leave him to an awful fate. But his death was, at any rate, a merciful one. I heard the Zulus asking him questions, as he tried to tear off his bandages and escape.

Reverend Smith stated

> The native of Umlunga's tribe, who had been shot through the thigh at Sihayo's kraal, was lying unable to move. He said that he was not afraid of the Zulus but wanted a gun. When the end room in which he lay was forced, Private Hook heard the Zulus talking with him; next day his charred remains were found amongst the ruins.'

2nd Battalion, 3rd Regiment, Natal Native Contingent

Friederich Schiess

Ferdnand Christian Schiess was born at Bergedorf in Canton Berne, Switzerland on 7 April 1856, the son of Niclaus Schiess, a stone cutter, and his wife Anna (formerly Ruchti). His father was known locally as 'Bernese Schiess'. Their parents having died while they were young, Ferdnand and his sister Anna

Corporal Schiess was said to have fought like a lion at Rorke's Drift, which was recognised by the award of Victoria Cross.

Marie were brought up at the Municipal Orphanage at Herisau in Canton Apenzell. 'Friederich', as he became known, left the orphanage at fifteen. The Franco-Prussian War began in 1870, so he joined General Bourbaki's French Legions. In 1877 he boarded the *Adele* at Hamburg bound for South Africa, arriving in East London on 21 August 1877. He was a strong, stocky young man, and was able to find work as a general labourer.

He served with distinction as a volunteer in the Cape Frontier War, and when colonial forces were being mustered for the campaign against the Zulus, Colonel Anthony Durnford of the Royal Engineers appointed him a corporal in the 2nd Battalion, 3rd Regiment, Natal Native Contingent. A colonial identified as 'J M', stated 'A corporal of ours (was) left behind on account of him having a severely blistered foot. He was a young foreigner – Swiss, I believe.' Consequently, Corporal Schiess was a patient in the hospital at Rorke's Drift on 22 January, but chose to take his place at the barricade when the Zulu attack began.

Lieutenant Chard:

Corporal Schiess, Natal Native Contingent, who was a patient in the Hospital with a wound in the foot, which caused him great pain, behaved with the greatest coolness and gallantry throughout the attack, and at this time [the retreat to the biscuit boxes] creeping out a short distance along the wall we had abandoned, and slowly raised himself, to get a shot at some of the enemy who had been particularly annoying, his hat was blown off by a shot from a Zulu on the other side of the wall. He immediately jumped up, bayoneted the Zulu, and shot a second, and bayoneted a third who came to their assistance, and then returned to his place.

Reverend Smith:

> One fellow fired at Corporal Schiess of the Natal Native Contingent, the charge blowing his hat off. He instantly jumped upon the parapet and bayoneted the man, regained his place and shot another, and then, repeating his former exploit, climbed upon the sacks and bayoneted a third. A bullet struck him on the instep early in the fight, but he would not allow that his wound was sufficient reason for leaving his post, yet he has suffered most acutely from it since.

Henry Harford:

> Some of the men of the 24th told me that he fought like a tiger. At one time, when some Zulus actually managed to clutch hold of his bayonet, he got it out of their hands, and springing over the parapet bayoneted some six or seven straight away.

He became the first man serving with South African forces under British command to be awarded the Victoria Cross, when his VC citation, the last for the defence of Rorke's Drift, appeared in the *London Gazette* of 29 November 1879.

> For conspicuous gallantry in the defence of Rorke's Drift post on the night of 22 January 1879, when, in spite of his having been wounded in the foot a few days previously, greatly distinguished himself when the Garrison were repulsing, with the bayonet, a series of desperate assaults made by the Zulus, and displayed great activity and devoted gallantry throughout the defence.
>
> On one occasion when the Garrison had retired to the inner line of defence, and the Zulus occupied the wall of mealie bags which had been abandoned, he crept along the wall, without any order, to dislodge a Zulu who was shooting better than usual and succeeded in killing him, and two others, before he returned to the inner defence.

He served throughout the Zulu War, and he was with the British square at Ulundi on 4 July 1879 to witness the final defeat of the Zulu Army. For his serv-

A Natal Native Contingent officer wearing an infantry officer-style patrol jacket and buff coloured cord riding breeches. The slouch hat has a red rag, or *puggree*, around the crown.

ices in the campaign he also received the South Africa Medal with 1877-8-9 clasp. When the Natal Native Contingent was disbanded he joined Lonsdale's Horse on 24 January 1880. He received his Victoria Cross from Garnet Wolseley at a special parade in Pietermaritzburg on 3 February 1880.

He left Lonsdale's Horse and gained employment in the telegraph office at Durban. However, by 1884 he was unemployed and had become destitute. He spent most of his time desperately trying to gain some kind of Government work in Natal, the colony he had fought so bravely to defend. Towards the end of the year he was found in tragic circumstances on the streets of Cape Town suffering from the effects of exposure to the elements and malnutrition. The Royal Navy offered him a trip to England on the *Serapis*, the cost of his rations being paid for by a public fund. Sadly, his health deteriorated and he died on board ship off the coast of Angola, West Africa. He was buried at sea 1,376 kilometres north-east of St Helena in the Atlantic Ocean. (latitude 13.00 south – longitude 07.24 west). His Victoria Cross is believed to have been found on his person, and is now at the National Army Museum, and there is a bronze plaque at the Rorke's Drift Memorial Museum in Natal.

Several other men of the 2nd Battalion, 3rd Regiment, NNC were patients in the hospital at Rorke's Drift when the Zulu attack began. Some, such as Corporals William Anderson, William Doughty, Carl (Charles) Scammel and

John Wilson were probably suffering from bowel disorders caused by drinking bad water. Anderson was killed by British fire before the Zulus attacked, and Scammel was wounded by a Zulu slug in the shoulder during the battle. John Chard stated that 'Corporal Scammel, who was badly wounded through the shoulder, staggered out under fire again from the Store building where he had been put, and gave me all his cartridges, which in his wounded state he could not use.' Corporal James B. Welson, known as John Wilson, was born at Hay-on-Wye, Herefordshire, in about 1848. He died in South Africa. Lieutenant Thomas Purvis had received a severe wound when a Zulu slug went through his arm during the skirmish at Sihayo's Kraal on 12 January. He died in South Africa in about 1923. Corporal Jessy Mayer had been caught below the knee by a Zulu assegai during the same engagement at Sihayo's Kraal.

Bibliography

Attwood, Corporal Francis, letters written while on active service in South Africa, November 1878–December 1879, The Royal Corps of Transport Museum

Bancroft, James W., *Rorke's Drift*, Tunbridge Wells, 1988

Bancroft, James W., *The Zulu War VCs*, Eccles, 1992

Bancroft, James W., *Gallantry Awards At Rorke's Drift*, Eccles, 2007

Bancroft, James W., *Zulu War Heroes, 24th Regiment VCs*, Eccles, 2009

Bancroft, James W., *Zulu War Heroes, The Defence of Rorke's Drift*, Eccles, 2009

Baynham-Jones, Alun, 24th Regiment Ongoing Updates and Amendments, The South Wales Borderers Museum

Bourne, Colonel Frank, letter naming survivors of the Rorke's Drift action, *Daily Mail*, 24 August 1932, PRO, WO 100/46 f 149A

Bourne, Colonel Frank, 'I Was There', *The Listener*, 30 December 1936

Chard, Lieutenant John, official report, 25 January 1879, PRO, WO 32/7737

Chard, Lieutenant John, 'An account submitted to Her Majesty Queen Victoria at Windsor Castle on 21 February 1880', Royal Archives, Windsor

Connolly, Private John, statement made to Captain Liddell, RN aboard the troopship *Tamar*, 3 May 1879, The South Wales Borderers Museum

Dunne, Commissary Walter, 'Reminiscences of Campaigning in South Africa, 1877–81', *Journal of the Army Service Corps*, February 1892

Head, Private 'Bob', letter from Rorke's Drift to his family, The South Wales Borderers Museum

Hitch, Private Frederick, statement made on admittance to Netley Military Hospital, *The Cambrian*, 13 June 1879

Hitch, Private Frederick, eyewitness account, The South Wales Borderers Museum

Holme, Norman, *The Noble 24th*, London, 1999

Hook, Private Henry, 'How They Held Rorke's Drift', *Royal Magazine*, February 1905

Hook, Private Henry, 'Stories of the Victoria Cross, Told by Those who have Won it', *The Strand*, January/June 1891

Howard, Gunner Arthur, letter, *Daily Telegraph*, 25 March 1879

Jobbins, Private John, letter from Rorke's Drift dated 6 February 1879, *Hereford Times*, 29 March 1879

Jones, Private Robert, 'Stories of the Victoria Cross, Told by Those who have Won it', *The Strand*, January/June 1891

Jones, Private William, 'Stories of the Victoria Cross, Told by Those who have Won it', *The Strand*, January/June 1891

Lugg, Trooper Henry, 'A Young O'ktonian at Rorke's Drift', *North Devon Herald*, 24 April 1879

Lyons, Corporal John, statement made on admittance to Netley Military Hospital, *The Cambrian*, 13 June 1879

Mason, Private Charles, letter from Rorke's Drift dated 8 February 1879, National Army Museum

Orchard, Private George, letter from Rorke's Drift dated 29 January 1879, *Bristol Observer*, 29 March 1879

Pitt, Private Samuel, press interview, *Western Mail*, 11 May 1914

Reynolds, Surgeon James, account in the appendix to the Report of the Army Medical Department, 1878, The Royal Army Medical Corps Museum

Savage, Private Edward, interview at Brecon, *Manchester Weekly Post*, 19 July 1879

Smith, Sergeant George, letter from Rorke's Drift to his wife in Brecon, *Brecon County Times*, 24 January 1879

Smith, Reverend George, account, 3 February 1879, *Royal Army Chaplains' Department Journal*, July 1936, Royal Army Chaplains' Department Museum
'The Defence of Rorke's Drift by an Eyewitness', *Natal Mercury*, 7 April 1879

'Victoria Cross Citations', *London Gazette*, 2 May, 17 June, 17 November and 29 November 1879

Waters, Private John, statement on admittance to Netley Military Hospital, *The Cambrian*, 13 June 1879

Wheatley, Kris, *Legacy, Heroes of Rorke's Drift* (Volume One), Eccles, 2006
Legacy, Heroes of Rorke's Drift (Volume Two), Eccles, 2006
Legacy, Heroes of Rorke's Drift (Volume Three), Eccles, 2007
Legacy, Heroes of Rorke's Drift (Volume Four), Eccles, 2007
Legacy, Heroes of Rorke's Drift (Volume Five), Eccles, 2007
Legacy, Heroes of Rorke's Drift (Volume Six), Eccles, 2008
Legacy, Heroes of Rorke's Drift (Volume Seven), Eccles, 2009

Wood, Private Caleb, 'Rorke's Drift, Story of Valour Retold by Ilkeston Veteran Who Was There', *Ilkeston Pioneer*, 26 December 1913

Index

Cardiff 42, 44, 118, 122, 136, 158, 202

Carmarthenshire 115

Casualties 10, 15, 39, 42, 43, 51, 58, 71, 75, 88, 96, 99, 108, 114, 148, 150, 160, 162, 163, 169, 172, 173, 174, 180, 181, 196, 202, 208, 209, 210

Cetshwayo 9 17

Channel islands 192

Chard VC, John Rouse Merriott 10, 13–19, 20, 21, 36, 37, 50, 55, 71, 75, 122, 164, 192, 195, 198, 205, 209, 211

Cheshire 69, 129–130, 131, 133, 134, 151, 152

Chester, Thomas 73–74

Chick, James 172–173

Clare, County, Ireland 167

Clayton, Thomas 74–75

Cole, Robert Edward 177–178

Cole, Thomas 75, 98, 99

Commissariat and Transport 7, 8, 193–202

Cork, County, Ireland 21, 39, 40, 89, 128, 129, 168, 173, 179, 181, 184, 198

Cornwall 13

Collins, Thomas 76–77

Connolly, John 99, 179–181

Connors, Anthony 77

Connors, Timothy 78

Cooper, William 117, 167, 178–179

Dalton VC, James Langley 192, 193–198, 202

Davies, George 78

Davis, William Henry 78–79

Daw, Thomas 79–80

Deacon, George (Power) 80–81

Deane, Michael 82

Denbighshire 176

Derbyshire 37, 118, 166, 167

Desmond, Patrick 39–40

Devon 13, 14, 17, 18, 32, 47, 149, 158, 159, 191, 201, 206

Dick, James William 82

Dicks, William 82, 83

Distinguished Conduct Medal 27, 28, 46, 64, 141, 201

Doughty, William 213

Driscoll, Thomas 84

Dublin, County, Ireland 26, 36, 48, 50, 65, 70, 131, 132, 138, 149, 174, 184, 185, 187, 198

Dunbar, William 84–85

Dunne, Walter Alphonsus 54, 194, 198–200

Durban 27, 61, 69, 85, 128, 130, 207

Edwards, George (Orchard) 85–87, 117

Egypt and the Sudan 29, 44, 190, 191, 192, 199, 203, 205

Essex 41, 81, 170

Evans, Abraham 28–30, 31

Evans, Thomas 183–184

Exeter 14, 17, 149

Fagan, John 88

French, John Barker 88–89

Galgey, Patrick J 173–174

Gallagher, Henry Edward 89–92

Gee, Edward 92

Glamorganshire 43, 74–75, 92, 106, 118, 136, 137, 149, 176, 183

Gloucestershire 42, 51, 73, 74–75, 98, 100, 101, 168, 169

Graham, James (Daniel Sheehan) 184

If history were taught in the form of stories, it would never be forgotten.

Rudyard Kipling